Mathematics 12

Workplace and Everyday Life

AUTHOR

Steve Etienne
B.Sc., B.Admin., Ed.Cert.
District School Board of Niagara

CONSULTANTS

Ian Charlton
B.Sc., Ed.Cert.
Thames Valley District School Board

Jodi Clarke
B.Sc., B.Ed.
Trillium Lakelands District School Board

Margaret Nesbitt
B.Math., B.Ed.
Ottawa-Carleton District School Board

ADVISORS

Doris Galea
Dufferin-Peel Catholic District School Board

John Gardiner
Math Consultant
Huntsville, Ontario

Chris Wadley
Grand Erie District School Board

Peter Wright
Grand Erie District School Board

Toronto Montréal Boston Burr Ridge, IL Dubuque, IA Madison, WI New York
San Francisco St. Louis Bangkok Bogotá Caracas Kuala Lumpur Lisbon London
Madrid Mexico City Milan New Delhi Santiago Seoul Singapore Sydney Taipei

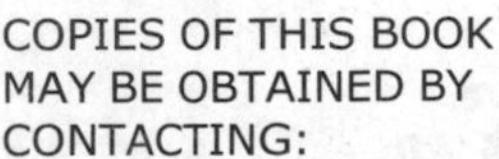

McGraw-Hill
Ryerson Limited

A Subsidiary of The **McGraw·Hill** *Companies*

COPIES OF THIS BOOK MAY BE OBTAINED BY CONTACTING:

McGraw-Hill Ryerson Ltd.

WEB SITE:
http://www.mcgrawhill.ca

E-MAIL:
orders@mcgrawhill.ca

TOLL-FREE FAX:
1-800-463-5885

TOLL-FREE CALL:
1-800-565-5758

OR BY MAILING YOUR ORDER TO:
McGraw-Hill Ryerson
Order Department
300 Water Street
Whitby, ON L1N 9B6

Please quote the ISBN and title when placing your order.

Mathematics 12 Workplace and Everyday Life

ISBN-13: 978-0-07-090894-9

ISBN-10: 0-07-090894-X

http://www.mcgrawhill.ca

3 4 5 6 7 8 9 MP 1 9 8 7 6 5

Printed and bound in Canada

PUBLISHER: Kristi Clark
PROJECT MANAGER: Helen Mason
DEVELOPMENTAL EDITORS: Christine Arnold, Sarah Rowe, Rita Vanden Heuvel
MANAGER, EDITORIAL SERVICES: Crystal Shortt
SUPERVISING EDITOR: Janie Deneau
COPY EDITOR: Laurel Sparrow
EDITORIAL ASSISTANT: Erin Hartley
MANAGER, PRODUCTION SERVICES: Yolanda Pigden
TEAM LEAD, PRODUCTION: Jennifer Hall
COVER DESIGN: Michelle Losier
MAIN COVER IMAGE: © Media Bakery
COVER IMAGES (LEFT TO RIGHT): Tanya Constantine/Getty Images; Blend Images/ColorBlind Images/Getty Images; Ron Levine/Getty Images

Acknowledgements

Reviewers

The author and editors of McGraw-Hill Ryerson Mathematics 12 Workplace and Everyday Life *wish to thank the following educators for their thoughtful comments and creative suggestions about what would work best in Workplace classrooms. Their input has been invaluable in making sure that the text and its related Teacher's Resource meet the needs of students and teachers in Ontario.*

John Cino
Niagara Catholic District School Board

Heather Curl
Lambton Kent District School Board

Terri Farha
Hamilton-Wentworth Catholic District School Board

Chris Graham
Rainbow District School Board

Steve Gunson
Simcoe County District School Board

Paul Higgins
Greater Essex County District School Board

Warren Hill
Waterloo Region District School Board

Amanda Kirk
Ottawa Carleton District School Board

Mark Kubisz
Toronto District School Board

Amanda Lee
Dufferin-Peel Catholic District School Board

Linda LoFaro
Ottawa Catholic District School Board

Linda McLaren
Catholic District School Board of Eastern Ontario

Judy Mendaglio
Peel District School Board

Reshida Nezirevic
Toronto Catholic District School Board

Pierre Periera
Upper Canada District School Board

Kenneth R. Rubin
York Region District School Board

Mary Schofield
Thames Valley District School Board

Laura Theoret
Halton District School Board

Liz Wood
Upper Grand District School Board

Contents

Probability Glossary 1

Chapter 1 Probability 3

Skills Practice 1: Fractions, Decimals, and Percents 4

1.1 What's the Chance? 6

1.2 In a Perfect World 10

Tech Tip: Experimenting with a Random Number Generator 14

Skills Practice 2: Equivalent Fractions 16

1.3 Roll the Bones 18

1.4 Heads, Heads, Heads 24

1.5 Free Coffee 28

Tech Tip: Using the Random Number Generator in a TI-83/84 Graphing Calculator 31

1.6 What Are the Odds? 34

Chapter 1 Review 40

Chapter 1 Practice Test 42

Task: Play Klass Kasino 44

Money Matters Glossary 45

Chapter 2 Budgets 51

Tech Tip: Using the TVM Solver 52

2.1 Savings Plans 54

2.2 Slicing Up the Pie 58

Tech Tip: Using a Spreadsheet 64

2.3 Track Your Spending 66

2.4 Living Expenses 70

2.5 Managing Change 74

Chapter 2 Review 78

Chapter 2 Practice Test 80

Task: Out of Control 82

Chapter 3 Renting Accommodations . . . 83

Tech Tip: Research Accommodations . . . 84

3.1 What's Available? . . . 86

3.2 Preparing to Move . . . 92

Skills Practice 3: Comparing Rental Prices . . . 100

Skills Practice 4: Writing a Cheque for Rent . . . 102

3.3 Looking for the Better Buy . . . 104

3.4 Rights and Responsibilities . . . 108

Skills Practice 5: Reading a Lease . . . 112

3.5 Some Other Living Expenses . . . 114

Tech Tip: Adding Percent to a Number . . . 118

Skills Practice 6: Reading a Utility Bill . . . 120

Chapter 3 Review . . . 122

Chapter 3 Practice Test . . . 124

Task: Leaving Town . . . 126

Chapter 4 Filing A Tax Return . . . 127

4.1 Income and Payroll Deductions . . . 128

Tech Tip: Using the CRA Payroll Calculator . . . 130

4.2 The T4 and the T1 . . . 134

4.3 Tax Deductions and Tax Credits . . . 142

Skills Practice 7: Identifying Tax Deductions and Tax Credits . . . 146

Tech Tip: Using an Online Income Tax Calculator . . . 147

4.4 Completing a Simple Tax Return . . . 148

Skills Practice 8: Completing a Tax Return . . . 152

4.5 Self Employed? . . . 154

Chapter 4 Review . . . 158

Chapter 4 Practice Test . . . 161

Task: Tax Planning . . . 164

Chapter 5 Owning A Home 165

5.1 Home Search 166

Tech Tip: Using the TVM Solver to Calculate Mortgage Payments 170

5.2 Buying a Home 172

5.3 The Cost of Owning a Home 178

Chapter 5 Review 182

Chapter 5 Practice Test 184

Task: Buying Your Dream Home 186

Measuring and Designing Glossary 187

Chapter 6 Measuring and Estimating 189

6.1 Length 190

6.2 Capacity 196

6.3 Estimating Large Numbers 202

Skills Practice 9: Converting Between Imperial Measures 208

Skills Practice 10: Converting Between Metric Measures. 210

6.4 Converting Units 211

Skills Practice 11: Using Ratio and Proportion to Convert Measurements 216

6.5 Converting Between Systems 218

6.6 Measurement Systems at Work and at Home 224

Chapter 6 Review 228
Chapter 6 Practice Test 230
Task: Plan A Shopping Trip 232

Chapter 7 Measurement and Design 233

7.1 2-D Scale Drawings 234
Skills Practice 12: The 3–4–5 Method of Checking for a 90° Angle 240
Skills Practice 13: Start Square and You'll Finish Square 241
7.2 Perimeter and Area Applications 243
7.3 Estimating the Cost of a Project 250
Skills Practice 14: Calculating Surface Area 256
7.4 3-D Scale Models 259
7.5 Capacity and Volume Applications 264
7.6 Composite Shapes and Figures 270
Chapter 7 Review 274
Chapter 7 Practice Test 277
Task: Home Renovations 280

Glossary 281

Centimetre Grid Paper 286
Formulas 290
Conversion Tables 291

Date ______________________

Probability Glossary

Glossary

Write the definition for each key term as you learn about it. Provide an example.

Key Terms		
equivalent fractions	population	sample
experimental probability	random number generator	simulate
odds		theoretical probability

Term	Definition

Date

Term	Definition

978-0-07-090894-9

1 Probability

- Contests, lotteries, and games offer the chance to win just about anything. You can win a cup of coffee. Even better, you can win cars, houses, vacations, or millions of dollars.
- Games of chance are designed so that the customer loses most of the time.
- For example, the chance of winning a lottery where you pick 6 numbers out of 49 is 1 in almost 14 million! You have a better chance of being struck by lightning.

1. a) List contests, lotteries, or games that you have entered.

b) How often have you won?

Chapter 1

Skills Practice 1: Fractions, Decimals, and Percents

1. a) You have several quarters. Write the amount shown in 2 ways.

Use a cents symbol ______ Use a dollar sign ______

b) Write the amount as a fraction of a dollar. Show the fraction in 2 ways.

______ = ______

c) Percent means "out of ______." The amount shown in part b) is _____% of a dollar.

2. This measuring tape shows 1 foot.

a) One foot equals ______ inches.

b) Half a foot is ______ inches.

c) How many inches are in $\frac{1}{4}$ foot? __________

Another way of saying one-fourth is one-__________.

d) How many inches are in $\frac{3}{4}$ foot? __________

e) Show 6 inches as a percent of 1 foot. __________

f) Express 1 inch as a fraction of 1 foot. __________

 978-0-07-090894-9

3. Without using a calculator, complete the table.

Fraction	Decimal	Percent
$\frac{1}{2}$		
$\frac{1}{4}$		
$\frac{3}{4}$		
	0.2	
	0.3	
		80%
		85%
$\frac{1}{3}$		
$\frac{2}{3}$		
	0.01	
	0.05	
		8%
		13%
$\frac{0}{10}$		
$\frac{10}{10}$		

Date

1.1 What's the Chance?

Focus: theoretical probability, number sense

Chapter 1

Warm Up

1. a) How many weeks are in 1 year? ______ **b)** How many weeks are in half a year? ______	**2. a)** How many seasons are in 1 year? ______ **b)** Each season is the same length. How many weeks are in each season? ______
3. Add. **a)** 0.1 + 0.2 + 0.3 + 0.4 = ______ **b)** 20% + 25% + 30% + 15% = ______ **c)** $\frac{20}{100} + \frac{13}{100} + \frac{27}{100} + \frac{40}{100}$ = ______	**4.** What fraction of a dollar is each coin?  =  =  =

Calculating Theoretical Probability

1. There are 52 cards in a standard deck of cards.
- There are 4 different suits.
- Two suits have red symbols. These are the hearts and diamonds.
- Two suits have black symbols. These are the clubs and spades.
- Each suit has numbered cards from 2 to 10, plus a jack, a queen, a king, and an ace.

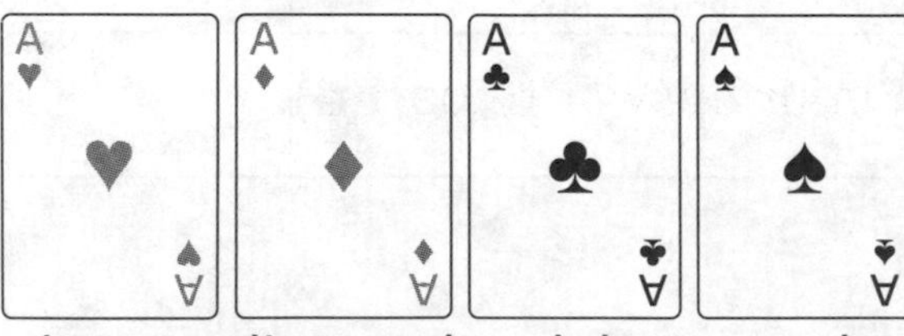

heart diamond club spade

You have a full deck of cards. What is the probability of picking the following card?

a) a heart ______ **b)** a black card ______

c) a red card ______ **d)** an ace ______

 978-0-07-090894-9

- The chance of something happening is its **theoretical probability**.

Go to pages 1–2 to write the definition for **theoretical probability** in your own words.

2. Use your answers from #1 to show the probability of picking the following cards. Show each probability 3 ways.

	Write as a Fraction	Write as a Decimal	Write as a Percent
a) A Heart			
b) A Black Card			
c) A Red Card			
d) An Ace			

3. a) What is the probability of picking a club from a full deck of cards? Write your answer as a percent. ________

b) What is the probability of picking a diamond? Write your answer as a percent. ________

c) Create a bar graph showing the probability of picking any 1 suit if you pull only 1 card from a full deck.
- Include a title for the graph.

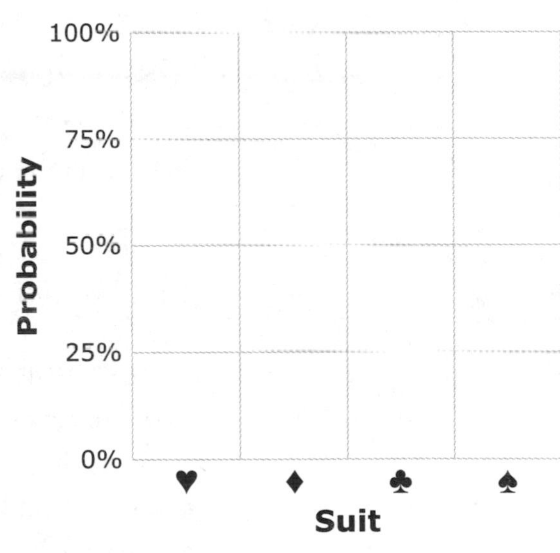

d) What is the probability of picking a club, a spade, a heart, or a diamond from a full deck? Write your answer as a percent.

____

____

e) Explain your answer to part d).

____

____

____

____

Date ______

4. a) What does this roll of a die show? ______

b) What is the probability of rolling a 2 with 1 die?

Write your answer as a fraction. ______

Die is the singular form of the word ______

c) What is the probability of rolling a 5? ______

d) Create a bar graph showing the probability of rolling each number when you roll 1 die.
- Include a title for the graph.
- Label each axis.

e) What is the probability of rolling a die and getting a 7? ______

f) Explain your answer to part e).

______

5. You flip a coin. Create and label a circle graph showing the probability of getting heads or tails.
- Include a title.
- Label each sector.

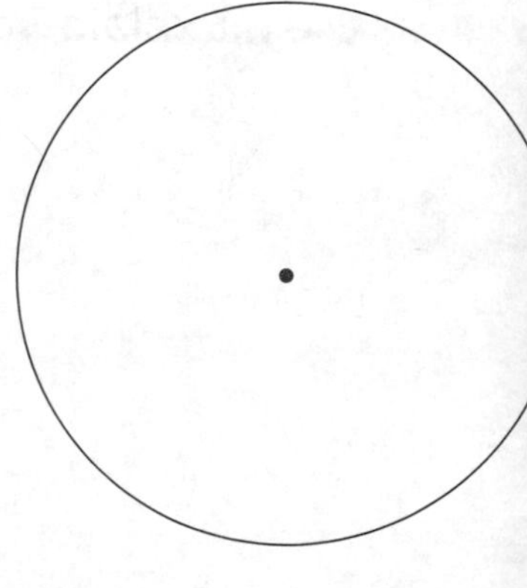

978-0-07-090894-9

Chapter 1

6. a) State the probability of the spinner below landing on each colour. Write your answer as a percent.

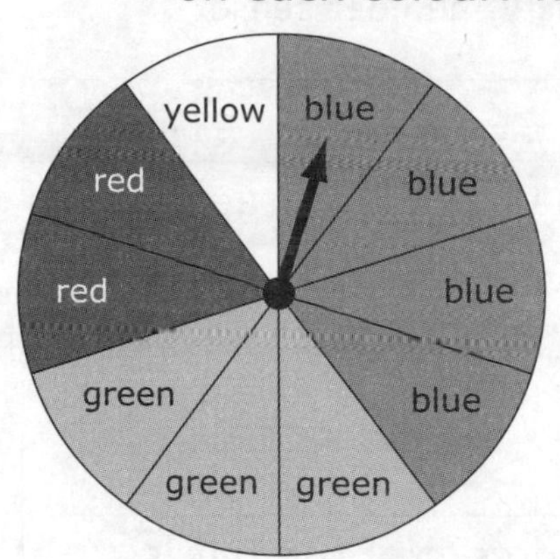

Blue: ______

Green: ______

Red: ______

Yellow: ______

b) What is the probability of the spinner landing on yellow or blue? ______

c) What is the probability of the spinner landing on green or blue? ______

d) What is the probability of the spinner *not* landing on blue? ______

☑ Check Your Understanding

1. Fill in each blank with the appropriate phrase.
It will happen. It is not likely to happen.
It is likely to happen. It will not happen.
It might happen, it might not.

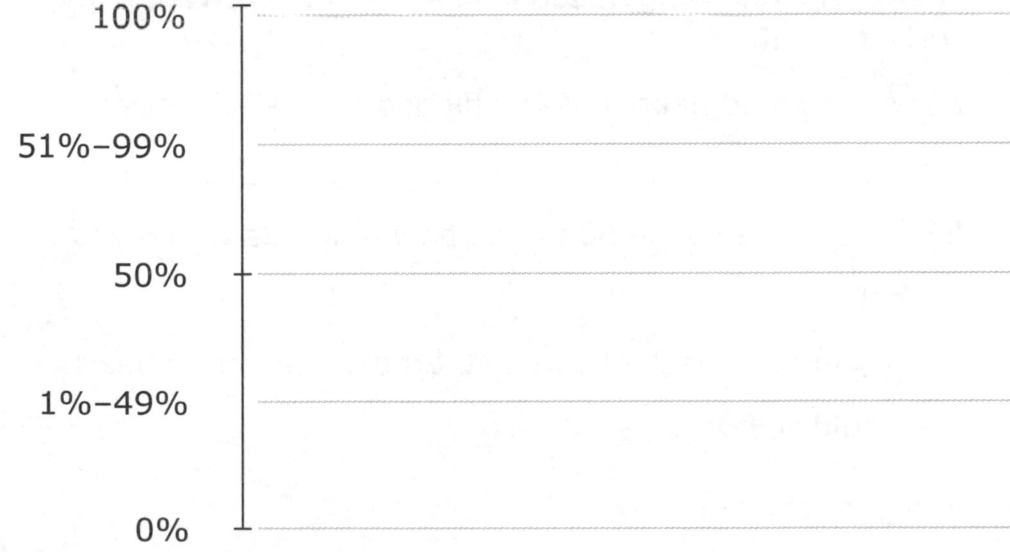

Date

1.2 In a Perfect World

Focus: theoretical probability, experimental probability, number sense

Chapter 1

Warm Up

1. Write $\frac{10}{40}$ in lowest terms. $\frac{10}{40} =$	**2.** Write 3 equivalent fractions for $\frac{1}{2}$. $\frac{1}{2} =$
3. Write 90% as a fraction in lowest terms.	**4.** What percent of the bar is shaded? 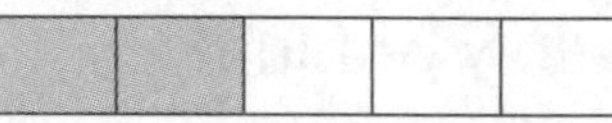
5. Shade 75% of the cylinder. 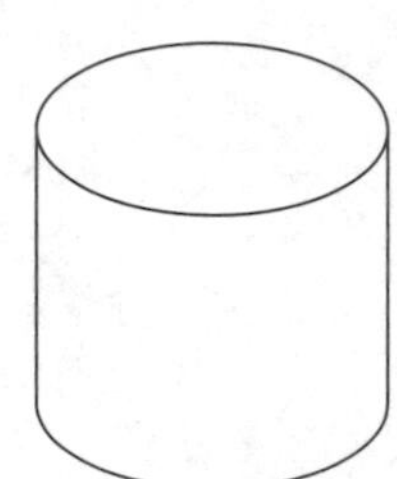	**6.** What is the chance of picking a king from a deck of 52 cards? Show your answer as a fraction in lowest terms.

Collecting Data to Calculate Probability

Imagine flipping this penny 10 times. In a perfect world you would get 5 heads and 5 tails. This is theoretical probability.

1. Answer the following questions as though you were in a perfect world.

a) What would happen if you flipped a coin 50 times?

____

b) If you rolled a die 60 times, how many 3s would you get? ______

c) If you cut a deck of cards 40 times, how many hearts would you get? ______

2. In a perfect world, the ______________ ______________ of flipping heads is 50%.

 978-0-07-090894-9

Date

- **Experimental probability** is the chance of something happening based on experimental results.
- After collecting data, it is useful to compare experimental probability with theoretical probability.

Go to pages 1–2 to write the definition for **experimental probability** in your own words.

3. a) Create and label a bar graph showing the "perfect world" results for rolling a die 60 times.
- Title the graph.

b) Roll a die *exactly* 60 times. Record your results in the tally chart.

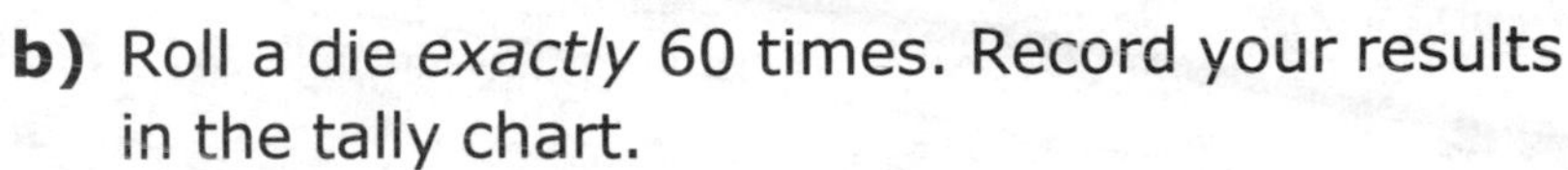

c) Create and label a bar graph showing your results in part b).

1	
2	
3	
4	
5	
6	

d) For each of your results, express the experimental probability as a fraction.

1 = ______ 2 = ______ 3 = ______

4 = ______ 5 = ______ 6 = ______

Date

Chapter 1

4. a) Create and label a bar graph showing the "perfect world" results for cutting a deck of cards 40 times.
   - Title the graph.
   - Label each axis.

b) Record the results for obtaining each of the 4 suits when you cut a deck of cards *exactly* 40 times.

c) Create and label a bar graph showing your results in part b).

d) For each of your results, express the experimental probability as a fraction and then a percent.

Clubs: ____________ or ____________ %

Spades: ____________ or ____________ %

Hearts: ____________ or ____________ %

Diamonds: ____________ or ____________ %

978-0-07-090894-9

5. a) Create and label a circle graph showing the "perfect world" results for flipping a coin 50 times.
   - Include a title.
   - Label each sector.

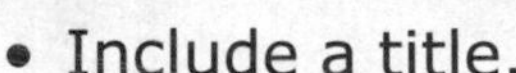

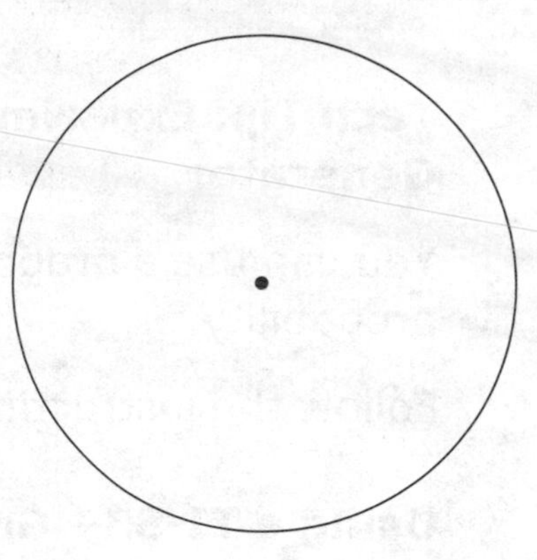

b) Flip a coin *exactly* 50 times. Record your results in the tally chart.

Heads	**Tails**

c) Create and label a circle graph for the results obtained in part b).

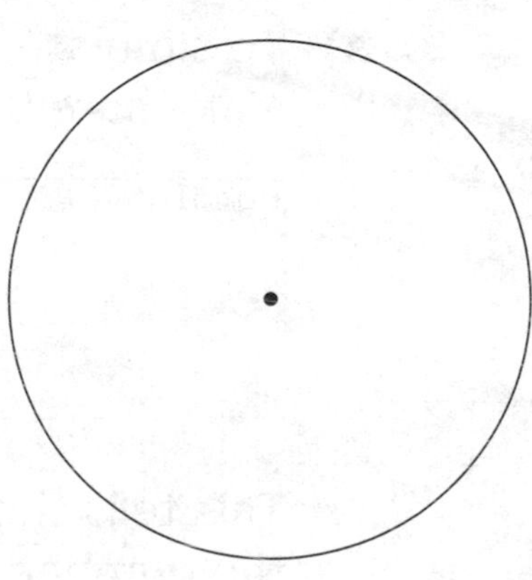

☑ Check Your Understanding

1. a) Did anyone in the class get "perfect world" results for all 3 of the experiments? YES ____ NO ____

b) Explain why few, if any, people in the class received "perfect world" results for all 3 of the experiments.

Date

Tech Tip: Experimenting with a Random Number Generator

You can use a graphing calculator to simulate experimental probability.

Follow the instructions to check out several different applications.

Chapter 1

Using a TI-83+ Graphing Calculator

1. Press **MATH**. Scroll right so that PRB is highlighted.
2. Press **5** to select **5:randInt(**.
   This command tells the calculator to generate random integers.

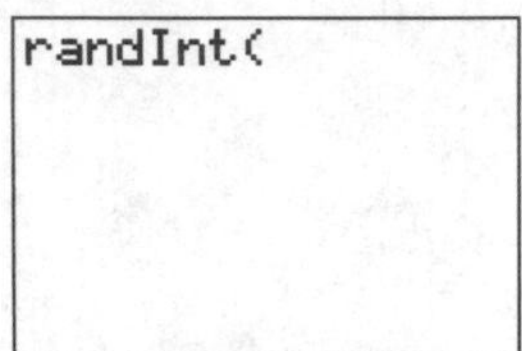

3. **a)** To simulate flipping coins, enter **1,2)**.
   Make sure there are no spaces between the characters.

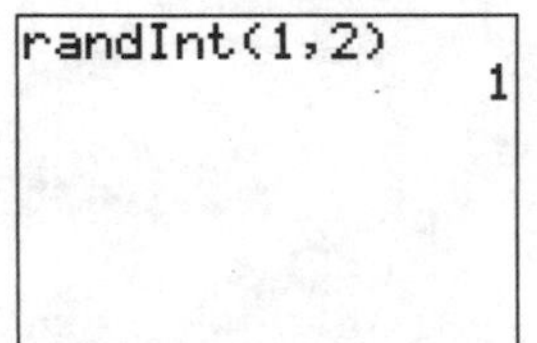

This tells the calculator to select either the number 1 or the number 2.
Mentally assign heads or tails to each number. For example, 1 is heads, 2 is tails.
Continue pressing the **ENTER** key to generate more random tosses.

978-0-07-090894-9

b) To simulate selecting the suit of a card, enter **1,4)**. Make sure there are no spaces between the characters.

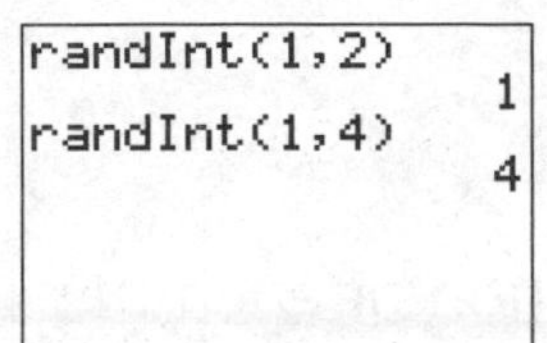

This tells the calculator to select an integer from 1 to 4. Mentally assign 1 suit to each of the 4 numbers. Continue pressing the **ENTER** key to generate more random suits.

c) To simulate selecting the value of a card, enter **1,____)**.

d) To simulate selecting the exact card, enter **1,____)**.

e) To simulate rolling 1 die, enter **1,____)**.

4. Press **ENTER**. A random integer from the acceptable range of values will be displayed. Continue pressing **ENTER** to generate more random numbers.

Date ______________

Skills Practice 2: Equivalent Fractions

The word "equivalent" comes from 2 smaller words.
"equi" = equal
"valent" = value

Equivalent fractions are fractions that have the same value.
The top number of a fraction is called the numerator.
The bottom number of a fraction is called the denominator.

$\frac{3}{4}$ ← numerator / ← denominator

Chapter 1

Go to pages 1–2 to write the definition for **equivalent fractions** in your own words. Give an example.

Example

Look at the 3 bars below. Write the fraction of each bar that is shaded.

In this example, the same amount of each bar is shaded. These visuals show ______________ ______________.

______ = ______ = ______

1. a) Write the fraction of each bar that is shaded.

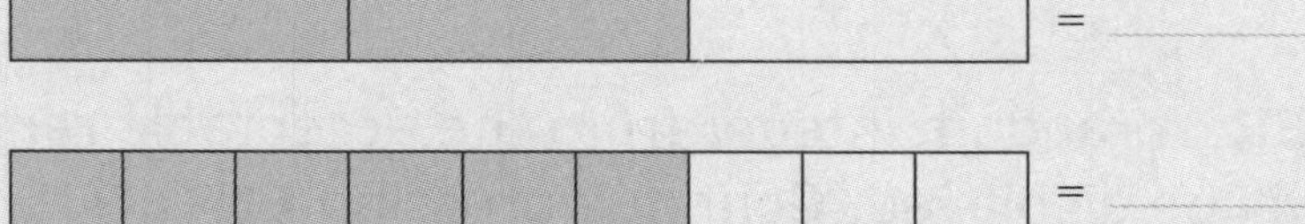

b) What is an equivalent fraction for $\frac{2}{3}$?

978-0-07-090894-9

Chapter 1

2. Write the fraction of each circle that is shaded.

a) 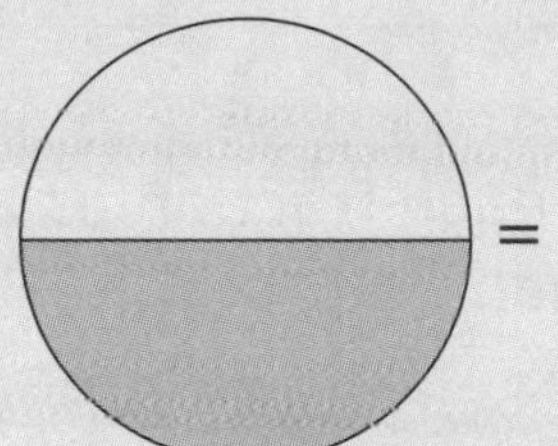 = ______

b) 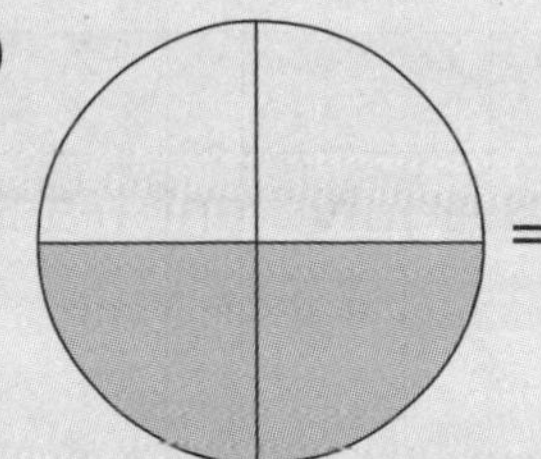 = ______

c) 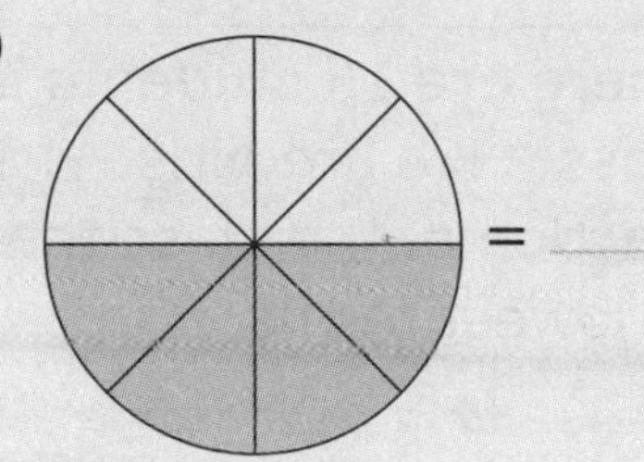 = ______

3. a) Write 4 equivalent fractions for $\frac{1}{2}$.

b) Explain or show how you developed the fourth fraction above.

____

____

4. a) Develop 3 visuals to show your own equivalent fractions.

b) Write the fractions.

5. Fill in the blanks to create equivalent fractions.

$$\frac{1}{2} = \frac{2}{\_\_} = \frac{\_\_}{6} = \frac{10}{\_\_} = \frac{20}{\_\_} = \frac{\_\_}{50} = \frac{\_\_}{100} = \frac{250}{\_\_}$$

Date

1.3 Roll the Bones

Focus: theoretical probability, experimental probability, number sense

Chapter 1

Warm Up

1. Write 3 equivalent fractions for $\frac{1}{4}$.	**2.** Write each fraction as a decimal. $\frac{1}{4} =$ $\frac{1}{5} =$
3. Write each fraction in lowest terms. $\frac{4}{12} =$ $\frac{6}{18} =$	**4.** There are 15 students in a class. Five are girls. Write the fraction of the class that is girls in lowest terms.

5. The bar graph shows attendance at a movie theatre for 1 week.

a) How many people saw the movie on Wednesday? ______

b) How many people saw the movie on Friday? ______

c) How many people saw the movie last week? ______

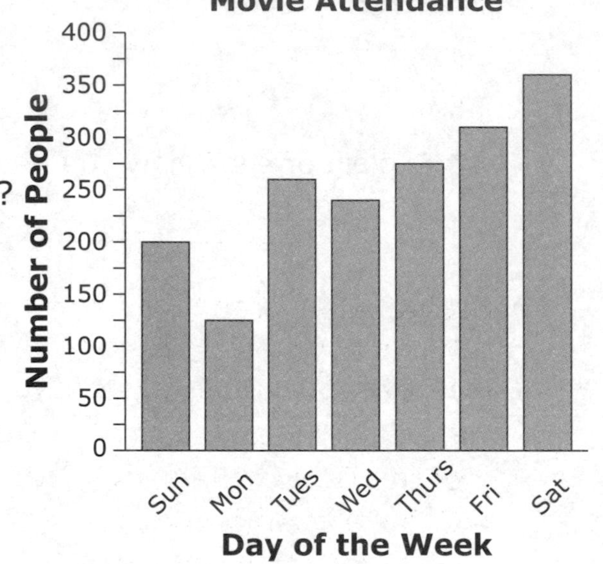

Rolling Dice

1. Suppose you roll 2 dice.

a) What is the smallest total you can get? ______

b) What is the greatest total you can get? ______

c) How many different totals are possible? ______

d) If you roll a pair of dice 50 times, predict the number of times that the total will be 7. ______

978-0-07-090894-9

Date ______________________

2. a) Roll 2 dice *exactly* 50 times. Add the 2 numbers showing. Record the number of times each total occurs.

Sum of the Dice	Tally	Total Times Rolled
2		
3		
4		
5		
6		
7		
8		
9		
10		
11		
12		

Chapter 1

b) Create a bar graph showing your results.

- Include a title.
- Title the *y*-axis, Total.
- Title the *x*-axis, Sum of the Dice.
- Choose an appropriate scale for the *y*-axis.

c) Did you roll each of the sums an equal number of times? YES ______ NO ______

d) Suggest some reasons for your answer.

____

____

- There is only 1 way to roll a 2 with 2 dice. You need a 1 on each die.
- There are 2 ways to roll a 3. You can have a 1 on the first die and a 2 on the other. Or, you can have a 2 on the first die and a 1 on the other.

3. a) Determine all the possible combinations for rolling 2 dice. Example:

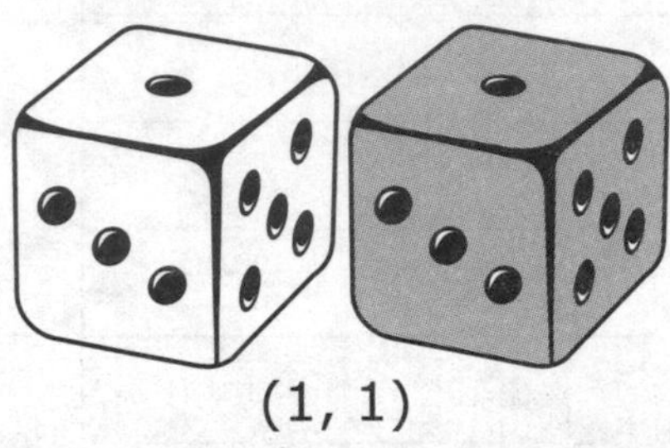

(1, 1)

Sum of the Dice	Possible Combinations	Number of Combinations
2	(1, 1)	1
3	(1, 2) (_____, _____)	2
4		
5		
6		
7		
8		
9		
10		
11		
12		
Total Number of Combinations		

 978-0-07-090894-9

b) Create a bar graph showing the Sum of the Dice versus Number of Combinations.

- Include a title.
- Title the *y*-axis, Number of Combinations.
- Title the *x*-axis, Sum of the Dice.
- Choose an appropriate scale for the *y*-axis.

c) Which sum has the highest theoretical probability of being rolled? ________

d) Does your answer to part c) match your experimental results? YES ______ NO ______

e) Why do you think this is the case?

____

____

____

4. When you roll 2 dice, list all of the combinations that make a sum of 7 or greater.

____

____

____

Date ____________________

5. **a)** Complete the table.
   - Write the fractions in lowest terms.
   - Round each percent to the nearest whole number.

Sum of the Dice	Number of Combinations	Fraction of the Total Number of Combinations	Percent of the Total Number of Combinations
2	1	$\frac{1}{36}$	2.777 = 3%
3	2		
4			
5			
6			
7			
8			
9			
10			
11			
12			
Total			

Chapter 1

Tech Tip: Suppose that you made 5 rolls. You rolled 2 twice. Use your calculator to show $\frac{2}{5}$ as a percent. If your calculator has a (%) key, enter 2 (÷) 5 (%) 2 is 40% of 5.

b) List the pairs of sums that have the same theoretical probability of occurring.

____

c) The likelihood of rolling a total of 3 with 2 dice is the same as the *total* of the likelihood of rolling 2 other combinations. What are those 2 combinations?

_____ and _____

d) As a percent, what is the chance of rolling 2 dice and obtaining a total of 7 or greater? _____

 978-0-07-090894-9

Date ____________

6. **a)** Add all of the class's results from #2a) and record the data in the appropriate row of the tally column. Calculate the percent of the total for each sum.

Sum of the Dice	Class Tally	Percent of Total
2		
3		
4		
5		
6		
7		
8		
9		
10		
11		
12		
	Total For Class Results	

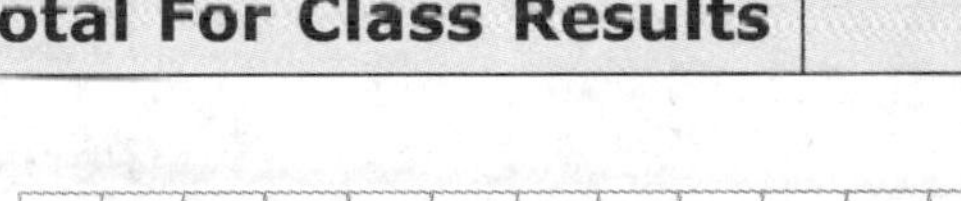

b) Graph the results.
- Include a title.
- Title the *y*-axis, Percent of Total.
- Title the *x*-axis, Sum of the Dice.

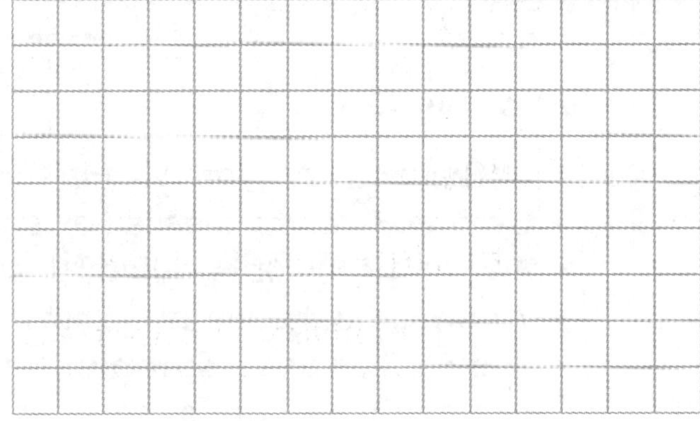

☑ Check Your Understanding

1. Which graph is closer in shape to the graph in #3?

   The graph in #2 or the graph in #6? ________

2. Why do you think this is so?

   ____

   ____

Date ____________

1.4 Heads, Heads, Heads

Focus: experimental probability, number sense

Warm Up	
1. What is the theoretical probability of flipping a coin and getting tails?	**2.** If you flipped a coin 40 times, how many tails would you expect to get?
3. A weather forecast states that there is a 30% chance of rain. Is it likely or not likely to rain?	**4.** Write $\frac{3}{4}$ as a decimal and as a percent. Decimal: ____________ Percent: ____________
5. What is the theoretical probability of picking a heart from a standard deck of cards? Write your answer as a fraction and a percent. Fraction: ____________ Percent: ____________	**6.** You flip a coin 25 times and get 8 heads. What is the experimental probability of getting heads? Write your answer as a fraction and a percent. Fraction: ____________ Percent: ____________

Flipping Coins

- In this activity, you will flip 3 coins at the same time.
- Getting 3 heads is called a "successful" result.
- Any other result is called "unsuccessful."
- You will flip the set of 3 coins exactly 40 times.
- The 40 flips are a **sample**. A sample is a small group of results taken from a larger group. A sample is easy to analyse. You could flip the coins 8 million times. That would be a much larger sample.

Go to pages 1–2 to write the definition for **sample** in your own words.

1. a) You are going to flip 3 coins 40 times. How many successful results do you expect? ________

b) Explain your answer to part a).

____

____

 978-0-07-090894-9

Date ______________________

2. a) Flip all 3 coins *exactly* 40 times. Record your results in the table.

	Successful (Got 3 heads)	Unsuccessful (Did not get 3 heads)
Tally		
Total		

b) How many successful results did you get? ______

Show this as a fraction of the total sample. ______

c) State the number of successful results as a percent. ______

3. In the chart below, list or draw all of the possible outcomes for flipping 3 coins at once.

First Coin	Second Coin	Third Coin

4. a) What is the theoretical probability of a successful result? Show your answer as a fraction and a percent.

b) What is the theoretical probability of an unsuccessful result? Show your answer as a fraction and a percent.

Chapter 1

Chapter 1

5. a) Record the individual results of the class from #2a) in the table. Add the class results for "Successful" and "Unsuccessful."

	Successful					Unsuccessful				
Individual Results										
Total										

b) How many flips are in this sample?

_____ students × 40 flips each = _______ flips

c) Calculate the overall percent of successful results.

d) Create a circle graph showing the results from part a).

- Estimate the size of each fraction of the circle.
- Include a title.
- Label each sector.

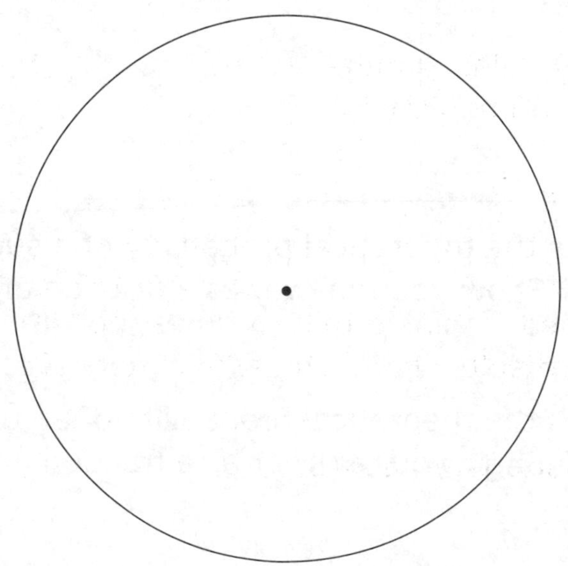

978-0-07-090894-9

Date

☑ Check Your Understanding

1.

a) The cartoon shows the results of the boy's first flip.

Do you agree with his comment? YES ______ NO ______

b) Explain your answer to part a). Use the term sample in your explanation.

______

2. a) Which class member had the greatest number of successful results in the sample in #2? ______

b) What was the percent of successful flips? ______

3. a) Which class member had the lowest percent of successful results in #2? ______

b) What was the percent of successful flips? ______

4. How do you think sample size relates to theoretical probability?

______

______

5. If you flipped 3 coins 8 million times, how many successful results would you expect to get?

6. Explain your answer to #5. ______

______

Date ____________________

1.5 Free Coffee

Focus: experimental probability, simulation

Chapter 1

Warm Up

1. The theoretical probability of winning a prize in a lottery is 1 in 5. Write this as a fraction and a percent.	**2.** The weather report says there is a 70% chance of snow. Write the probability of it snowing as a decimal and a fraction.
3. You roll 2 dice. Circle the probability of rolling a sum of 7. Impossible Not Likely Likely Very Likely Certain	**4.** Explain your answer to #3.
5. What is the theoretical probability of rolling a 5 with 2 dice? Write your answer as a fraction and a percent.	**6.** If you flip a coin 10 times, what is the theoretical probability of flipping heads? Write your answer as a fraction and a decimal.
7. Flip a coin 10 times. What is the experimental probability of flipping heads? Write your answer as a fraction and a decimal.	**8.** What is the difference between theoretical and experimental probability?

978-0-07-090894-9

Date ______________________

It's On the Cup

1. A coffee shop promotion offers prizes in specially marked cups. The chance of winning is 1 in 9.

a) In your own words, explain the meaning of "The chance of winning is 1 in 9."

____

____

Chapter 1

b) List 2 words that mean the same as "chance."

______________________ ______________________

c) What experiment that you completed recently has the same theoretical probability as getting a winning cup?

Check out the table you completed on page 23.

____

2. a) How can you **simulate** the coffee cup promotion without actually using coffee cups? To simulate means to model with an experiment. Describe or draw what you will do.

Go to pages 1–2 to write the definition for **simulate** in your own words.

____

____

____

b) If you run this simulation 100 times, how many "winners" should you get? __________

c) Explain how you determined your answer to part b).

____

____

____

Chapter 1

d) Test your hypothesis. Do the simulation *exactly* 100 times. Tally the results below.

Winner	
Non-Winner	

e) Write your winning results 3 ways.

As a percent of the total: ______

As a fraction of the total: ______

As a decimal: ______

f) Some people like to show data like this on a graph. Use a circle graph to display your results.

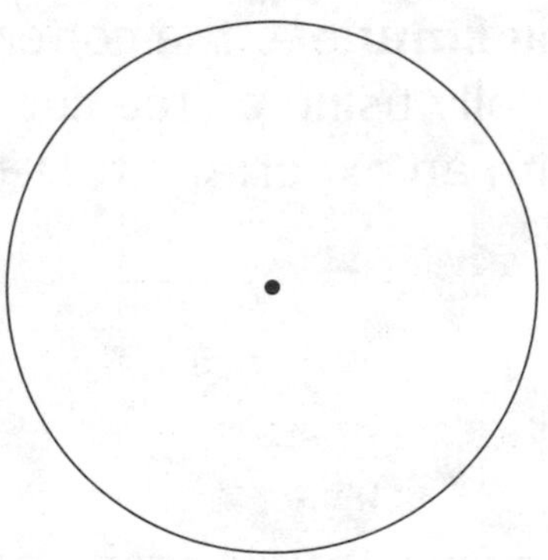

g) Did your experiment match the theoretical probability of the promotion?

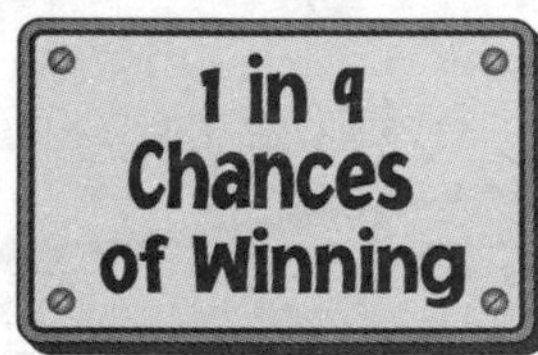

YES ______ NO ______

h) If not, explain why.

______

______

______

978-0-07-090894-9

- Another way to run this kind of simulation is to use a device that generates random numbers.
- A **random number generator** is a tool that picks numbers so that each number has an equal probability of coming up on each try.
- A graphing calculator can be set up to work as a random number generator. It can then model the previous experiment.

Go to pages 1–2 to write the definition for **random number generator** in your own words.

Tech Tip: Using the Random Number Generator in a TI-83/84 Graphing Calculator

1. Press **MATH**. Scroll right so that PRB is highlighted.
2. Press **5** to select **5:randInt(**.
   The command **randInt(** tells the calculator to generate random integers.

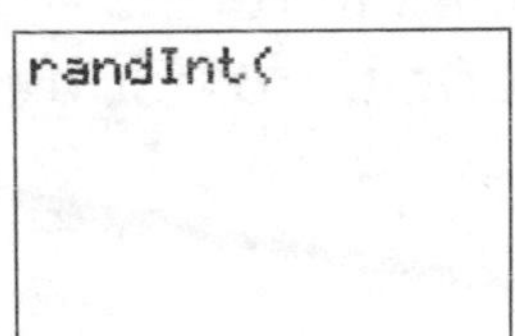

3. Type **1,9)**.
   Make sure there are no spaces between the characters.
   This tells the calculator to select numbers between 1 and 9.
4. Press **ENTER**. An integer from 1 to 9 will be displayed.
   Continue pressing **ENTER** to generate more random integers.

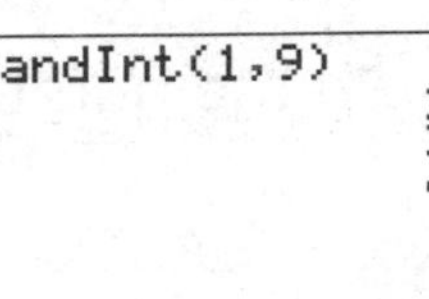

Chapter 1

3. a) Select a target number from 1 to 9 for this experiment. ______

Every time the random generator comes up with that number, you are a winner.

b) Use a random number generator to select exactly 100 numbers ranging from 1 to 9. Tally the results below.

Winner	
Non-Winner	

c) How many times did the number you selected in part a) appear? ______

d) State your winning percent. ______

e) Explain your results in terms of simulating winning a prize from the coffee promotion.

______

______

4. a) Repeat the experiment another 100 times. Tally the results below.

Winner	
Non-Winner	

b) Add these results to you totals from #3b).

How many times did the number you selected in #3a) appear? ______

c) State your winning percent. ______

d) Is your result closer to the theoretical probability you calculated in #2b)? YES ______ NO ______

e) Explain your answer to part b). ______

______

 978-0-07-090894-9

5. a) Collect the number of winning simulations in #4b) from everyone in your class.

Number of Winning Simulations for Each Member of the Class									
Total Number of Winners in the Class = ______									

b) What is the total number of random numbers generated by the class? ______

c) Calculate the class's winning percent.

☑ Check Your Understanding

1. According to the theoretical probability of the promotion, how many winning results should your class have had?

2. Explain why your individual results and the whole class's results may have differed.

3. Is the coffee shop's ad accurate? Explain.

Date ______________

1.6 What Are the Odds?

Focus: probability, media, number sense

Chapter 1

Warm Up	
1. The probability of picking the 7 of clubs from a deck of cards is 1 in ____.	**2.** The probability of picking any red card from a deck of cards is 1 in ____.
3. What is the probability of flipping "tails, tails, tails" with 3 coins?	**4.** Reduce the following fractions to lowest terms. **a)** $\frac{5}{10}$ **b)** $\frac{70}{100}$

What Are Odds?

You flip a coin.

The probability of flipping heads is

$$\frac{\text{\# of chances of winning}}{\text{\# of possible flips}} = \frac{1}{2}.$$

Another way of showing this is 1:2.
heads↑ ↑tails

Go to pages 1–2 to write the definition for **odds** in your own words.

The **odds** of flipping heads are $\frac{\text{\# of chances of winning}}{\text{\# of chances of losing}} = \frac{1}{1}$.

Another way of showing this is 1:1.
heads↑ ↑tails

This can be confusing because the term **odds** is often used in the media as another word for probability or chance.

978-0-07-090894-9

- An ad such as the following really means that the *probability* of winning is 1 in 10 (or 10%).

The odds of winning are 1 in 10!

- The odds of winning would be 1:9.

chance of winning↑ ↑chance of not winning

1. a) Calculate the odds of drawing a red card from a deck of cards.

$$\frac{\text{How many red cards are in the deck? \_\_\_\_}}{\text{How many not red cards are in the deck? \_\_\_\_}} = \_\_\_\_$$

Odds are shown as a ratio. The odds are 1:____.

b) What are the odds of drawing a spade from a deck of cards? The odds are 1: ____.

c) What are the odds of drawing an ace from a deck of cards?

d) What are the odds of drawing a jack, queen, or king from a deck of cards?

e) What are the odds of rolling a 3 with one die?

f) What are the odds of flipping "heads, heads" with 2 coins?

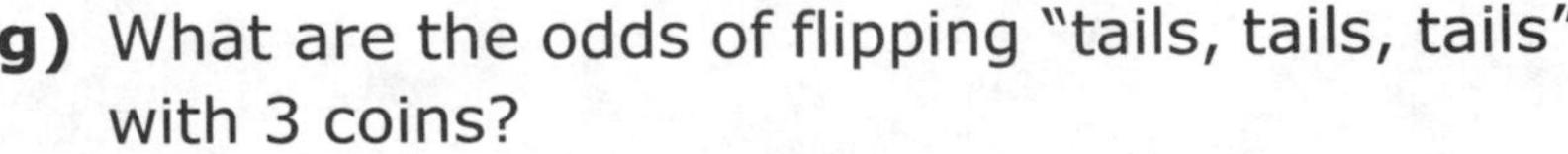

g) What are the odds of flipping "tails, tails, tails" with 3 coins?

Date ______

Chapter 1

Populations

2. Collect the following data.
   a) What is the student population of your school? ______
   b) What is the grade 9 population? ______
   c) What is the grade 10 population? ______
   d) What is the grade 11 population? ______
   e) What is the grade 12 population? ______
   f) How many teachers are there? ______
   g) How many teachers are male? ______
   h) How many teachers are female? ______
   i) How many other people work in the school? ______
   j) Therefore, what is the total **population** of the school? ______

You have now worked with your school's population. Go to pages 1–2 to write a definition for **population** in your own words.

Look at the glossary for help.

3. What are the odds that the next teacher to walk past your classroom will be male?

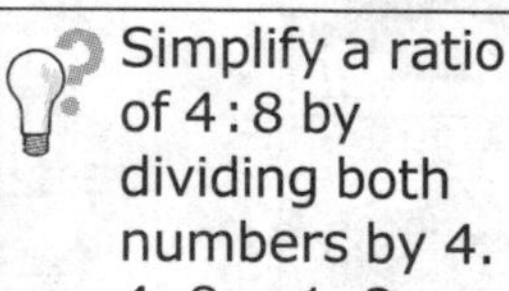

Simplify a ratio of 4 : 8 by dividing both numbers by 4.
4 : 8 = 1 : 2

4. Determine the following ratios. Whenever possible, write the ratios in simplest form.
   a) The ratio of grade 9s to grade 10s: ______
   b) The ratio of grade 9s to grade 12s: ______
   c) The ratio of grade 11s to grade 12s: ______
   d) The ratio of students to teachers: ______
   e) The ratio of teachers to other people who work in the school: ______

978-0-07-090894-9

Date ______________________

Samples

The school principal wants to do a survey about starting and finishing the school day 3 hours later than the current start and end times.

5. a) This would make your school day start at ______ and finish at ______.

b) Explain why the principal might not wish to survey the entire population of the school.

____

____

- The principal decides to survey a sample of the school population.
- A sample is part of a population.
- A good sample represents the entire population.

6. The principal is trying to decide which of the following samples would best represent the school's population.
   - Consider your school's population.
   - Read the description of each proposed sample.
   - Decide which ones are potentially good samples.
   - Which ones are potentially bad samples?

Proposed Sample	Good Sample	Bad Sample
a) Survey all of the grade 9s.		
b) Survey all of the teachers.		
c) Survey 10 students from each grade and ask 10 teachers.		
d) Survey 10% of the population.		
e) Survey only those old enough to vote.		
f) Survey 10% of the population of each grade, the teachers, and the other staff.		
g) Survey the students in the cafeteria.		

Date

7. Choose 1 proposed sample you classified as a "Bad Sample." Explain your thinking.

Chapter 1

8. a) Describe a good sample of your school's population.

b) Discuss your sample idea with several other students. Listen to their coaching to make sure that your sample plan represents the school's population. Revise your sample if necessary.

c) Using the sample, conduct a small survey to determine whether the odds are likely or unlikely that your school's population is in favour of starting and finishing the school day 3 hours later. Record your results.

In Favour	
Not in Favour	

d) What can you conclude from your survey?

Probability in the Media

Many people read long-term forecasts before making plans.

- Can we play volleyball outside on Monday?
- Will it be warm enough to ride our bikes on Wednesday?
- Should we plan a weekend beach party?

The long-term forecast on the next page shows the type of information the media provide.

978-0-07-090894-9

Date ____________

Long-Term Forecast

	Monday Sept. 13	Tuesday Sept. 14	Wednesday Sept. 15	Thursday Sept. 16	Friday Sept. 17	Saturday Sept. 18
	Cloudy With Sunny Breaks	**Showers**	**Isolated Showers**	**Mostly Sunny**	**Sunny**	**Sunny**
P.O.P.	40%	80%	60%	20%	20%	10%
High	18°C	16°C	17°C	18°C	21°C	22°C
Low	11°C	13°C	9°C	14°C	16°C	18°C
24-Hr Rain	close to 1 mm	close to 10 mm	close to 5 mm			

9. a) What does P.O.P. stand for?

> **Hint:** P.O.P. has two *P*s. One stands for the topic of this chapter. The other is another word for rain.

b) How can it help you plan outdoor jobs or events?

c) Which day, in your opinion, would be best for a family barbecue? Explain why.

d) You work for a company that paves driveways. List the days you think you will be able to work this week.

☑ Check Your Understanding

1. Jack says, "The odds of a 6-day forecast being right are slim to none." What might he mean by this?

Date ____________________

Chapter 1 Review

Chapter 1

1. Define theoretical probability.

____

____

2. What is the probability of each of the following?

a) picking the 9 of clubs from a deck of cards ________ (fraction)

b) flipping heads with a coin ________ (decimal)

c) picking a diamond from a deck of cards ________ (percent)

d) rolling a 3 with 1 die ________ (fraction)

e) rolling an even number with 1 die ________ (decimal)

f) flipping heads or tails with a coin ________ (percent)

3. a) How many combinations can be obtained by rolling 2 dice? ________

b) List all of the combinations for rolling a 7 with 2 dice.

____

c) Write the probability of rolling a 7 as a fraction of the total.

4. Define experimental probability.

____

____

5. Pick 10 cards from a deck of 52.

a) How many spades did you pick? ________

b) Write the number of spades you got as a fraction, a decimal, and a percent.

________ = ________ = ________

fraction decimal percent

978-0-07-090894-9

6. Complete the table.

Fraction	Decimal	Percent
a) $\frac{1}{2}$		
b) $\frac{1}{10}$		
c)	0.3	
d)	0.7	
e)		90%
f)		95%

7. a) Create and label a bar graph for the "perfect world" results for obtaining each suit when you cut a deck of cards 40 times.

b) The graph in part a) shows ______________ probability.

8. A department store offers "scratch and win" tickets to its customers. The store claims that 25% of the tickets result in customers paying no taxes on purchases.

a) Write the probability of getting a winning ticket as a fraction. ______

b) If the store prints 10 000 tickets, how many winning tickets are there?

c) What are the odds of getting a winning ticket?

Date ____________

Chapter 1 Practice Test

Chapter 1

1. Explain the difference between theoretical probability and experimental probability.

____

____

____

2. What is the theoretical probability of each of the following?

a) picking a club from a deck of cards ________ (fraction)

b) picking a spade or a heart from a deck of cards ________ (fraction)

c) flipping tails with a coin ________ (percent)

d) rolling a 7 with 1 die ________ (percent)

e) rolling an odd number with 1 die ________ (decimal)

3. a) How many combinations can you get by rolling 2 dice? ________

b) List all of the combinations for rolling 10, 11, or 12 with 2 dice.

____

____

c) Write the probability of rolling a 10 or greater as a fraction of the total.

d) Write the answer to part c) in lowest terms. ________

4. Roll a die 20 times.

a) How many 6s did you roll? ________

b) Write the number of 6s that you rolled as a fraction, a decimal, and a percent.

________ = ________ = ________

fraction decimal percent

c) This is an example of ________________ probability.

978-0-07-090894-9

5. Complete the table.

Fraction	Decimal	Percent
a) $\frac{1}{4}$		
b) $\frac{1}{5}$		
c)	0.4	
d)	0.65	
e)		80%

6. Create and label a bar graph for the "perfect world" results for rolling 2 dice exactly 36 times. What totals do you get?

7. a) You flip 4 coins at the same time. What different ways can the coins land? List all combinations.

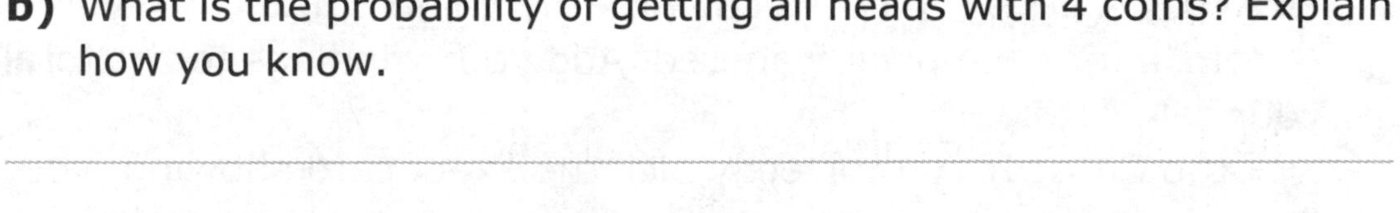

b) What is the probability of getting all heads with 4 coins? Explain how you know.

Task: Play Klass Kasino

The following activity is designed to simulate the way that many games of chance are set up. You don't have to play.

The goal of any lottery, casino, or other gambling game is to have some winners and a *lot* of losers. While the games are designed to entertain, their main goal is to make money. Lots of it.

In this game, each student who wishes to participate has a calculator and enters the number 100. This represents the maximum number of points each student has to wager.

- You have 100 points to wager. Enter 100 in a calculator.
- For each round, you choose how many points you wish to wager.
- In this game, your teacher will cut a deck of cards to reveal 1 card.
- You can play 1 of 4 games on each cut of the cards. The games are:
  - Pick the Colour
  - Pick the Suit
  - Pick the Value
  - Pick the Card
- Each game has a different set of point values.
  - Pick the Colour: If you correctly pick the colour of the card showing, you win **1 point** for each point wagered. Add your winnings to the total on your calculator.
  - Pick the Suit: If you correctly pick the suit of the card, you win **2 points** for each point wagered. Add your winnings to the total on your calculator.
  - Pick the Value: If you correctly pick the value of the card, you win **8 points** for each point wagered. Add your winnings to the total on your calculator.
  - Pick the Card: If you correctly pick the exact card showing, you win **20 points** for each point wagered. Add your winnings to the total on your calculator.
- If you lose a game, **deduct the number of points wagered** from the total on your calculator.

978-0-07-090894-9

Date ______________________

Money Matters Glossary

Write the definition for each key term as you learn about it. Provide an example.

Key Terms		
amortization period	fixed term	Schedule 1
balanced budget	gross pay	T1
budget	landlord	T4
budget template	lease	taxable income
Canada Pension Plan (CPP)	lessee	tax credit
	lessor	tax deduction
Canada Revenue Agency (CRA)	mortgage	TD1
	net pay	tenancy agreement
deposit	non-essential expenses	tenant
down payment		term
Employment Insurance (EI)	ON428	unit price
	parties	utilities
essential expenses	post-dated cheque	variable expenses
fixed expenses	premium	variable rate mortgage
fixed rate mortgage	real estate	

Glossary

Term	Definition

Date ____________________

Term	Definition

978-0-07-090894-9

Date ______________________

Term	Definition

Glossary

Date ______________________

Term	Definition

Glossary

978-0-07-090894-9

Date

Term	Definition

Glossary

Date

Term	Definition

Glossary

978-0-07-090894-9

Date

2 Budgets

Chapter 2

1. Why can't the boy on the right go to the movie?

2. How could this situation be avoided?

Tech Tip: Using the TVM Solver

Since these calculations involve money, turn on the graphing calculator and press **MODE, ↓→→→, ENTER** to set all calculations to 2 decimal places.

Press **APPS, ENTER, ENTER** to access the TVM solver.

```
N=0.00
I%=0.00
PV=0.00
PMT=0.00
FV=0.00
P/Y=1.00
C/Y=1.00
PMT:END BEGIN
```

Example 1:
Esteban and Suzanne want to take their sons on a vacation to Florida in 1 year. They estimate the trip will cost $2500. They have an account that pays 3% interest per year, compounded monthly. Determine the amount they will need to deposit into the account at the end of each month to reach their goal.

- N is the number of payments, so N = ______.
- I% is the interest rate in percent, so I% = ______.
- PV is the Present Value (or the amount today), so PV = ______.
- PMT stands for Payment. PMT is the number we want to calculate, so for now, let PMT = 0.
- FV is the ________________________, so FV = ______.
- P/Y is for payments per year, so P/Y = ______.
- C/Y is the number of times the interest is compounded in 1 year, so C/Y = ______.
- The last line deals with when payments are made, so END needs to be highlighted. For all problems in this unit, payment will be made at the end of the pay period.

After you set all of the variables, the calculator does the work. Scroll up to PMT and press **ALPHA, ENTER**. This directs the calculator to SOLVE for the payment. PMT = $ ________.

Notice that the answer is negative. The TVM solver distinguishes between money received (+) and money given (−). The negative value makes sense since each payment is money that Esteban and Suzanne give up.

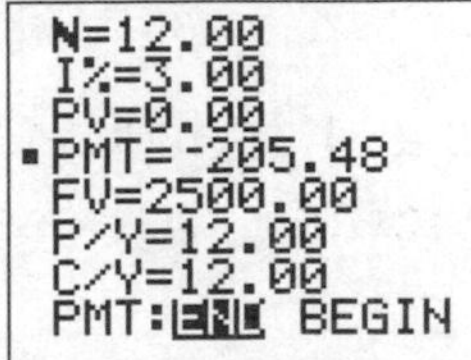

 978-0-07-090894-9

Practice

1. Jesse wants to have a party for his girlfriend's birthday in 6 weeks. He estimates it will cost him $500 for snacks, drinks, and entertainment. His savings account pays 2% interest per year, compounded monthly. How much money does he need to save weekly? PMT = $ ________.

2. Tatiana wants to buy a surround-sound system for her TV. She wants it in time for her vacation, in 4 months. It costs $1100. Her account pays 1.8% interest per year, compounded monthly. How much does she need to save each month?

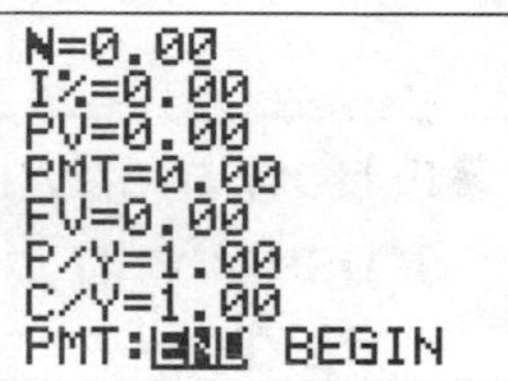

PMT = $ ______________.

Example 2:

Carrie and Bill want to build a deck and landscape their backyard. They estimate it will cost $4000. Their account pays 2.5% interest per year, compounded monthly. They can afford to save $325 per month.

```
▪N=12.17
 I%=2.50
 PV=0.00
 PMT=-325.00
 FV=4000.00
 P/Y=12.00
 C/Y=12.00
 PMT:END BEGIN
```

- N stands for ________________________ (skip for now)
- I% stands for ________________________, so I% = ______.
- PV stands for ________________________, so PV = ______.
- PMT stands for ________________________, so PMT = ______.
- FV stands for ________________________, so FV = ______.
- P/Y stands for ________________________, so P/Y = ______.
- C/Y stands for ________________________, so C/Y = ______.

Practice

3. a) How long will it take Carrie and Bill to save $4000? N = ______.

b) What payment would they need to make if they already had $1000 saved? PMT = $ ________.

c) If the interest rate is lowered to 1.4%, how long will it take? N = ______.

d) If the interest rate is 1.4% and they only have 8 months to save, how much would they need to save each month?

PMT = $ ________.

Date

2.1 Savings Plans

Focus: percent, using technology, planning, goal setting

Warm Up	
1. About how many days are in 6 months? ______	**2.** What is 10% of **a)** 70? ______ **b)** 120? ______
3. How many pay periods are usually in 1 year if you are paid **a)** weekly? ______ **b)** bi-weekly? ______ **c)** monthly? ______	**4.** What is 10% of **a)** 238? ______ **b)** 119.20? ______ **c)** 473.92? ______
5. What do the following TVM solver abbreviations stand for? **a)** PV ______ **b)** FV ______	**6.** Explain the difference between the 2 variables in #5. ______ ______ ______ ______

Chapter 2

Planning for the Future

- Long-term financial goals help you manage your money.
- You need to plan ahead to buy a house, go on vacation, get out of debt, or go back to school.

1. a) What are your financial goals in the next 5 years?

______

______

b) What major purchases do you see in your future?

______

______

978-0-07-090894-9

c) Investigate the cost of 1 of these goals or purchases.

d) List the steps you could start taking right now to reach this goal.

e) Compare your goals and plans with a partner.

2. Jaspreet is saving for a vacation to Halifax with her friends. She puts $2 a day into a glass jar on her night table.

a) Approximately how much will Jaspreet save in 30 days?

b) Approximately how much will she save in 6 months?

c) How much will she have in 1 year?

d) State 1 advantage and 1 disadvantage of Jaspreet's savings method.

3. Jasira is going to college next year to study culinary arts. She has 1 year to save $3000. Calculate the amount she needs to save from each paycheque if she is paid

a) weekly

b) bi-weekly

c) monthly

4. Caleb needs to buy snow tires for his truck. They will cost $1000.

a) If he saves $120 each week, will he have enough to buy the tires in 6 weeks?

____

____

____

b) How much will Caleb have to save each week in order to buy the snow tires in 6 weeks?

____

____

Chapter 2

5. In 9 months, Rob wants to purchase a $1200 snowboard. He has an account that pays 2.5% interest per year, compounded monthly. Use a TVM solver to determine how much he should put in the account each month.

N: ________, **I%:** ________, **PV:** ________, **PMT:** ____________,
FV: ________, **P/Y:** ________, **C/Y:** ________, **PMT: END BEGIN**

6. a) Find an article about financial planning on the Internet or in a print resource. Read the article.

b) Describe the attitude of the author toward financial planning.

____

____

c) How does the author use statistics to promote the ideas in the article?

____

____

Go to pages 45–50 to write the definitions for **gross pay** and **net pay** in your own words.

- **Gross pay** is an employee's total earnings before deductions, such as income tax, are taken off. An employee who makes $9.50/h and works 10 hours has a gross pay of $95.
- **Net pay** is gross pay after all deductions are taken off.

 978-0-07-090894-9

7. Last spring, Rhys started working after school. The table shows the amounts of his first 4 paycheques.

Pay Date	Net Pay	Amount Saved
March 17	$212.98	$21.30
March 31	$244.30	
April 14	$192.09	
April 28	$263.87	

a) Rhys saved 10% of his net pay. Calculate the amount he saved from each paycheque. Write your answers in the chart. The first one is done for you.

b) Estimate the average amount Rhys can save each month.

____

c) Rhys is saving for a $1500 motorcycle. Use a TVM solver to determine how many months it will take him to reach his goal. He has an account that earns 2% interest, compounded monthly.

N: ________, **I%:** ________, **PV:** ________, **PMT:** ____________,
FV: ________, **P/Y:** ________, **C/Y:** ________, **PMT: END BEGIN**

☑ Check Your Understanding

1. Jackson works part-time and earns about $450 every 2 weeks. He wants to buy a $6000 motorcycle. Design a savings plan for Jackson. He wants to buy his motorcycle within 1 year.

N: ________, **I%:** ________, **PV:** ________, **PMT:** ____________,
FV: ________, **P/Y:** ________, **C/Y:** ________, **PMT: END BEGIN**

Date ______________________

2.2 Slicing Up the Pie

Focus: number sense, proportional reasoning, interpreting and displaying data

Warm Up

1. Solve without a calculator.

a) 40 is what percent of 80? ______

b) 20 is what percent of 80? ______

c) 10 is what percent of 80? ______

d) 50 is what percent of 80? ______

2. Complete the chart.

Fraction	Percent	Decimal
$\frac{9}{10}$		
	35%	
		0.08

3. Solve without a calculator.

a) 22% of $100 ______

b) 22% of $200 ______

c) 22% of $300 ______

4. What is 10% of

a) $212.60? ______

b) $348.71? ______

5. An employee being paid bi-weekly receives ______ or ______ pays per month.

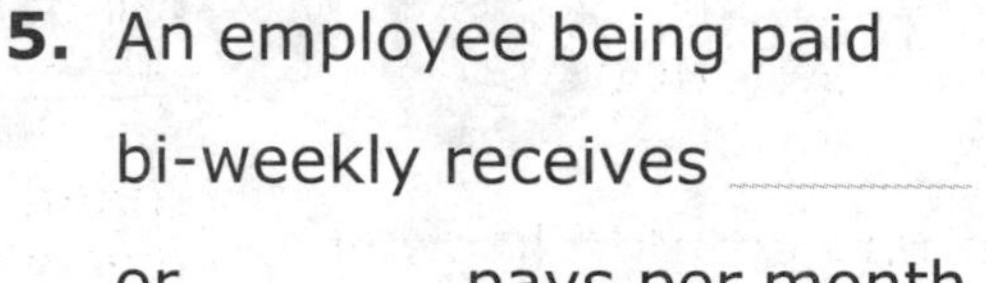

6. Explain why there are 2 possible answers for #5.

____

____

Chapter 2

Managing Your Money

- Many people spend more time planning a party than managing their money.
- Whether you rent a basement apartment or own a large house, you can predict and manage most of your income and many of your expenses.

1. Brainstorm some household and living expenses you or your family might pay in a typical month.

____

____

____

978-0-07-090894-9

Date ______________________

- **Essential expenses** are not optional. These include such things as groceries.
- **Non-essential expenses** *are* optional. Going to the movies or out to dinner is a non-essential expense.

Go to pages 45–50 to write the definitions for **essential expense** and **non-essential expense** in your own words. Give an example of each.

2. Classify your list of expenses from #1 as either essential or non-essential.

Essential Expenses		Non-Essential Expenses	

Chapter 2

- **Fixed expenses** are paid at the same time each week or each month. They are generally the same amount from payment to payment.
- **Variable expenses** are expenses that can change in their frequency or their amount.

Go to pages 45–50 to write the definitions for **fixed expenses** and **variable expenses** in your own words. Give an example of each.

3. Classify your list of expenses from #1 as either fixed or variable.

Fixed Expenses		Variable Expenses	

4. Dylan graduated from high school last year and works full-time at a job that pays $11.25/h. He lives with his parents. He drives his own car, which will be paid in full in about 1 year.

a) Assuming he works 40 hours per week, calculate Dylan's bi-weekly gross income.

b) Dylan's net earnings are about 85% of his gross earnings. What is his approximate bi-weekly net pay?

c) Dylan saves 10% of his net pay in a long-term savings account. How much does he put into the account each pay?

d) Estimate the amount that he will deposit into this account in 1 year.

e) Most months, Dylan's total take-home pay is $ ________.

f) Some months, his total take-home pay is $ ________.

g) Dylan pays his parents $300 per month to help with household expenses. In a 2-pay month, $300 is approximately ____% of Dylan's net earnings.

h) In a 3-pay month, $300 is approximately ____% of his net earnings.

i) List Dylan's possible car-related expenses. Circle the fixed expenses.

978-0-07-090894-9

- A **budget** is an organized income and spending plan.

Go to pages 45–50 to write the definition for **budget** in your own words.

5. a) Hafeeza lives with her young son. Her monthly expenses are listed in the chart below. Determine the percent of her total income for each expense. Round all calculations to the nearest percent.

Item	Amount ($)	Calculation	Percent of Income
Rent	635		
Food	250		
Daycare	300		
Savings	100		
Phone	50		
Car loan	115		
Car insurance	105		
Gas & other car expenses	180		
Gifts, charities	50		
Vacation fund	50		
Clothing	100		
Entertainment	75		
Total			

b) Circle the non-essential items in Hafeeza's budget. Draw a rectangle around the fixed items.

c) What is the total amount budgeted for

essential items? $________ variable items? $________

d) Hafeeza is planning a trip with her son to Montreal to visit family. She estimates the vacation will cost $1000. If she starts the vacation fund today, when will she have enough saved?

Chapter 2

6. Kaylee works part-time after school and on weekends. She earns $120 per week. She is learning how to manage her money by tracking her expenses.

a) Determine Kaylee's total expenses for each week in October. Then, calculate the total of each item for all 4 weeks.

Week of →	**October 1–7**	**October 8–14**	**October 15–21**	**October 22–28**	
Item ↓	**Amount ($)**				**Total**
Lunches	25.00	20.00	19.00	23.00	
Clothes		32.75		45.60	
Mom	20.00	20.00	20.00	20.00	
Going out	18.00	12.00	35.00	32.00	
Phone			44.30		
Miscellaneous	17.54	16.00	20.00	13.50	
Saving	39.46	19.25	−18.30	−3.50	
Total					

b) Explain the negative amounts in Kaylee's savings.

c) Explain "Miscellaneous."

d) Make 3 suggestions that Kaylee can use in November to improve her situation.

Chapter 2

 978-0-07-090894-9

Date

e) Determine the average amount spent each week for each category. Then, determine the percent of Kaylee's total income spent in each category. Round calculations to the nearest percent.

To find the weekly average, divide the 4-week total by 4.

Item	4-Week Total	Weekly Average	Percent of Total Income
Lunches			
Clothes			
Mom			
Going out			
Phone			
Miscellaneous			
Savings			

Chapter 2

f) Some people prefer to see data in a graph. Create a circle graph showing the Percent of Total Income column. Estimate the size of each pie slice.

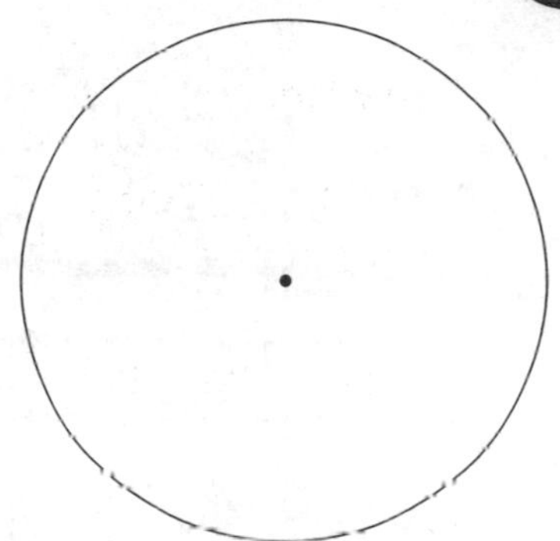

g) Use the Tech Tip on pages 52–53 to create a spreadsheet that displays Kaylee's expenses on a circle graph. Compare the accuracy of your sketch to the graph created by the computer.

☑ Check Your Understanding

1. You have organized Kaylee's budget information in several ways.

a) How can a circle graph help you interpret how you spend your money? ______________________

____

b) How can a spreadsheet help you interpret how you spend your money? ______________________

____

Tech Tip: Using a Spreadsheet

The following instructions are for use with Microsoft Excel. Other spreadsheet programs will use similar commands.

1. Open the program so that a blank sheet appears.

2. In this Tech Tip, you will use the data in #6 on pages 62–63.

a) Type "Week of" in cell A1. Press **Tab** to move 1 cell to the right (to B1). Type "Oct 1–7," press **Tab**, and continue entering the rest of the data in that row.

Save your work.

b) Press **Enter** and you should move directly to cell A2. Otherwise, move the cursor to A2. You can leave out the "Item, Amount, Total" row. Enter the rest of the data. Enter 0 where you see blanks to indicate no spending.

3. Your spreadsheet should now look like this.

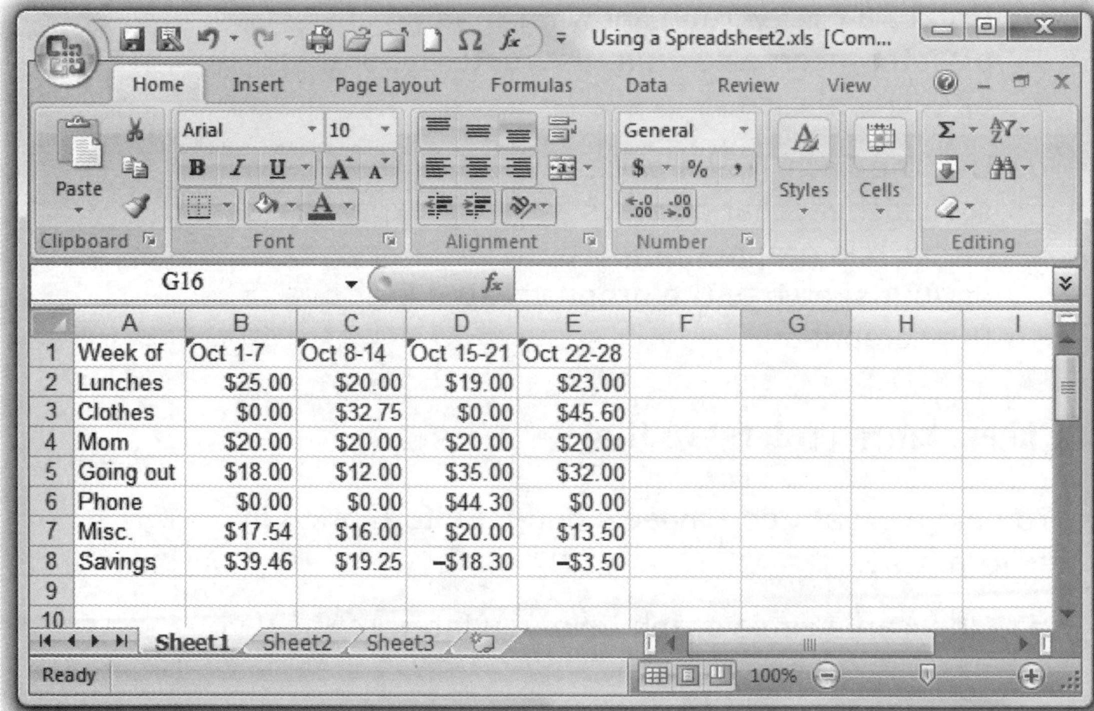

	A	B	C	D	E
1	Week of	Oct 1-7	Oct 8-14	Oct 15-21	Oct 22-28
2	Lunches	$25.00	$20.00	$19.00	$23.00
3	Clothes	$0.00	$32.75	$0.00	$45.60
4	Mom	$20.00	$20.00	$20.00	$20.00
5	Going out	$18.00	$12.00	$35.00	$32.00
6	Phone	$0.00	$0.00	$44.30	$0.00
7	Misc.	$17.54	$16.00	$20.00	$13.50
8	Savings	$39.46	$19.25	–$18.30	–$3.50

a) Bring the cursor above the letter B. The plus-sign cursor should change to a downward pointing arrow. Click and drag to highlight columns B through F.

 978-0-07-090894-9

b) Right click, select **Format Cells**, and click on **Currency**. Make sure that Decimal places is 2 and the Symbol is $. Click **OK**. Your spreadsheet will now display the data as money values.

Save

4. a) Click on cell **B9**. Click on the **Σ** symbol in the top toolbar. The cells B1 to B8 should be highlighted. Press **Enter**. $120.00 should appear in B9.
Alternatively, click and drag to highlight the cells you wish to add, and then click **Σ**.

Some spreadsheet programs will show a small triangle in the top corner of the cell. This shows you that the cell has been programmed for a specific function.

b) Program the spreadsheet to total the data on the rows *and* columns so that there are appropriate values in cells C9 to E9 and cells F2 to F8.

c) Program F9 to total the cells above it or to its left. $480.00 should appear.

Save

5. To create a circle graph, click and drag to highlight cells A2 to A8. Hold the **Ctrl** key while you highlight cells F2 to F8.

6. a) Click **Insert** and select **Pie** or **Chart**. Select the first option under 2-D Pie.

b) Click anywhere on the graph to highlight. Click **Layout**, **Data Labels**, **More Data Label Options**. Select the options of your choice. Try different displays or combinations. Print your finished graph.

7. Click on **Sheet 2** and create a circle graph with the following data.

a) In A1 type "Month." In A2 to A13 type the months of the year in order.

b) In B1 type "Gasoline." In B2 to B13 enter $75, $66, $112, $90, $123, $109, $265, $134, $122, $180, $105, $127.

c) Try other displays, for example, a bar graph or a line graph. Look at the displays of other students. Which display do you like best for this type of data? ______

Date

2.3 Track Your Spending

Focus: planning, goal setting, number sense, interpreting and displaying data

Warm Up	
1. You have been keeping track of your spending for several weeks. How much did you spend on entertainment?	**2.** What forms of entertainment did you spend money on?
3. What is an advantage to tracking your expenses?	**4.** Add. **a)** \$134 + \$26 = \$ **b)** \$21 + \$72 = \$ **c)** \$56 + \$29 = \$

Chapter 2

Analysing Your Data

- Now that you have been tracking your spending, you should have a good understanding of how you spend your money.

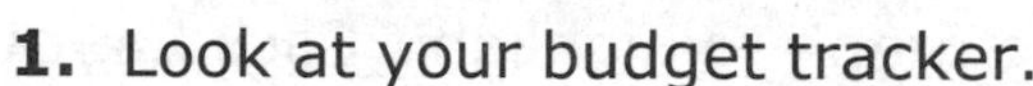

1. Look at your budget tracker.

a) List the essential items you have purchased.

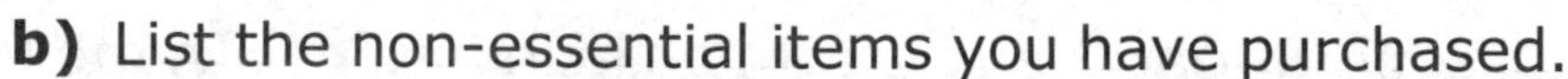

b) List the non-essential items you have purchased.

2. Discuss your list with several peers.

a) What items do you consider essential that one of the others considers non-essential?

b) What items do you consider non-essential that one of the others considers essential?

 978-0-07-090894-9

Date ______________________

3. a) What regular payments do you make?

____

b) Which of these are fixed?

____

c) Which of these are variable?

____

- Many people group their expenses by category.
- Housing, transportation, and food make up the largest amount of many budgets.
- Some people think that clothing, entertainment, and gifts are even more important.
- Create a number of categories to group similar items that you spent money on. Refer back to Section 2.2 for some additional examples.

4. Determine the total spent for each category. Use the table below as an organizer.

Week of						
Category	**Amount ($)**					**Total**
Total						

5. **a)** Enter the data from the table in a spreadsheet.

   b) Program the spreadsheet to calculate all totals.

   c) Create a circle graph showing the percent value of each category.

   d) Print and attach a copy of the circle graph.

Chapter 2

   e) Looking at this graph, are there areas where you might reduce your spending? List them.

   f) Are there areas where you would like to increase your spending?

6. **a)** Have you identified any spending patterns that you would like to change?

   b) State 3 things that you will do during the next month to improve your financial situation.

978-0-07-090894-9

- Many people make changes to their budget when they are saving for something important.
- Keeping a visual reminder of how much they have saved helps some people keep saving.

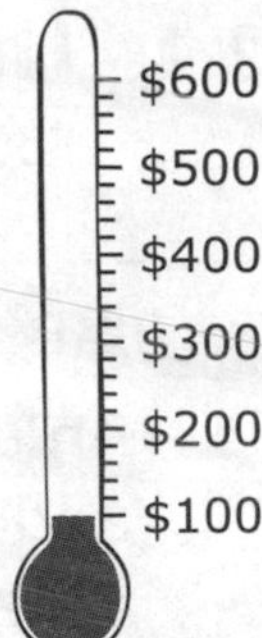

Goal: Fly to the Dominican Republic

7. a) You want to make a large purchase. Perhaps you want to buy a stereo system. Maybe you want to take a vacation in the Caribbean or visit family in another country. Research the cost of that purchase.

b) How could you change your spending habits to allow you to save for that goal?

c) How much could you save each month by taking the actions in part b)?

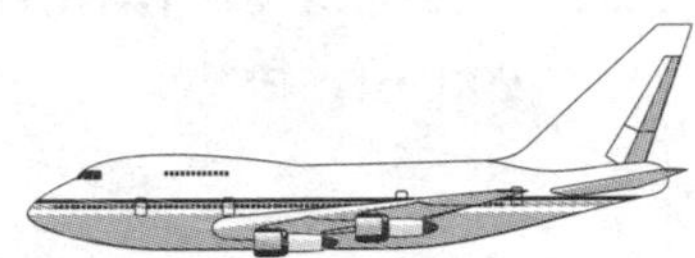

d) Predict how long it will take you to reach your goal.

8. a) With your goal in mind, set up a spreadsheet or paper template to track next month's expenses.

b) What is your goal?

c) What steps do you plan to take in the next month to help reach it?

☑ Check Your Understanding

1. Re-assess your budget in a month. Did you accomplish what you planned in #7b)?

2. What changes could you make to help you achieve your goal in the next month?

978-0-07-090894-9

Date

2.4 Living Expenses

Focus: number sense, income versus expenses

Warm Up	
1. An employee is paid weekly and was last paid April 6. When are the next 2 paydays?	**2.** An employee is paid bi-weekly and was last paid April 6. When are the next 2 paydays?
3. Round to the nearest $10. **a)** $128.75 **b)** $62.45 **c)** $206.90	**4.** Add the rounded values from #3.
5. State 2 common fixed living expenses.	**6.** State 2 common variable living expenses.

Chapter 2

Using Your Budget Template

- The car. The kids. Groceries. Saving for a house. Taking care of your living expenses doesn't have to be overwhelming.
- You need to keep track of what money comes in and manage what money goes out.
- Save some of what you make. Invest some. Give some away.

Go to pages 45–50 to write the definition for **budget template** in your own words.

1. One way of organizing your expenses is to use a **budget template**. This is a list of common sources of income and expenses. You can get them from banks, financial planners, or the Internet.

a) Go to **www.mcgrawhill.ca/books/workplace12** and follow the links to budgeting. Look at 2 different budget templates. Choose a template that looks easy to use.

b) Look at the templates collected by classmates. Discuss why each of you chose the template that you did.

978-0-07-090894-9

Date ______________________

2. Below is a list of expenses from a typical budget template.

Home	Daily Living	Transportation	Entertainment
Mortgage/rent	Groceries	Car payments	Cable or satellite TV
Utilities	Child care	Fuel	Video/DVD rentals
Home/cell phone	Dry cleaning	Insurance	Movies/plays
Internet	Dining out	Repairs	Concerts/clubs
Home repairs	Housecleaning	Car wash	Books
Home decorating	Clothing	Parking	Music: MP3s, CDs, etc.
Home security	Gifts	Public transit	
Garden supplies	Salon/barber/stylist		
Property tax	Credit card/loan payments		
Health and Recreation	**Vacations**	**Saving/ Investing**	**Dues/ Subscriptions**
Club/team/gym memberships	Travel: bus, car, plane, train	Savings accounts	Magazines
Insurance	Accommodations	RRSP	Newspapers
Prescriptions	Food	RESP	Religious organizations
Over-the-counter drugs	Souvenirs	Stocks	Charity
Veterinarians/pet medicines	Child/pet care	Other investments	
Life insurance			
Sports equipment			
Toys/child gear			

a) Circle the items that apply to you now.

b) Draw a rectangle around the items that might apply to you next year.

c) Highlight 5 essential and 5 non-essential expenses.

d) Use different colours to highlight 5 fixed expenses and 5 variable expenses.

Chapter 2

Date

3. Stephanie works part-time after school and some weekends. Her monthly budget for February is shown.

Income ($)		**Expenses ($)**			
Feb 2–16	312.61	Save for college	200	Clothes	95
Feb 17–Mar 3	290.09	Room and board	160	Cell phone	20
		Spending money	100		
Total Income =		**Total Expenses =**			
Balance (Income − Expenses) =					

a) What is Stephanie's total income? $

b) What are her total expenses? $

c) Determine Stephanie's balance. $

d) Explain the meaning of her monthly balance.

Chapter 2

4. Mario moved out of his parents' house into a 2-bedroom apartment 4 months ago. He has recorded some of his expenses on a piece of paper.

Jan 1 - first and last months' rent - $1180
Jan 7 - activate cable - $65
Jan 19 - top up cell phone - $40
Feb 1 - rent - $590
Feb 18 - gas bill - $117.40
Feb 22 - hydro bill - $86.23
Mar 1 - rent - $590
Mar 11 - cable bill - $103.06
Mar 18 - gas bill - $123.64
Mar 29 - top up cell phone - $50
Apr 1 - rent - $590
Apr 18 - gas bill - $93.68
Apr 22 - hydro bill - $92.91

978-0-07-090894-9

Date

a) Total Mario's expenses by month and by item.

Month ($)		Item ($)	
Jan	1180 + 65 + 40 = ____	**Rent**	1180 + 590 + 590 + 590 = ____
Feb		**Cable**	
Mar		**Cell phone**	
Apr		**Gas**	
		Hydro	

b) Which expenses do you think will decrease over the next few months? Explain your answer.

Which expenses will change between winter and spring?

c) Look at your budget template or the one on page 71. List expenses that Mario has left out of his budget.

d) If 1 month's rent should not exceed 1 week's net income, approximate the minimum weekly net income that Mario needs in order to be able to afford to live in this apartment.

☑ Check Your Understanding

1. a) Create a list of living expenses that a couple with a baby would have that a couple living alone would not.

b) Suggest ways the couple might adjust their budget to pay for these extra expenses.

978-0-07-090894-9

Date

2.5 Managing Change

Focus: number sense, balancing a budget

Warm Up	
1. George earns $14.50/h and works 36 hours per week. What is his bi-weekly gross income?	**2.** If George's net income is 80% of his gross income, what is his bi-weekly net income?
3. If George's monthly expenses are $1450, what is his balance in a 2-pay month?	**4.** How much money do you think George should save each month? Why?

Chapter 2

Developing a Balanced Budget

- A budget is **balanced** when the money coming in equals the money going out. The money going out can include savings and investments.

Go to pages 45–50 to write the definition for **balanced budget** in your own words.

1. a) Luca is in grade 12 and works part-time after school. His weekly earnings average $125. Write each week's earnings in the Income column below.

Income ($)	Expenses (approximate $)	
Total Income =	**Total Expenses =**	
Monthly Balance (Income − Expenses) =		

b) Each month, Luca saves $200. His car is paid for. His car insurance costs about $125. He spends about $75 on gas and about $100 on entertainment. Write the data in the Expenses column.

978-0-07-090894-9

Date ______________________

c) Complete the last 2 rows of the table for Luca's balance.

d) Luca's budget is BALANCED/NOT BALANCED because his ______________________ equals his ______________________.

- Bill is a single, 28-year-old man.
- He has a full-time job with regular bi-weekly take home pay of about $750.
- He has income from a second job of about $200 per month.
- He rents a 1-bedroom apartment for $634 per month.

- He does not own a car and uses public transportation. A transit pass costs $75 per month.
- Bill has a personal loan, which costs him $238 monthly.
- He spends about $100 per week in groceries.

Look at Section 2.4 or your budget tracker from Section 2.3.

2. a) In the table below, list other expenses that Bill might have. Estimate the monthly cost of each expense.

b) Calculate Bill's total income for a month in which he receives 2 pays from his full-time job ______________________.

c) Balance Bill's monthly budget. Keep a running total of his remaining income by deducting each expense from the total calculated in part b). How much does Bill have left for savings at the end of the month?

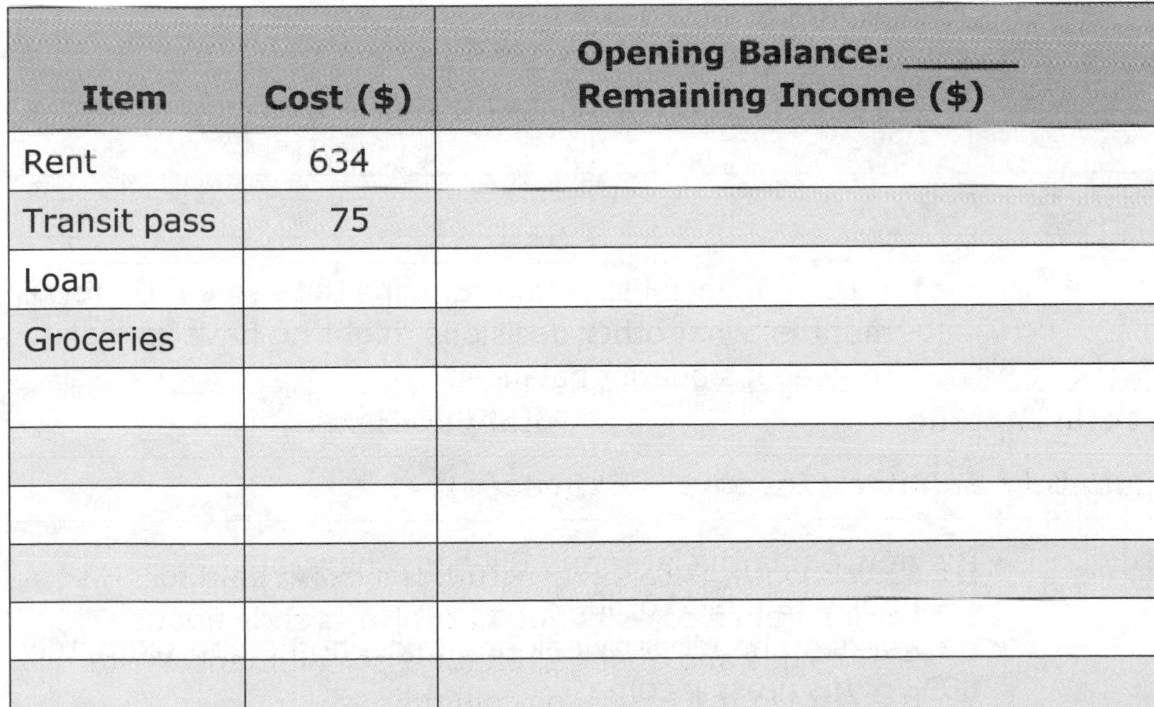

Item	Cost ($)	Opening Balance: ______ Remaining Income ($)
Rent	634	
Transit pass	75	
Loan		
Groceries		

Chapter 2

- Bill is losing his part-time job at the end of the week.

3. a) If next month is also a 2-pay month at his full-time job, calculate Bill's total income for next month ____________.

b) Which item(s) from the table in #2c) must stay the same?

____

c) Which item(s) from the table in #2c) can change?

____

d) Design a balanced budget for Bill's reduced income.

Item	Cost ($)	Opening Balance: ______ Remaining Income ($)
Rent	634	
Transit pass	75	
Loan		
Groceries		

Chapter 2

e) If Bill's financial situation remains the same for a few months, what other decisions might he have to make to keep his budget balanced?

____

____

- It's now 6 months later and Bill has a new job.
- His hourly rate is $16.50.
- He works 40 hours per week and takes home approximately 80% of his gross income.

 978-0-07-090894-9

Date ______________________

4. **a)** Calculate Bill's new weekly net income ______________.

   b) Calculate his monthly net income for a 4-pay month and for a 5-pay month ______________.

   c) If there is money left over after paying for all of his monthly expenses, what could Bill do? Prioritize your choices. ______________________

   d) Design a balanced budget for Bill with the information you know for a 4-pay month. Include the same items as you did in #2c). Feel free to add new items.

Item	Cost ($)	Opening Balance: ______ Remaining Income ($)
Rent	634	
Transit pass	75	
Loan		
Groceries		

☑ Check Your Understanding

1. Brainstorm some life changes that could affect a budget. Describe how you would adjust the budget for each life change.

Chapter 2

Date ________________

Chapter 2 Review

1. Martin wants to go to college in 1 year to study landscaping design. He needs to save $2500. Calculate the amount Martin needs to save from each paycheque if he is paid

   a) weekly

   b) bi-weekly

2. **a)** Tanika and Avi are saving $400 per month for a down payment on a house. They have an account that pays 3% interest per year, compounded monthly. In approximately how many months will they have $8000 saved?

   N: _____, **I%:** ______, **PV:** __________, **PMT:** _________,

   FV: _______, **P/Y:** _____, **C/Y:** _____, **PMT: END BEGIN**

   b) If Avi and Tanika wanted to have the $8000 down payment saved in exactly 1 year, how much would they need to save each month?

   N: _____, **I%:** ______, **PV:** __________, **PMT:** _________,

   FV: _______, **P/Y:** _____, **C/Y:** _____, **PMT: END BEGIN**

3. **a)** State 2 common fixed expenses.

   ________________ ________________

   b) State 2 common variable expenses.

   ________________ ________________

   c) State 2 common non-essential expenses.

   ________________ ________________

   d) State 2 common essential expenses.

   ________________ ________________

 978-0-07-090894-9

Date

4. Marina works part-time after school and some weekends. Her monthly budget for April is shown.

Income ($)		**Expenses ($)**			
Apr 2–16	164.55	Save for own car	100	Clothes	50
Apr 17–May 1	182.09	Spending money	75	Cell phone	20
		Car insurance	40	Gas	40
Total Income =		**Total Expenses =**			
Balance (Income − Expenses) =					

a) What is Marina's total income for April? $________

b) What are her total expenses? $________

c) Calculate her monthly balance. $________

d) Explain what is meant by having a balanced budget.

____

____

e) Marina's hours at work have been cut. She expects to lose about half of her monthly income. Estimate her income for May.

$________

f) Change Marina's budget to create a balanced budget for May.

Item	**Cost**	**Remaining Income**

Chapter 2

Date ______________________

Chapter 2 Practice Test

1. Karina plans to attend a community college in 1 year to study culinary arts. She thinks that she will need to save $4000. Calculate the amount Karina needs to save from each paycheque if she is paid

a) bi-weekly

b) weekly

2. Circle the fixed expenses. Draw a box around the non-essential expenses.

Groceries	*Car payments*	*Electricity*
Gym membership	*Bus pass*	*Pet food*
Lottery tickets	*Rent*	*Car insurance*
Digital cable TV	*Golf clubs*	*Clothing*

Chapter 2

3. Trevor holds 2 jobs. He works part-time after school and on weekends. His monthly budget for October is shown.

Income ($)		**Expenses ($)**			
Oct 4–18	272.59	Car insurance	110	Clothes	70
Oct 19–Nov 2	287.09	Money to Mom	100	Cell phone	70
		Gas	80	Saving	50
		Spending money	80		
Total Income =		**Total Expenses =**			
Balance (Income − Expenses)					

a) What is Trevor's total income for October? $__________

b) What are his total expenses? $__________

c) Calculate his monthly balance. $__________

d) Explain the meaning of a balanced budget.

____

____

978-0-07-090894-9

e) Trevor's hours at work have been cut. He expects to lose about $75 per pay. Estimate his income for next month. $________

f) Change the amount spent on each item in Trevor's budget as necessary to create a balanced budget for November.

Item	Cost	Remaining Income

4. a) A couple is saving $200 per month in an account so they can replace the roof of their house as soon as possible. The account pays 2% interest per year, compounded monthly. In approximately how many months will they have $6000 saved?

N: _____, **I%:** ______, **PV:** __________, **PMT:** _________,

FV: ________, **P/Y:** _____, **C/Y:** _____, **PMT: END BEGIN**

b) If the couple wants to have the $6000 saved in 2 years, how much would they need to save each month?

N: _____, **I%:** ______, **PV:** __________, **PMT:** _________,

FV: ________, **P/Y:** _____, **C/Y:** _____, **PMT: END BEGIN**

c) Is fixing the house roof an essential or a non-essential expense? Why do you think so?

____

____

Date

Task: Out of Control

Chapter 2

- Terry is a 43-year-old divorced man with 2 children.
- His take-home pay is $4123 per month.
- He pays $1250 per month in child support.
- He pays $1600 per month for his mortgage.
- His house insurance is about $85 monthly.
- His car insurance costs $113 every month.
- His car lease payment is $245 monthly.
- Terry has an $8500 loan. He pays $95 per month to cover the interest.
- Terry has a golf membership which costs approximately $6000 per year. He makes monthly payments.

1. Create a monthly budget for Terry. Estimate his other expenses, such as food, gas, utilities, and household items.

2. Make 2 suggestions that might help Terry improve his financial position.

 978-0-07-090894-9

Date

3 Renting Accommodations

1. What are some freedoms that come with living on your own?

2. What are some financial responsibilities that come with living on your own?

3. What issues not related to money might you have to deal with when you live on your own?

978-0-07-090894-9

Date

Tech Tip: Research Accommodations

In the past, most people used newspaper ads to look for a place to rent. Sometimes, people who had a place to rent would post a sign in the window of the building. Today, many people search the Internet for a place to rent.

1. Go to the search engine of your choice.
- Type "rent" and the name of your town/city. In most instances, this will give you a number of websites to choose from.
- If you live in a small community, you may need to enter the name of the closest city.
- Select a website and begin your search.

Name of town/city:
Websites used:

Chapter 3

2. Some websites will allow you to do an advanced search. Narrow your search according to the price, the location, the number of bedrooms, or any other criteria that are important to you.
Some criteria I will consider:
-
-
-

3. Save the information for those places that interest you. Write down several questions you might want to ask the owner.

 978-0-07-090894-9

Date ______________________

4. You may wish to walk or drive by each place that interests you. This will allow you to look at the neighbourhood and the condition of the building. Take your time. Make a list of 3 places that you would consider renting.

Possible Places	Reason

5. When you are actually in the market for a place to rent, set up appointments to view places that meet all of your criteria.
   - Take a friend or family member with you. Two or three people can notice more than you can by yourself.
   - Ask the advice of people who have experience with renting or with living on their own.

   I would like ______________ and ______________ to come with me to view apartments because

   ____

   ____

   ____

   ____

6. Do not agree to rent if you feel pressured or if you get a negative feeling from the people you are dealing with. Renting an apartment is like buying a used car. There will always be another one to choose from.

Chapter 3

Date

3.1 What's Available?

Focus: research, rental prices, percent

Warm Up	
1. Someone who earns $15 per hour earns $_______ in a 30-hour work week.	**2.** Someone who earns $15 per hour earns $_______ in a 40-hour work week.
3. What is 25% of the amount in #1?	**4.** What is 30% of the amount in #2?
5. Double the following amounts. **a)** $600 _______ **b)** $745 _______ **c)** $890 _______	**6.** Complete the following. **a)** 300 is _______% of 1000. **b)** 400 is _______% of 1600. **c)** _______ is 20% of 2000.
7. Someone with a net income of $720 per week earns $_______ in a 4-pay month.	**8.** Someone with a net income of $720 per week earns $_______ in a 5-pay month.

Chapter 3

What Are Your Choices?

1. There are many types of places to rent.
- Check off the types that might be available in your community.
- Check your local newspapers or brainstorm to add any types that are missing.

☐ detached house ☐ semi-detached house
☐ high-rise apartment ☐ basement apartment
☐ condominium ☐ room in a home
☐ _______ ☐ _______
☐ _______ ☐ _______
☐ _______ ☐ _______
☐ _______ ☐ _______
☐ _______ ☐ _______

978-0-07-090894-9

2. a) Often, people choose where to live based on their current needs. These needs can change throughout life. Check the boxes that are important to you when choosing a place to live now.

- ☐ close to schools
- ☐ close to a college
- ☐ 1 bedroom
- ☐ 2 bedrooms
- ☐ close to work
- ☐ close to shopping
- ☐ close to public transit
- ☐ parking available
- ☐ close to a highway
- ☐ close to main roads
- ☐ close to downtown
- ☐ close to parks
- ☐ close to family
- ☐ close to friends
- ☐ in the city
- ☐ on a quiet street
- ☐ ____________
- ☐ ____________

b) What streets or neighbourhoods in your community would best suit your choices from part a)?

c) What life events could make you re-evaluate your choices from parts a) and b)?

Chapter 3

3. a) Describe your dream place. Include things that are important to you, such as the size of your room or being close to stores or friends.

b) Which of the things in part a) are the most important to you? Explain your answer.

978-0-07-090894-9

- Some financial planners suggest that monthly rent should not be greater than your net weekly income.

4. For a 4-pay month, monthly rent should not be greater than _____% of your net monthly income.

5. a) To be able to afford $600 in monthly rent, you would need to earn __________ net per week.

b) If you work 40 hours per week, you would need a job that pays you __________ per hour.

c) If you work 30 hours per week, you would need a job that pays __________ per hour.

d) Complete the chart.

Monthly Rent	Weekly Earnings Needed	Wage Needed If Working 40 Hours Per Week	Wage Needed If Working 30 Hours Per Week
$500			
$800			
$1000			

e) State 2 ways in which someone who does not earn $600 per week could afford a place that costs $600 per month.

____

____

6. a) Jacob earns $800 net per week. What is his net monthly income in a 4-pay month?

b) Jacob lives alone in a 1-bedroom apartment. His monthly rent is $700. What percent of his net monthly income is spent on rent? Assume a 4-pay month.

978-0-07-090894-9

Date

7. a) Simone earns $800 net per week. What is her net monthly income in a 4-pay month?

b) Simone lives alone in a 2-bedroom townhouse. Her monthly rent is $950. What percent of her net monthly income is spent on rent? Assume a 4-pay month.

c) What could Simone do to make her monthly rent more affordable?

8. a) Joey and Michel share a 2-bedroom basement apartment. The monthly rent is $900. What fraction of the monthly rent must each pay? Explain your thinking.

b) Calculate the amount of rent each boy must pay, based on your answer for part a).

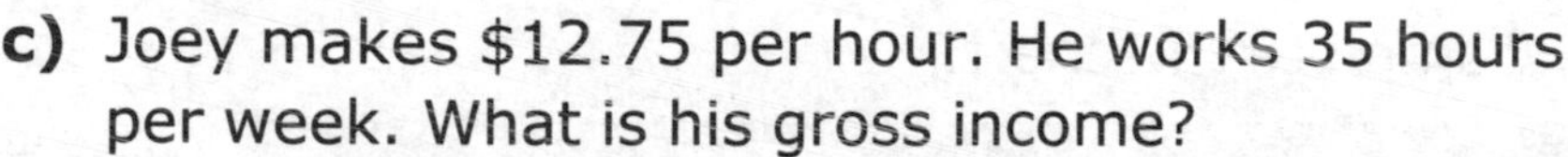

c) Joey makes $12.75 per hour. He works 35 hours per week. What is his gross income?

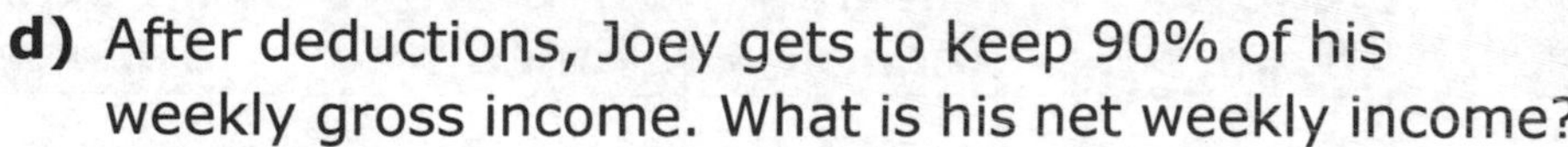

d) After deductions, Joey gets to keep 90% of his weekly gross income. What is his net weekly income?

e) What is Joey's net monthly income? Assume a 4-pay month.

f) What percent of Joey's net monthly income is spent on rent?

g) Explain why having a roommate can help make a place to live more affordable.

9. Dinara and Sharon rent a 2-bedroom house. Dinara earns $500 net per week. Sharon earns $650 net per week. Their monthly rent is $1200. Each pays $600 per month in rent.

a) What percent of Dinara's monthly net income is spent on rent?

b) What percent of Sharon's monthly net income is spent on rent?

c) Is it fair that each pays $600 per month in rent? Why or why not?

____

____

____

____

Chapter 3

10. a) What is your current total monthly income? If you do not have a monthly income, use an amount of $1600. __________

b) Complete the chart.

20% of My Monthly Income	25% of My Monthly Income	30% of My Monthly Income	35% of My Monthly Income	40% of My Monthly Income

c) What is the minimum amount you would consider spending on rent each month? Explain your thinking.

____

____

____

 978-0-07-090894-9

Date

d) What is the maximum amount you would consider spending on rent each month? Explain your thinking.

☑ Check Your Understanding

1. Use a local publication (newspaper, rental magazine) or go to **www.mcgrawhill.ca/books/workplace12** and follow the links to rental accommodation websites.

- Select 3 places in your community that you would consider renting.
- Describe each place.
- Justify your choices based on your answers to #2, #3, and #4.

Choice 1.

Choice 2.

Choice 3.

Chapter 3

Date ______________

3.2 Preparing to Move

Focus: proportional reasoning, estimation

Warm Up	
1. A package of 6 rolls of paper towels costs $2.29. What is the cost of a single roll? This is also called the unit price.	**2.** A package of 12 rolls of paper towels costs $3.99. What is the unit price?
3. Based on #1 and #2, which package is the better buy?	**4.** The combined tax on most purchases in Ontario is ________ % of the total cost.
5. Calculate the tax on the package of paper towels that is the better buy.	**6.** What is the total cost of the package of paper towels that is the better buy?

Chapter 3

Start With a Checklist

- You need to do some planning before you move out on your own.
- Your plan might consist of a checklist of things to do or to buy before, during, or after moving.
- You will also need to budget for the move so that you can pay for moving expenses.

1. a) If you currently live with your family, start by listing the items you could take with you if you moved out tomorrow. If you currently live on your own, list the items you had when you first moved out.

____

____

____

b) Describe 2 ways that having a moving plan can make moving easier.

____

____

978-0-07-090894-9

Date ____________________

2. a) Go to **www.mcgrawhill.ca/books/workplace12** and follow the links to moving checklists. Select a checklist that you like. Read through the checklist and circle items you might need to plan for before you move. Save an electronic copy of the checklist, or print a copy.

b) Some of the items that you selected in part a) may cost money. These could include:

- having Canada Post forward your mail to your new address
- renting a van to move your furniture
- having keys cut

Enter these items and their estimated costs in the chart. Estimate the total cost of the items.

Item	Estimated Cost
Total Estimated Cost	

c) Is there a way you could reduce the estimated costs of the items in the chart? Explain.

____

____

____

Date ______________________

3. You find the following ad in the local newspaper.
- Use the floor plan of the apartment and the information in the ad to decide what items you will need if you move there.
- List the items below or write directly on the diagram. Circle the items you already have.
- Do not include everyday items such as groceries or cosmetics.

____

____

____

____

Apartments For Rent: $800 Per Month

Clean, bright, unfurnished, 2-bedroom apartments for rent

- Balcony overlooking a park
- Blinds on all windows and sliding doors
- Plenty of storage space
- Large walk-in closet
- Large bathroom with tub/shower combination, sink, and toilet
- New laminate flooring in all rooms

Rent includes:
- 2 appliances (refrigerator and stove)
- Utilities (heat, electricity, and water)

Located at 123 Main Street
Close to schools, shopping, and public transit

Laundry and gym facilities in basement of building
Parking available

Pets not allowed

Call (555) 555-6203 for a viewing

 978-0-07-090894-9

Date

Chapter 3

Date

- Setting up your first apartment can be expensive.
- You will need to buy everyday items such as personal care items and groceries.
- You will also need kitchen or bathroom items such as cleaning supplies, towels, and pots and pans.
- If you rent an unfurnished apartment, you may also need to buy furniture such as a bed, couch, and chairs.

4. a) Where could you go to buy items to set up your apartment?

b) Browse flyers and websites for the locations you identified in part a). Find 10 kitchen or bathroom items you will need to buy to set up the apartment from #3. Complete the chart with the information you have found.

Chapter 3

Item	Estimated Cost
Total Estimated Cost	

978-0-07-090894-9

5. a) If you had a budget of $1000 to furnish your apartment, what would you buy? Complete the Item and Estimated Cost columns in the chart.

Item	Estimated Cost	Location	Actual Cost
Total Estimated Cost		**Total Actual Cost**	

b) Research the actual cost of each item from various locations. Decide where you would make your purchases. Complete the Location and Actual Cost columns in the chart.

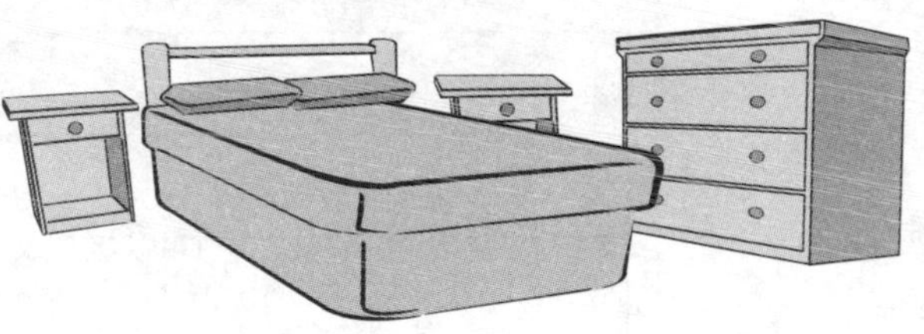

c) Was your budget of $1000 enough to purchase all the items you wanted in part a)? ____________

d) What are some ways you could get some of the items from part a) that you did not have enough money to buy?

____

____

Chapter 3

Go to **www.mcgrawhill.ca/books/workplace12** and follow the links to Classified Ads to access several sources of used or free furniture online.

- It may be cheaper to borrow, rent, or buy used items such as furniture when you are setting up your apartment.
- Items can be borrowed, rented from rental centres, or bought used at a thrift store or through a classified ad.

6. a) Take a second look at the items you chose in #5. Research the cost of renting, borrowing, or buying used from various locations. Complete the chart.

Item	Cost to Buy New	Location	Cost to Borrow, Rent, or Buy Used
Total Cost New		**Alternative Cost**	

b) Calculate how much money you could save by borrowing, renting, or buying these items used.

7. a) What items do you own that you could not store inside the apartment?

978-0-07-090894-9

b) Where could you store the item(s) listed in part a)?

☑ Check Your Understanding

1. State 2 advantages and 2 disadvantages of living on your own.

2. State how you could calculate the monthly rent you would be able to afford.

3. What math skills do you think are an important part of being able to manage living on your own?

4. Create a list of all of the people, businesses, and organizations that you would give a Change of Address notice to.

Skills Practice 3: Comparing Rental Prices

Fields Rental Properties
Best prices around!
Two-bedroom apartments starting from $775/month, plus utilities.
Parking extra.

Harbour Side Apartments
2-bedroom apartments from $895/month.
Heat, hydro, water, and parking included!

- Compare these two ads.
- Which advertises the lower monthly price?

1. a) What is the rent for the lowest-priced apartment at Harbour Side Apartments? ________

b) What is the cost of the following extras at Harbour Side Apartments?

heat ________ water ________

hydro ________ parking ________

c) What is the total cost of renting the least expensive 2-bedroom apartment at Harbour Side Apartments? ________

2. a) Different companies have different billing schedules for their customers. Leo rents an apartment at Fields Rental Properties. The chart lists his monthly expenses and billing frequency. Complete the chart.

Expense	Billing Frequency	Rounded Amount per Bill	Annual Total Cost	Average Monthly Cost
Hydro	Bi-monthly	$130		
Heat	Monthly	$90		
Water	Quarterly	$220		
Parking	Monthly	$25		

 978-0-07-090894-9

b) What is the total monthly cost of renting an apartment at Fields Rental Properties? ______

3. a) Which ad appears to advertise the lower monthly price?

______

b) Which ad actually offers the lower monthly price?

______

c) Suggest reasons why the place that appears to be less expensive is actually more expensive.

______

______

______

d) Rewrite both ads. Use more accurate wording.

Skills Practice 4: Writing a Cheque for Rent

- There are many ways to pay for things, including writing a cheque.
- A cheque is a substitute for cash.

A Blank Cheque

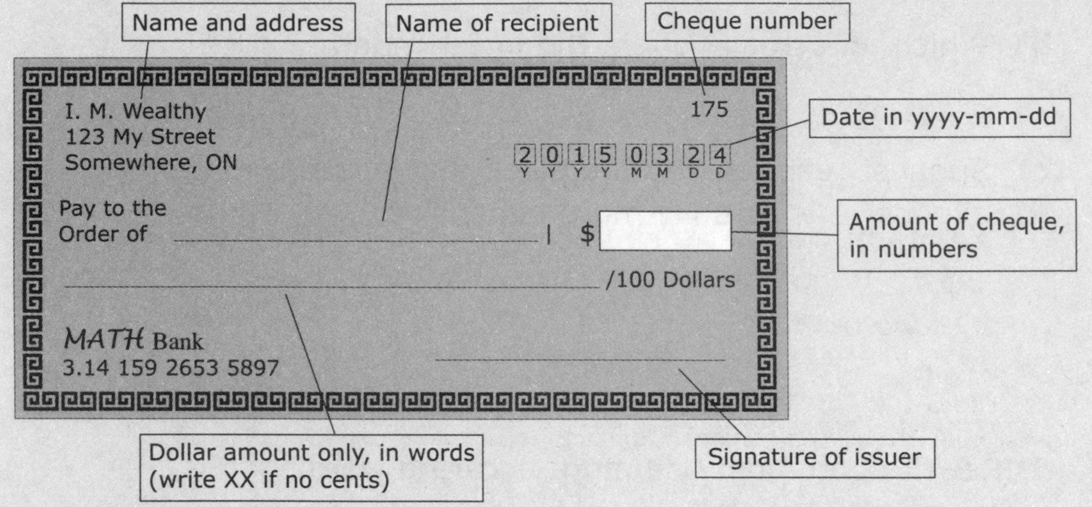

Example of a Completed Cheque

The **issuer** is the person who writes the cheque.
The **recipient** is the person or business who receives the money.

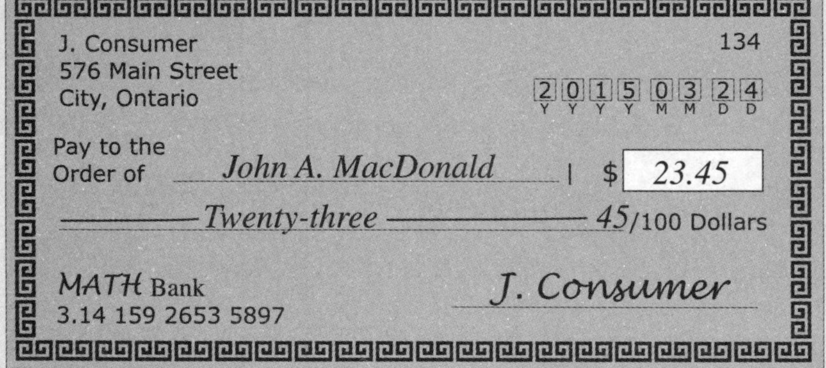

1. a) Who is the issuer of the completed cheque? ______

b) Who is the recipient of the completed cheque? ______

c) What amount is the cheque for? ______

2. Why is the amount on the cheque written in numbers and in words? ______

______

978-0-07-090894-9

Date

3. On some cheques, the date is shown in numerical form. For example, yyyy/mm/dd.

The numerical form of a date can have a different order on some cheques. For example, mm/dd/yyyy.

   a) What do these letters represent?

   b) Write August 19 of this year in yyyy/mm/dd format.

   c) Write May 8 of this year in yyyy/mm/dd format.

4. You want to rent an apartment for $650 per month.

   a) Your first cheque will be for the first and last month's rent. Calculate how much you need to pay and complete the cheque below.

   b) Write the cheque below for the second month's rent.

190
2 0
Y Y Y Y M M D D
Pay to the
Order of
$
/100 Dollars
MATH Bank
3.14 159 2653 5897

Date _______________

3.3 Looking for the Better Buy

Focus: unit price, unit conversion, decision making

Warm Up	
1. List 3 grocery items sold by weight. **a)** ____________ **b)** ____________ **c)** ____________	**2.** List 3 grocery items sold by volume. **a)** ____________ **b)** ____________ **c)** ____________
3. List 3 items found in a grocery store that are perishable. **a)** ____________ **b)** ____________ **c)** ____________	**4.** Solve without using a calculator. **a)** $750 \div 1000 =$ ______ **b)** $7200 \div 1000 =$ ______ **c)** $250 \div 1000 =$ ______
5. Complete the following unit conversions. **a)** 1 L = ______ mL **b)** 1 kg = ______ g **c)** 500 mL = ______ L **d)** 100 g = ______ kg	**6.** Solve without using a calculator. **a)** $0.355 \times 1000 =$ ______ **b)** $1.89 \times 1000 =$ ______ **c)** $1.14 \times 1000 =$ ______ **d)** $0.473 \times 1000 =$ ______

Chapter 3

How to Determine the Better Buy

- Sometimes, you have to stock up on items, especially if this is your first time living on your own. Stock up on the things you use regularly. This can include paper towels, razor blades, soap, toothpaste, and toilet paper.
- Stores have many different choices. How can you tell which one to buy? One way is by using the **unit price**. The unit price represents the cost of a single item in a group, even when a single item cannot be purchased.
- It may be just as effective to estimate total costs and compare.
- Sometimes, money doesn't enter into the decision. It depends on what you want, and why you want it.

Go to pages 45–50 to write the definition for **unit price** in your own words. Provide one example.

 978-0-07-090894-9

Date ______________

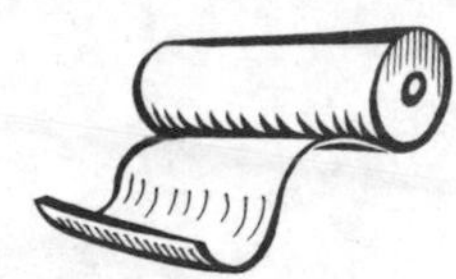

1. Ravi's Grocer grocery store sells a roll of paper towels for 79¢. Independent Mart sells 3 rolls for $2.29.

   a) Calculate the price of 3 rolls of paper towels at Ravi's Grocer.

   b) Calculate the unit price of the paper towels at Independent Mart.

   c) Which calculation do you prefer making, a) or b)? ______

   d) Would a lower unit price affect what paper towels you bought? Explain. ______________________

   ____

   e) Would a lower unit price affect where you bought paper towels? Explain. ______________________

   ____

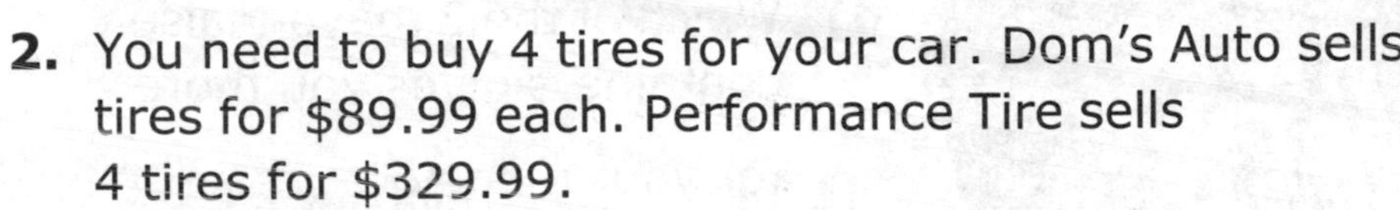

2. You need to buy 4 tires for your car. Dom's Auto sells tires for $89.99 each. Performance Tire sells 4 tires for $329.99.

   a) Calculate the price of 4 tires at Dom's Auto.

   b) Calculate the unit price of the 4 tires at Performance Tire.

   c) Which calculation do you prefer making, a) or b)? ______

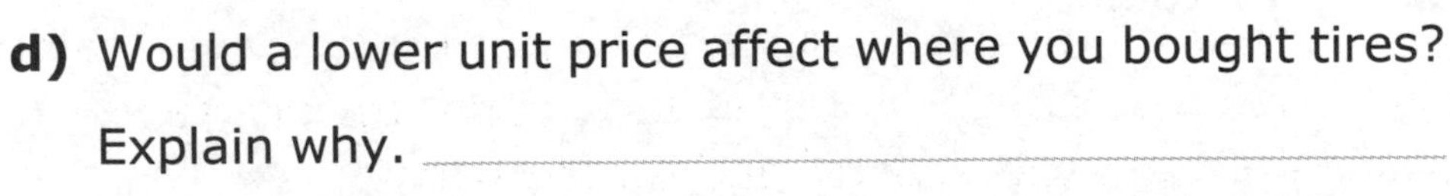

   d) Would a lower unit price affect where you bought tires? Explain why. ______________________

   ____

   e) How could a simple estimate have been used in part a)?

   f) Estimate the cost of 4 tires at Dom's Auto. ______

Date

How Much Do You Need?

3. A 2-L jar of mayonnaise sells for $4.49. A 500-mL squeezable plastic bottle of the same brand of mayonnaise costs $2.79. Each bottle advertises a best-before date approximately 6 months from now.

a) What does the best-before date mean to the retailer?

b) What does the best-before date mean to the consumer?

c) Calculate the unit price, per litre, for each bottle.

2-L jar:

500-mL plastic bottle:

d) Which of the 2 mayonnaise containers gives you more for your money?

e) Explain how you might be able to determine the better buy without calculating the price per litre for each bottle.

f) If you planned on buying mayonnaise on your next trip to the grocery store, which bottle would you buy? Explain why.

Chapter 3

978-0-07-090894-9

Date

Use the Easier Unit

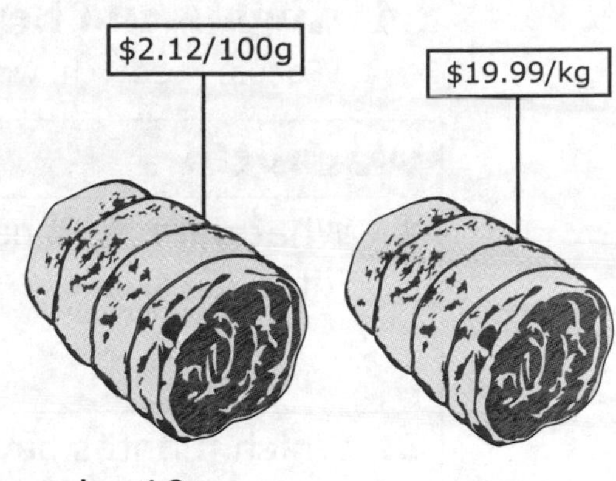

4. Two grocery stores advertise in weekly flyers. One sells sandwich meat at \$2.12/100 g. The other sells the same sandwich meat at \$19.99/kg.

a) Calculate the larger unit. One kilogram equals 1000 grams. Therefore, there are ten 100-g units in each kilogram. Multiply the price advertised by the first store by 10 to get the price per kg.

b) Calculate the smaller unit. Divide the price advertised by the second store by 10 to get the price per 100 g.

c) Which store has the better buy?

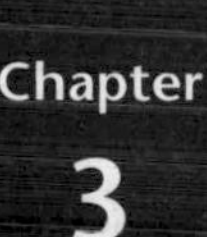

5. A discount department store sells toilet paper in packages of 45 rolls for \$14.99. A grocery store sells toilet paper at \$6.99 for 12 rolls.

a) Calculate the price per roll at each store.

b) What factors other than price might influence your choice of toilet paper?

☑ Check Your Understanding

1. You need to buy 500 sheets of printer paper. Paper is sold in different quantities. An office supply store sells a package of 250 sheets for 79¢ and a package of 500 sheets for \$1.79. Determine the better buy. Show your calculations.

Date ______

3.4 Rights and Responsibilities

Focus: research, writing cheques

Warm Up	
1. What date is 14 days after June 23?	**2.** What date is 60 days after March 15?
3. Which months have 31 days? ______ ______ ______	**4.** Without using a calculator, determine the following amounts. **a)** 900 ÷ 2 = ______ **b)** 900 ÷ 3 = ______ **c)** 900 ÷ 4 = ______
5. Calculate: **a)** 10% of \$800 ______ **b)** 1% of \$800 ______ **c)** 2% of \$800 ______	**6.** What is 12 × \$800?

Chapter 3

Go to pages 45–50 to write definitions for **tenancy agreement**, **lease**, **landlord**, and **tenant** in your own words.

Tenants, Landlords, and Leases

- A **tenancy agreement** is a contract between a landlord and a tenant. It can be oral or written. A written agreement is also called a **lease**.
- The **landlord** provides the rental unit.
- The **tenant** pays rent to the landlord and lives in the rental unit.

Go to pages 112–113. Use **Skills Practice 5: Reading a Lease** to learn about the type of rental agreement tenants often sign.

1. Each statement in the chart on the next page is about the rights and responsibilities of landlords and tenants in Ontario. Record whether you think each statement is true or false.

978-0-07-090894-9

Statement	True/False
a) Landlords and tenants must have a written lease.	
b) A landlord may charge a deposit for allowing someone to rent a unit.	
c) A landlord can refuse to rent to a person who has a pet.	
d) A landlord can ask a person applying for a rental unit to provide information about income or rental history.	
e) The landlord is responsible for maintaining the unit and ensuring that it is in a good state of repair.	
f) A tenant can withhold rent if the landlord isn't properly maintaining the building.	
g) If the tenant withholds rent, the landlord can give the tenant a notice of termination.	
h) The tenant is responsible for keeping the unit clean, up to the standard that most people consider normal cleanliness.	
i) The tenant is responsible for repairing or paying for any damage to the rental property caused by the tenant, their guests, or another person living in the rental unit.	
j) If a landlord provides heat, the landlord is required to keep the unit to at least 20 °C from September 1 to June 15.	
k) If a landlord provides air conditioning, the landlord is required to keep the unit at no more than 20 °C from June 15 to September 1.	
l) The landlord is required to update a rental unit with renovations like painting before a tenant moves in.	

2. Go to **www.mcgrawhill.ca/books/workplace12** and follow the links to the Landlord and Tenant Board. Research the answers for the statements in the chart. Correct any incorrect answers.

Date

3. a) Kendra has found an apartment that she wants to rent. The monthly rent is $845. When she signs the lease, Kendra is required to pay the first month's rent plus a **deposit** equal to 1 month's rent. Calculate the total she must pay when she signs the lease.

A deposit is often referred to as paying "first and last month's rent."

b) Complete the cheque for the amount in part a). Date the cheque for the first day of next month. Make the cheque payable to "ABCDE Incorporated."

191

2 0 Y Y Y Y M M D D

Pay to the Order of $

/100 Dollars

MATH Bank
3.14 159 2653 5897

Chapter 3

c) Complete the cheque for the amount of 1 month's rent. Date the cheque for the first day of the month after the cheque in part b). This is known as a **post-dated cheque**.

Go to pages 45–50 to write a definition for **post-dated cheque**.

192

2 0 Y Y Y Y M M D D

Pay to the Order of $

/100 Dollars

MATH Bank
3.14 159 2653 5897

d) How much rent will Kendra pay in 1 year?

e) Kendra wishes to spend no more than 25% of her net income on rent. How much will she need to earn each year to meet her goal?

978-0-07-090894-9

4. Go to **www.mcgrawhill.ca/books/workplace12** and follow the links to the Landlord and Tenant Board. Research information about paying rent in Ontario. Fill in the blanks to complete the statements correctly. The statements are written in everyday English.

a) The landlord cannot increase the rent for a new tenant until ______ months after the tenant has moved in.

b) The landlord is allowed to increase the rent once every ______ months.

c) In order for a landlord to increase the rent, the landlord must give a written notice of rent increase to the tenant at least ______ days before the day the rent increase is to start.

d) A landlord gives a notice to a tenant who pays rent monthly and is late with payment. The tenant has ______ days to pay before the landlord can file an application for an order to evict the tenant.

e) A tenant who is persistently late paying monthly rent can be given a ______-day notice of eviction.

Chapter 3

☑ Check Your Understanding

1. The Landlord and Tenant Act outlines the rights and responsibilities of landlords and tenants in Ontario. Is there a reason that a landlord could ask tenants who have paid rent and maintained their unit to leave? Explain your answer.

Date ....

Skills Practice 5: Reading a Lease

A lease is a legal document. There are terms frequently used in the wording of a lease that you should become familiar with.

Lessor: The person or company that owns the rental unit. This is also called the landlord.

Lessee: The person paying for renting the unit. This is also called the tenant.

Parties: The people involved in the rental agreement, that is, the lessor(s) and the lessee(s).

Go to pages 45–50 to write definitions for **lessor**, **lessee**, **parties**, and **fixed term** in your own words.

Fixed Term: A set length of time, usually 1 year, for which the lease is in effect.

Rental agreements indicate the terms and conditions for both parties. All parties must agree to the terms and conditions. It is important to read and understand all parts of a lease before signing it.

Chapter 3

Sometimes, you will need to translate what you read into English that you understand.

Example

In consideration of the mutual benefits and promises herein, the parties agree that the lessee will rent from the lessor the residential premises located at 427 Main Street, Unit 217.

Translation

I agree to rent 427 Main Street, apartment 217.

Read the statements below. Translate each one into everyday English.

1. A security deposit in the amount of $100 has been or is to be paid by the lessee to the lessor. (Not to exceed 1 week's rent under weekly agreement; otherwise, 1 month's rent.)

____

____

 978-0-07-090894-9

2. The lessee and any person admitted to the premises by the lessee shall conduct themselves in such a manner as not to interfere with the possession, occupancy, or quiet enjoyment of other lessees.

3. The lessee shall be responsible for the ordinary cleanliness of the interior of the premises and for the repair of damage caused by any wilful or negligent act of the lessee or of any person whom the lessee permits, but not for damage caused by normal wear and tear.

4. When a lessee fails to pay rent in accordance with the rental agreement, the lessor may, on any day following the day the rent was due, serve the lessee with a notice of termination to be effective not earlier than 20 days after the date it is served.

5. A lessee may, within 10 days of being served with a notice of termination, deliver to the lessor all the rent due as of the date, whereupon the notice shall be void.

For examples of full rental agreements, go to **www.mcgrawhill.ca/books/workplace12** and follow the links to rental agreements.

Date

3.5 Some Other Living Expenses

Focus: research, percent

Warm Up	
1. Calculate **a)** 10% of $900 ____ **b)** 1% of $900 ____ **c)** 2% of $900 ____ **d)** 3% of $900 ____	**2.** Add each amount in #1 to $900. **a)** ____ **b)** ____ **c)** ____ **d)**
3. What is 12 × $900?	**4.** Calculate 12 times the answer to #2 d).
5. What is 1.03% of 1500?	**6.** Calculate a 3% increase on $850.

Chapter 3

Rent Increases

Each year, the Ontario government announces the province's rent increase guidelines for the next year.

- This is the maximum amount by which landlords are allowed to increase rent in that year.
- The increase is based on the cost of living.
- A positive rate of change in the cost of living is often called inflation.

1. In the 1970s, the annual rate of inflation was quite high. In 1975, the province set the annual percent rent increase at 8%. Complete the table.

Monthly Rent in 1974 ($)	Allowable Rent Increase ($)	Monthly Rent in 1975 ($)
$475		

978-0-07-090894-9

2. In the first decade of this century, the annual inflation rate was quite low. In 2005, the province sent the annual percent rent increase at 1.5%. Complete the table.

Monthly Rent in 2004 ($)	Allowable Rent Increase ($)	Monthly Rent in 2005 ($)
$860		

3. Go to **www.mcgrawhill.ca/books/workplace12** and follow the links to the Landlord and Tenant Board. Research the percent rent increase for this year and the last 2 years.

Year	Percent Rent Increase

Chapter 3

4. Three years ago, a 2-bedroom apartment rented for $970 per month. Use the data from the table in #3 to determine the possible monthly rent for the apartment this year.

Year	Previous Amount of Rent	Percent Rent Increase (%)	Amount of Increase ($)	Total Monthly Rent
	$970			

5. If you were a landlord, why would you charge the maximum rate of increase every year?

Insurance

Many renters choose to have their belongings insured against damage or theft. The amount of money people pay to the insurance company for insurance coverage is called a **premium**.

Go to pages 45–50 to write a definition for **premium**.

6. Moktar lives alone in a 1-bedroom basement apartment. Last year, the insurance on his belongings was $242. He could pay the entire premium at once, or in monthly installments.

a) Calculate Moktar's monthly insurance premium.

b) This year, Moktar's insurance premium will increase by 5%. Calculate his new monthly insurance premium.

Go to pages 45–50 to write a definition for **utilities**.

Utilities

Some rental units have certain expenses included with the rent. Water, electricity, and heating are often referred to as **utilities**. Some tenancy agreements require the tenant to pay for utilities.

7. a) Bianca and Sarah rent a semi-detached house. They pay for utilities as well as rent. Complete the chart to determine their estimated annual cost for utilities.

Item	Billing Frequency	Average Amount Billed	Estimated Annual Cost
Natural gas	Monthly	$118	
Electricity	Bi-monthly	$140	
Water	Quarterly	$120	
		Estimated Total Annual Cost	

b) A news report claimed that utility costs would rise by an average of 10% next year. Estimate how much Bianca and Sarah can expect to pay for utilities next year.

978-0-07-090894-9

8. a) Christine just moved into a 2-bedroom apartment. She pays $915 per month in rent. The costs of electricity, heat, and water are included. How much did Christine pay for first and last months' rent?

b) How much will Christine spend on rent in one year?

c) What other expenses might Christine have to pay for?

d) Christine keeps her apartment set to 27 °C during the winter because she says that she doesn't have to pay for heating. Is she right about not paying for heating? Explain.

☑ Check Your Understanding

1. What is meant by "annual percent increase in rent?"

2. List 2 things a tenant can do to lower the cost of heating, electricity, and water.

Heating:

Electricity:

Water:

3. If using simple conservation strategies can conserve resources by 15%, how much could a couple who spend $3000 annually on utilities save in 1 year?

Tech Tip: Adding Percent to a Number

Often, you will need to add a percent to a number.
- This is done to calculate the tax on a purchase.
- This can also be done to determine the amount of rent increase for your apartment.

Percent means "for each 100."

Example

Johanna wants to buy a CD for $17.99. What is the total cost of the CD, including 13% tax?

Solution

Method 1

Use the (%) key.

(C) 17.99 (+) 13 (%) (=) 20.3287

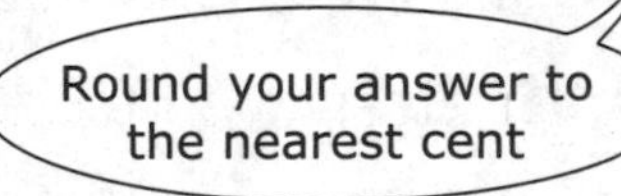

The total cost of Johanna's CD is $20.33.
Note: The method above will work with many calculators. If you have a scientific calculator, experiment to find out how the (%) key works.

Method 2

Multiply the cost by 1 plus the percent shown as a decimal.

(C) 17.99 (×) 1.13 (=) 20.3287

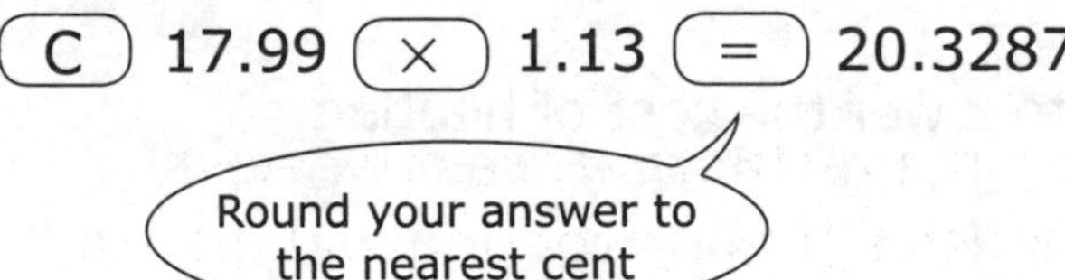

The total cost of Johanna's CD is $20.33.

Chapter 3

978-0-07-090894-9

1. The monthly rent for Theeben's apartment is $625. His landlord tells him that next year, the monthly rent will increase by 6%.

   a) Calculate Theeben's new monthly rent using Method 1.

   b) Calculate Theeben's new monthly rent using Method 2.

   c) Which method do you prefer to use? Why?

2. Hakim works 40 hours per week and currently earns $10.25 per hour at his job. His supervisor tells him that next month, he will receive a 7% pay increase.

   a) Calculate Hakim's new hourly pay.

   b) How much will Hakim earn per month after the increase? Assume a 4-pay month.

3. Niko's monthly car insurance premium is $165, and will increase by 10% next year. How much will he pay per month next year?

4. Natasha works as a server in a restaurant. Last week she earned $460 in wages. Natasha enjoys working with people and often gets large tips. Last week, she received an amount equal to 80% of her wages in tips. How much did she bring in last week?

Chapter 3

Date ______________________

Skills Practice 6: Reading a Utility Bill

Select Hydro Company
P.O. Box 1234, Capital, Ontario
Electricity Bill

Billing Period from May 12, 20__, to July 12, 20__

Your Electricity Charges

Energy Charge	2580.3 kWh @ 0.033	$85.15
Provincial Benefit		$32.75
Delivery		$48.88
Regulatory Charges		$6.52
Debt Retirement Charge		$6.88
Total Electricity Charges		$180.18
GST		$9.01
Sub Total		$189.19
Prior Balance		$5.00
Total Amount You Owe		$194.19

Payment Due on August 28, 20__

Your Electricity Usage for this Period

Meter Number	Days	Start Reading	End Reading	Usage
2546719	60	27363	28365	1002.5

JOE CONSUMER
Account #: 714033-002-5050
Service Address:
14 CITY CIRCLE, CAPITAL, ON
Date Your Bill Was Prepared:
July 28, 20__
Thank You For Your Payment:
$187.90

CONSERVATION TIP: Turn off lights, computers, and appliances when you are not using them.

Your Historical Electricity Usage (kWh per day)

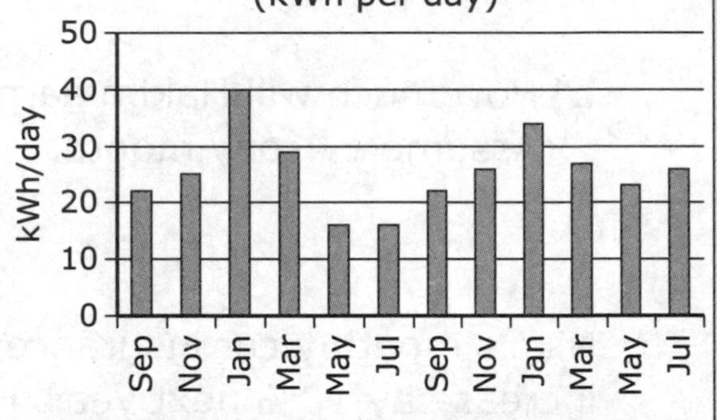

There is a lot more information on a utility bill than how much you owe! You can use information about historical usage, conservation tips, and rates to help you save money on utilities.

1. a) What are the beginning and end dates of the billing period?

beginning date ______________________

end date ______________________

 978-0-07-090894-9

b) A bill with the frequency in a) is referred to as a ______________ expense.

c) How many times per year will this customer be billed? ______

d) On what date is payment due? ______________

2. What is the customer's account number? ______________

3. a) What is the unit price of 1 kilowatt hour (kWh)?

b) What is the average number of kilowatt hours used per day in this billing period?

c) How many kilowatt hours of electricity would this customer use in a 4-month period? Assume that their consumption remains the same.

d) How much would this customer spend on electricity consumption in the 4-month period in part c)?

4. Read the box titled Conservation Tip. Suggest 3 other ways of using less electricity.

____

____

____

Date ______________________

Chapter 3 Review

1. Name 2 types of living accommodations that can be rented.

______________________ ______________________

2. a) To be able to afford $800 in monthly rent, you would need to earn __________ per week. If you worked 40 hours per week, you would need a job that paid __________ per hour.

b) If you worked 30 hours per week, you would need a job that paid __________ per hour.

c) How else could you afford to pay $800 in monthly rent?

____

Chapter 3

3. Rhadika earns $600 per week and lives alone in a 1-bedroom apartment. Her monthly rent is $550. What percent of her month's income is spent on rent? Assume a 4-pay month.

____

4. Reid earns $14 per hour and works 44 hours per week. If he does not want to spend more than 30% of his income on rent, what is the maximum monthly rent that he can afford? Assume a 4-pay month.

____

5. a) Kelsey has just rented an apartment from Rental Properties Inc. The monthly rent will be $885. When she signs the lease, Kelsey must write a cheque for first and last months' rent. Calculate this amount.

b) Write a cheque for the amount in part a).

193

2 0 __ __ __ __ __ __
Y Y Y Y M M D D

Pay to the Order of ______________________ | $ ______

______________________ /100 Dollars

MATH Bank
3.14 159 2653 5897 ______________________

978-0-07-090894-9

6. Name 4 expenses, other than rent, that a renter may have.

____________________ ____________________

____________________ ____________________

7. The province of Ontario set the most recent annual percent rent increase at ________%. Suppose the percent rent increase remains the same next year. This year, an apartment has a monthly rent of $945. What will the cost of rent be for the same apartment next year?

8. The Smiths rent a semi-detached house for $1120 per month. They pay for utilities as well as rent.

a) How much will the Smiths pay in rent in 1 year?

b) Determine the estimated annual cost of some of their other expenses based on the following information.

Item	Billing Frequency	Average Amount Billed	Estimated Annual Cost
Natural gas	Monthly	$140	
Electricity	Bi-monthly	$190	
Water	Quarterly	$160	
		Estimated Total Annual Cost	

c) An economist predicts that utility costs could rise by 15% next year. How much can the Smiths expect to pay for utilities next year?

9. **a)** Toilet paper is on sale for 24 rolls for $4.99 at one store. Another store sells 4 rolls of toilet paper for $1.49. What is the unit price for each buy?

24 rolls: ____________________ 4 rolls: ____________________

b) Which toilet paper would you buy? Why? ____________________

____

Chapter 3

Date ____________________

Chapter 3 Practice Test

1. Name 2 types of places, other than an apartment, that can be rented.

____________________ ____________________

2. a) To be able to afford $900 in monthly rent, you would need to earn __________ per week.

b) If you worked 40 hours per week, you would need a job that paid you __________ per hour.

c) Give an example of the types of places in your community that could be rented for $900 per month.

____

3. Hunter earns $750 net per week. He lives alone in a 1-bedroom apartment. The monthly rent is $785. What percent of his monthly net income is spent on rent? Assume a 4-pay month.

Chapter 3

4. a) Yasmine earns $11.75 per hour and works 35 hours per week. She has a young child and feels that she cannot spend more than 30% of her income on rent. What is the maximum monthly rent that she should pay? Assume a 4-pay month.

b) Given your knowledge of the cost of housing in your community, suggest a strategy Yasmine could use to help her afford an apartment.

____

____

5. This year, the monthly rent for a condominium is $1060. If the annual percent rent increase for next year is set at 3.1%, what will be the monthly rent for the condominium next year?

978-0-07-090894-9

Date

6. a) Orlando has found an apartment he wants to rent. The monthly rent is $795. When he signs the lease, Orlando must write a cheque for first and last months' rent. Calculate this amount.

b) Write a cheque to "City Rental Inc." for the amount in part a). Use today's date.

196

2 0 _ _ _ _ _ _
Y Y Y Y M M D D

Pay to the Order of ______________ $

______________/100 Dollars

MATH Bank
3.14 159 2653 5897

7. Aimee's apartment is within walking distance of 2 grocery stores. She needs to buy milk, light bulbs, and paper towels.

Chapter 3

a) Complete the chart.

Item	Package and Price	Unit Price
Milk	$1.99 for 1-L carton	
	$4.99 for 4 L in bags	
Light Bulbs	$6.99 for 3	
	$19.99 for 12	
Paper Towels	99¢ for 2 rolls	
	$9.99 for 30	

b) Suggest which purchases Aimee should make. Explain your reasoning.

Task: Leaving Town

- You have just graduated from high school and landed a job in the community nearest you. Circle the community: Niagara Falls, Toronto, Windsor, Ottawa, Sudbury, Thunder Bay.
- Your starting wage will be $11.40 per hour and you will work 40 hours per week.
- If you decide to take the job, you need to move to that city.

1. Complete the chart. Round your calculations to the nearest dollar.

Weekly Gross Income	Weekly Net Income (Assume 85% of Gross Income)	Monthly Net Income (Assume a 4-Pay Month)

2. What is the maximum amount that you should consider spending for rent? $______

Explain why. ______

3. Use the Internet or a newspaper or magazine and select a rental accommodation. State your choice, and why you selected it.

______

______

 978-0-07-090894-9

Date

4 Filing a Tax Return

1. The first person said he could get back all the money he "loaned to the government." What do you think he meant?

2. Why might you look forward to filing a tax return?

3. Why might you *not* look forward to filing a tax return?

Chapter 4

Date

4.1 Income and Payroll Deductions

Focus: working with forms, number sense, data management

Warm Up	
1. Define gross income.	**2.** Jana earns about \$650 per week. Calculate her approximate annual gross income.
3. Define net income.	**4.** Calculate the annual net income for Jana in #2 if she takes home approximately 80% of her gross income.

Who Determines Deductions?

The **Canada Revenue Agency (CRA)** is the federal government agency that collects taxes. The taxes pay for federal and provincial programs and services, such as health care and education.

- The CRA determines what percent of your gross income you will contribute to the **Canada Pension Plan (CPP)** and to **Employment Insurance (EI)**.

The Canada Pension Plan provides income for retired workers.

Employment Insurance provides income for unemployed workers.

Chapter 4

Go to pages 45–50 to write definitions for **Canada Revenue Agency (CRA)**, **Canada Pension Plan (CPP)**, **Employment Insurance (EI)**, and **TD1** in your own words.

- The amount of federal income tax and provincial income tax that you pay depends on how much you earn, where you live, and a number of other factors.
- Your net income will be determined, in part, by how you complete the **TD1**. The TD1 is the form your employer uses to determine the amount of federal and provincial tax to deduct from your pay.

978-0-07-090894-9

Date ______

1. a) What is the basic personal amount this year? ______

b) What is the purpose of the basic personal amount?

______

You can earn at least this amount before you have to start paying income tax.

c) How much tax would be withheld from your gross pay if you earned less than the basic personal amount? ______

Gross pay is your total earnings before any deductions are taken off.

2. a) List any other amounts on the TD1 form that apply to you at present.

______

b) List any amounts on the TD1 form that may apply to you next year.

______

c) What is your total claim amount? ______

For the current federal TD1 form, go to **www.mcgrawhill.ca/books/workplace12** and follow the links.

3. a) List each of your sources of income. Beside each, record your expected gross income for this year.

______

______

______

Hint: Do you have more than 1 job? Do you receive income that is not taxed? For example, tips are taxable income, but tax is not deducted when you get the tips.

Chapter 4

b) What is your expected total gross income for this year from all sources? ______

c) Will your total gross income this year be more than your total claim amount? YES NO Explain.

______

______

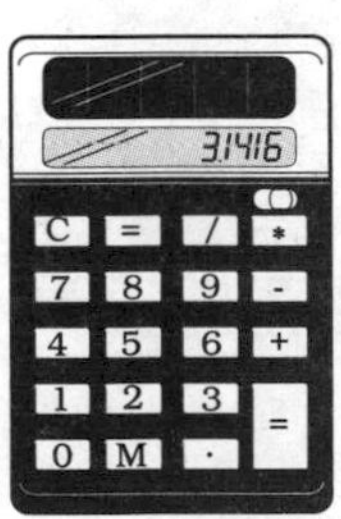

4. Complete the TD1 form for your present circumstances. Keep the completed form with your notes or attach it to this page.

Date

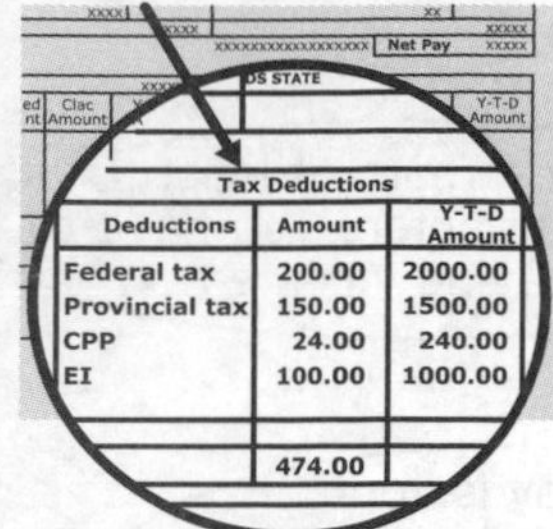

Calculating Net Income

- Many young adults can claim only the basic personal amount on the TD1. This is Tax Claim Code 1.
- The CRA has an online calculator that allows you to calculate net income.

Tech Tip: Using the CRA Payroll Calculator

Example

a) Anna has a weekly income of $300. What is her weekly net income after payroll deductions?

For the CRA payroll deductions online calculator, go to **www.mcgrawhill.ca/books/workplace12** and follow the links.

Go to the CRA payroll deductions online calculator.

- Select **Ontario** and then select **Weekly (52 pay periods a year)**. The calculator will default to Claim Code 1.
- Click on **Salary / Bonus / Retroactive / Pension calculation**.
- Click on **Determine Gross Income**. Enter Anna's gross income.
- Click **OK**. Then, scroll down and click **Calculate**.

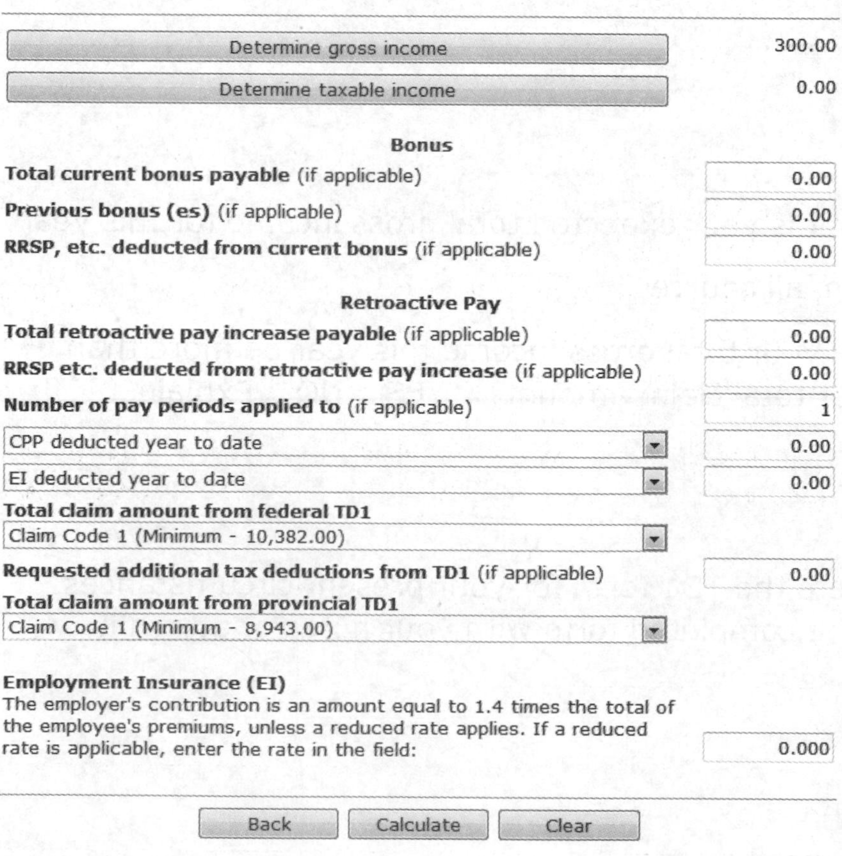

Determine gross income	300.00
Determine taxable income	0.00

Bonus

Total current bonus payable (if applicable)	0.00
Previous bonus (es) (if applicable)	0.00
RRSP, etc. deducted from current bonus (if applicable)	0.00

Retroactive Pay

Total retroactive pay increase payable (if applicable)	0.00
RRSP etc. deducted from retroactive pay increase (if applicable)	0.00
Number of pay periods applied to (if applicable)	1
CPP deducted year to date	0.00
EI deducted year to date	0.00
Total claim amount from federal TD1 Claim Code 1 (Minimum - 10,382.00)	
Requested additional tax deductions from TD1 (if applicable)	0.00
Total claim amount from provincial TD1 Claim Code 1 (Minimum - 8,943.00)	

Employment Insurance (EI)
The employer's contribution is an amount equal to 1.4 times the total of the employee's premiums, unless a reduced rate applies. If a reduced rate is applicable, enter the rate in the field: 0.000

Back | Calculate | Clear

 978-0-07-090894-9

Payroll Deductions Online Calculator

Results - Effective January 1, 2010

Employee's name	
Employer's name	
Pay period	Weekly (52 pay periods a year)
Pay period ending date	
Province of employment	Ontario
Federal amount from TD1	Claim Code 1 (Minimum - 10,382.00)
Provincial amount from TD1	Claim Code 1 (Minimum - 8,943.00)
Salary or wages for the pay period	300.00
Total EI insurable earnings for the pay period	300.00
Taxable income	300.00
Cash income for the pay period	300.00
Federal tax deductions	9.51
Provincial tax deductions	3.32
Requested additional tax deduction	0.00
Total tax on income	12.83
CPP deductions	11.52
EI deductions	5.19
Amounts deducted at source	0.00
Total deductions on income	29.54
Net amount	270.46

Back | New Calculation | Employer summary

Save Employee Results

Anna's net income after payroll deductions is ____________.

b) What percent of her gross income is Anna's net income? Express the answer to the nearest percent.

$$\frac{270.46}{300.00} \times 100 = \_\_\_\_\_\_ \%$$

Anna's net income is ________ of her gross income.

Chapter 4

1. Go to the CRA payroll deductions online calculator. Use the calculator to help complete the table.

- Determine the weekly net income for each weekly gross income.
- Calculate net income as a percent of gross income. Express the answer to the nearest percent.

Weekly Gross Income	Weekly Net Income	Net Income as a % of Gross Income
a) $200		
b) $400		
c) $600		
d) $800		

2. Using the online calculator, complete the pay stub for an employee with a gross income of $800 last week.

Week of:	
Gross Income	
Deductions	
• Federal tax	
• Provincial tax	
• CPP	
• EI	
Total Deductions	
Net Income	

Showing Net Income

5. Refer to the data for #1 on page 131. Shade the percent of the circle that is deducted from gross income. The first one is done for you.

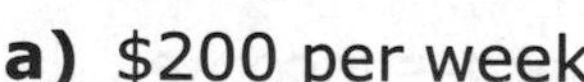

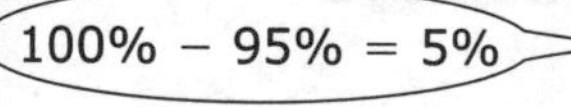

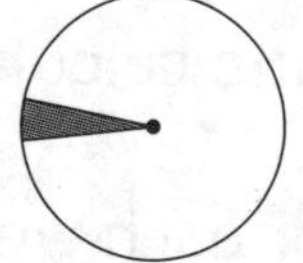

b) $400 per week

c) $600 per week

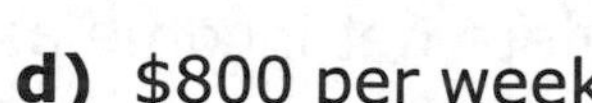

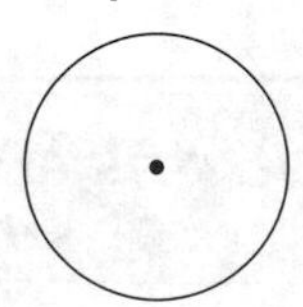

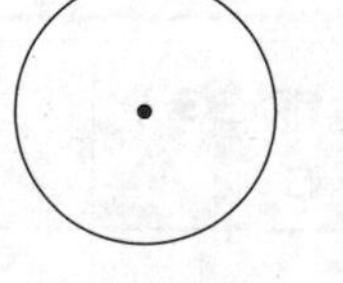

6. **a)** Refer to the circle graphs you completed above. What pattern do you observe about deductions and gross income? ____________________

b) Based on this pattern, in general, the more you earn, the ____________________ your ____________________.

978-0-07-090894-9

Date

7. a) Tyler holds 2 part-time jobs. He earns about $200 per week at 1 job and $300 per week at the other. Use the CRA online calculator to complete the table.

	Weekly Gross Income	Deductions					Weekly Net Income
		CPP	EI	Federal Tax	Provincial Tax	Total	
Job 1							
Job 2							
Total							

b) Slodjana works an average of 40 hours per week at $12.50 per hour. Use the CRA online calculator to determine her weekly deductions and her weekly net income.

Weekly Gross Income	Deductions					Weekly Net Income
	CPP	EI	Federal Tax	Provincial Tax	Total	

c) Compare the total deductions for Tyler and Slodjana. What financial risk is Tyler running?

d) Suggest two strategies for reducing this risk.

Chapter 4

☑ Check Your Understanding

1. Why do Canadians need to file a tax return?

2. Fill in the blanks with the missing terms.

______ Income = ______ Income − ______.

3. Why is it important to complete a TD1 accurately?

Date

4.2 The T4 and the T1

Focus: working with forms, filing income tax, number sense

Warm Up

1. What does CRA refer to?	**2.** What are the approximate gross annual earnings for Paul, who earns about $300 per week?
3. What are the approximate gross annual earnings for Ling, who earns about $700 per week?	**4.** What is the difference between gross income and net income?

What Is the T4?

Go to pages 45–50 to write a definition for **T4** in your own words.

- Your employer is required to submit payroll deductions to the CRA on your behalf.
- Your employer is responsible for giving you an annual record of all your earnings and deductions.
- The **T4** is used to record this information.

Chapter 4

Employer's name – Nom de l'employeur

Sports R Us

Canada Revenue Agency / Agence du revenu du Canada

T4

STATEMENT OF REMUNERATION PAID
ÉTAT DE LA RÉMUNÉRATION PAYÉE

Year / Année

Box	Field	Amount
14	Employment income – line 101 / Revenus d'emploi – ligne 101	31 200.00
22	Income tax deducted – line 437 / Impôt sur le revenu retenu – ligne 437	4680.00
54	Payroll Account Number (15 characters) / Numéro de compte de retenues (15 caractères)	
10	Province of employment / Province d'emploi	ON
16	Employee's CPP contributions – line 308 / Cotisations de l'employé au RPC – ligne 308	1371.15
24	EI insurable earnings / Gains assurables d'AE	
12	Social insurance number / Numéro d'assurance sociale	999 123 456
28	Exempt – Exemption: CPP/QPP (RPC/RRQ), EI (AE), PPIP (RPAP)	
29	Employment code / Code d'emploi	
17	Employee's QPP contributions – line 308 / Cotisations de l'employé au RRQ – ligne 308	
26	CPP/QPP pensionable earnings / Gains ouvrant droit à pension – RPC/RRQ	
18	Employee's EI premiums – line 312 / Cotisations de l'employé à l'AE – ligne 312	539.76
44	Union dues – line 212 / Cotisations syndicales – ligne 212	
20	RPP contributions – line 207 / Cotisations à un RPA – ligne 207	1650.00
46	Charitable donations – see over / Dons de bienfaisance – voir au verso	
52	Pension adjustment – line 206 / Facteur d'équivalence – ligne 206	
50	RPP or DPSP registration number / N° d'agrément d'un RPA ou d'un RPDB	
55	Employee's PPIP premiums – see over / Cotisations de l'employé au RPAP – voir au verso	
56	PPIP insurable earnings / Gains assurables du RPAP	

Employee's name and address – Nom et adresse de l'employé

Last name (in capital letters) – Nom de famille (en lettres moulées)	First name – Prénom	Initials – Initiales
Brown	Dan	A

Other information (see over) / Autres renseignements (voir au verso) T4

Box – Case	Amount – Montant	Box – Case	Amount – Montant	Box – Case	Amount – Montant

978-0-07-090894-9

Date

1. Dan's employer used the following record of his earnings and deductions to complete the T4.

Gross Income	$31 200.00
Payroll Deductions	
• Federal tax	$3135.60
• Provincial tax	$1544.40
• CPP	$1371.15
• EI	$539.76

Use the information above to help you interpret the T4 on page 134. In what box on the T4 is each value found?

a) Employment income

b) CPP contributions

c) EI premiums

d) Income tax deducted

Dan contributes to a registered pension plan for his retirement. This is a **tax deduction** that he can subtract from his income to determine his taxable income.

Go to pages 45–50 to write definitions for **tax deduction** and **T1** in your own words.

2. What is the value of Dan's registered pension plan (RPP) contribution on his T4?

Chapter 4

3. Dan will need the values on the T4 to complete the **T1**, which is the tax return. On what line of the T1 would he enter each of the following amounts?

a) Employment income

b) Income tax deducted

c) Union dues

What Is the T1 General?

The T1 General form includes 4 pages. The main parts of the T1 are

- Identification
- Total income
- Net income
- Taxable income
- Refund or balance owing

For the current T1 General form, go to **www.mcgrawhill.ca/books/workplace12** and follow the links.

Date

Dan's T1 General form appears on the following pages. Use it to answer the questions that follow.

4. Refer to page 1 of the T1 form. What is its main purpose?

5. Fill in the following information for Dan on page 1.
- Provide a full name, address, social insurance number, date of birth, language preference, marital status, and place of residence for Dan.
- Dan will give the CRA permission to give certain information to Elections Canada.
- Dan is eligible for the GST/HST credit since he is older than 19 and has a modest income.

Elections Canada uses the information to produce voters lists.

The GST/HST credit is a tax-free quarterly payment that helps people with low and modest incomes offset all or part of the GST or HST that they pay.

Canada Revenue Agency / Agence du revenu du Canada

T1 GENERAL

Income Tax and Benefit Return

Complete all the sections that apply to you in order to benefit from amounts to which you are entitled.

Identification

ON 1

Attach your personal label here. Correct any wrong information. If you are not attaching a label, print your name and address below.

First name and initial

Last name

Mailing address: Apt No – Street No Street name

PO Box | RR

City | Prov./Terr. | Postal code

Information about you

Enter your social insurance number (SIN) if it is not on the label, or if you are not attaching a label:

Enter your date of birth: Year Month Day

Your language of correspondence: / Votre langue de correspondance : English ☐ Français ☐

Tick the box that applies to your marital status on December 31, 2009: (see the "Marital status" section in the guide)

1 ☐ Married 2 ☐ Living common-law 3 ☐ Widowed
4 ☐ Divorced 5 ☐ Separated 6 ☐ Single

Information about your spouse or common-law partner (if you ticked box 1 or 2 above) **(see the guide for more information)**

Enter his or her SIN if it is not on the label, or if you are not attaching a label:

Enter his or her first name:

Enter his or her net income for 2009 to claim certain credits:

Enter the amount of Universal Child Care Benefit included on line 117 of his or her return:

Enter the amount of Universal Child Care Benefit repayment included on line 213 of his or her return:

Tick this box if he or she was self-employed in 2009: 1 ☐

Information about your residence

Enter your province or territory of residence on **December 31, 2009:**

Enter the province or territory where you **currently** reside if it is not the same as that shown above for your mailing address:

If you were self-employed in 2009, enter the province or territory of self-employment:

If you **became** or **ceased** to be a **resident of Canada in 2009**, give the date of:

entry Month Day or **departure** Month Day

Person deceased in 2009

If this **return** is for a **deceased person**, enter the date of death: Year Month Day

Do not use this area

Elections Canada (see the Elections Canada page in the tax guide for details or visit **www.elections.ca**)

A) Are you a Canadian citizen? .... Yes ☐ 1 No ☐ 2

Answer the following question **only if you are a Canadian citizen.**

B) As a Canadian citizen, do you authorize the Canada Revenue Agency to give your name, address, date of birth, and citizenship to Elections Canada for the National Register of Electors? .... Yes ☐ 1 No ☐ 2

Your authorization is valid until you file your next return. Your information will only be used for purposes permitted under the *Canada Elections Act* which includes sharing the information with provincial/territorial election agencies, Members of Parliament and registered political parties, as well as candidates at election time.

Goods and services tax/harmonized sales tax (GST/HST) credit application

See the guide for details.

Are you applying for the GST/HST or the Ontario Sales Tax (OST) credit? .... Yes ☐ 1 No ☐ 2

Chapter 4

978-0-07-090894-9

Date ______

6. a) Refer to page 2 of the T1 form. What will you calculate by the end of this page? ______

b) Describe income that someone might have that would not be recorded on a T4.

______

______

> As a Canadian resident, you have to report your income from all sources both inside and outside Canada. What do you think this statement means?

7. a) Dan does not have foreign income. Complete box 266.

b) Use Dan's T4 information to complete line 101 on page 2 below. Since Dan has no other income, you can complete line 150 for his total income.

2

Your guide contains valuable information to help you complete your return.
When you come to a line on the return that applies to you, look up the line number in the guide for more information.

Please answer the following question:

Did you own or hold foreign property at any time in 2009 with a total cost of more than CAN$100,000? (see the "Foreign income" section in the guide for details) .... 266 Yes ☐ 1 No ☐ 2

If **yes**, attach a completed Form T1135.

If you had dealings with a non-resident trust or corporation in 2009, see the "Foreign income" section in the guide.

As a Canadian resident, you have to report your income from all sources both inside and outside Canada.

Total income

Line		
Employment income (box 14 on all T4 slips)		101
Commissions included on line 101 (box 42 on all T4 slips)	102	
Other employment income		104+
Old Age Security pension (box 18 on the T4A(OAS) slip)		113+
CPP or QPP benefits (box 20 on the T4A(P) slip)		114+
Disability benefits included on line 114 (box 16 on the T4A(P) slip)	152	
Other pensions or superannuation		115+
Elected split-pension amount (see the guide and **attach** Form T1032)		116+
Universal Child Care Benefit (see the guide)		117+
Employment Insurance and other benefits (box 14 on the T4E slip)		119+
Taxable amount of dividends (eligible and other than eligible) from taxable Canadian corporations (see the guide and **attach** Schedule 4)		120+
Taxable amount of dividends other than eligible dividends, included on line 120, from taxable Canadian corporations	180	
Interest and other investment income (**attach** Schedule 4)		121+
Net partnership income: limited or non-active partners only (**attach** Schedule 4)		122+
Registered disability savings plan income (see the guide)		125+
Rental income	Gross 160	Net 126+
Taxable capital gains (**attach** Schedule 3)		127+
Support payments received	Total 156	Taxable amount 128+
RRSP income (from all T4RSP slips)		129+
Other income Specify:		130+
Self-employment income (see lines 135 to 143 in the guide)		
Business income	Gross 162	Net 135+
Professional income	Gross 164	Net 137+
Commission income	Gross 166	Net 139+
Farming income	Gross 168	Net 141+
Fishing income	Gross 170	Net 143+
Workers' compensation benefits (box 10 on the T5007 slip)	144	
Social assistance payments	145+	
Net federal supplements (box 21 on the T4A(OAS) slip)	146+	
Add lines 144, 145, and 146 (see line 250 in the guide).	=	▶ 147+
Add lines 101, 104 to 143, and 147. This is your total income.		150=

Chapter 4

Date ______________________

8. Refer to page 3 of the T1 form. What will you calculate on this page? ______________ and ______________

9. Follow the instructions to complete page 3.

- Re-enter the amount for line 150 on page 3 of the T1 form.
- Dan has a tax deduction on his T4. It is his ______________________. Enter the amount on line 207.
- Since Dan has no other tax deductions, you can complete lines 233, 234, and 236. Dan's net income is __________.
- The amount that is left after all tax deductions is called **taxable income**. In Dan's case, this is the same as his net income. Enter this amount on line 260.

Go to pages 45–50 to write a definition for **taxable income** in your own words.

Attach your Schedule 1 (federal tax) and Form 428 (provincial or territorial tax) here. Also attach here any other schedules, information slips, forms, receipts, and documents that you need to include with your return. 3

Net income

Enter your **total income** from line 150. 150

Pension adjustment (box 52 on all T4 slips and box 34 on all T4A slips) 206

Registered pension plan deduction (box 20 on all T4 slips and box 32 on all T4A slips) 207

RRSP deduction (see Schedule 7 and **attach** receipts) 208+

Saskatchewan Pension Plan deduction (maximum $600) 209+

Deduction for elected split-pension amount (see the guide and **attach** Form T1032) 210+

Annual union, professional, or like dues (box 44 on all T4 slips, and receipts) 212+

Universal Child Care Benefit repayment (box 12 on all RC62 slips) 213+

Child care expenses (**attach** Form T778) 214+

Disability supports deduction 215+

Business investment loss Gross 228 Allowable deduction 217+

Moving expenses 219+

Support payments made Total 230 Allowable deduction 220+

Carrying charges and interest expenses (**attach** Schedule 4) 221+

Deduction for CPP or QPP contributions on self-employment and other earnings (**attach** Schedule 8) 222+

Exploration and development expenses (**attach** Form T1229) 224+

Other employment expenses 229+

Clergy residence deduction 231+

Other deductions Specify: 232+

Add lines 207 to 224, 229, 231, and 232. 233= ► –

Line 150 minus line 233 (if negative, enter "0"). This is your **net income before adjustments**. 234=

Social benefits repayment (if you reported income on line 113, 119, or 146, see line 235 in the guide) Use the federal worksheet to calculate your repayment. 235–

Line 234 minus line 235 (if negative, enter "0"). If you have a spouse or common-law partner, see line 236 in the guide. This is your **net income**. 236=

Taxable income

Canadian Forces personnel and police deduction (box 43 on all T4 slips) 244

Employee home relocation loan deduction (box 37 on all T4 slips) 248+

Security options deductions 249+

Other payments deduction (if you reported income on line 147, see line 250 in the guide) 250+

Limited partnership losses of other years 251+

Non-capital losses of other years 252+

Net capital losses of other years 253+

Capital gains deduction 254+

Northern residents deductions (**attach** Form T2222) 255+

Additional deductions Specify: 256+

Add lines 244 to 256. 257= ► –

Line 236 minus line 257 (if negative, enter "0") This is your **taxable income**. 260=

Use your taxable income to calculate your federal tax on Schedule 1 and your provincial or territorial tax on Form 428.

Chapter 4

978-0-07-090894-9

Date

10. Refer to page 4 of the T1 form. What will you determine on this page?

You will learn how to do this in the next section.

Refund or balance owing

4

Net federal tax: enter the amount from line 55 of Schedule 1 (**attach** Schedule 1, even if the result is "0")	420	
CPP contributions payable on self-employment and other earnings (**attach** Schedule 8)	421+	
Social benefits repayment (enter the amount from line 235)	422+	
Provincial or territorial tax (**attach** Form 428, even if the result is "0")	428+	
Add lines 420 to 428. This is your **total payable.**	435=	•

Total income tax deducted (see the guide)	437	•
Refundable Quebec abatement	440+	•
CPP overpayment (enter your excess contributions)	448+	•
Employment Insurance overpayment (enter your excess contributions)	450+	•
Refundable medical expense supplement (use federal worksheet)	452+	•
Working Income Tax Benefit (WITB) (**attach** Schedule 6)	453+	•
Refund of investment tax credit (**attach** Form T2038(IND))	454+	•
Part XII.2 trust tax credit (box 38 on all T3 slips)	456+	•
Employee and partner GST/HST rebate (**attach** Form GST370)	457+	•
Tax **paid** by instalments	476+	•
Provincial or territorial credits (**attach** Form 479 if it applies)	479+	•
Add lines 437 to 479. These are your **total credits.**	482=	▶ −

Line 435 minus line 482 =

If the result is negative, you have a **refund**. If the result is positive, you have a **balance owing**.

Enter the amount below on whichever line applies.

Generally, we do not charge or refund a difference of $2 or less.

Refund 484 ________ •

Balance owing (see line 485 in the guide) 485 ________ •

Amount enclosed 486 ________ •

Attach to page 1 a **cheque** or **money order** payable to the Receiver General. Your payment is due no later than April 30, 2010.

Direct deposit – Start or change (see line 484 in the guide)

You do not have to complete this area every year. Do not complete it this year if your direct deposit information has not changed. **Refund, GST/HST credit, WITB advance payments, and any other deemed overpayment of tax** – To start direct deposit or to change account information only, **attach** a "void" cheque or complete lines 460, 461, and 462.

Notes: To deposit your **CCTB** payments (including certain related provincial or territorial payments) into the **same** account, also tick box 463. To deposit your **UCCB** payments into the **same** account, also tick box 491.

Branch number	Institution number	Account number	CCTB	UCCB
460 ______ (5 digits)	461 ______ (3 digits)	462 ______ (maximum 12 digits)	463 ☐	491 ☐

Ontario — **Ontario Opportunities Fund**

You can help reduce Ontario's debt by completing this area to donate some or all of your 2009 refund to the Ontario Opportunities Fund. Please see the provincial pages for details.

Amount from line 484 above			1
Your donation to the Ontario Opportunities Fund	465−		• 2
Net refund (line 1 minus line 2)	466=		• 3

I certify that the information given on this return and in any documents attached is correct, complete, and fully discloses all my income.

Sign here ________

It is a serious offence to make a false return.

Telephone – – Date

490 **For professional tax preparers only**

Name:

Address:

Telephone: – –

Date ____________________

Your Turn

Get a copy of the most recent T1 General form. Use it to answer the following questions.

11. a) Explain how you will answer the questions on page 1 of the T1 about
- Elections Canada

____

- GST/HST credit application

____

b) Complete page 1 on your copy of the T1.

12. a) On page 2, highlight the lines about the sources of income that apply to you this year.

b) How many lines other than Total Income on line 150 did you highlight? ____

c) Survey 5 class members. Other than Total Income, how many lines did each student highlight?

____ ____ ____ ____ ____

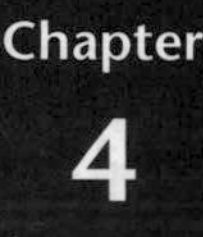

d) Compare the results. What do you notice?

____

____

e) You have information about the number of lines that you and 5 of your class members highlighted on page 2 of the T1. Is this a large enough sample to draw conclusions about how many lines teenagers fill in on page 2 of the T1? YES NO Explain.

____

f) Estimate and record the income for each line that you highlighted on page 2. Enter your total estimated income on line 150.

978-0-07-090894-9

13. a) On page 3, highlight the tax deductions that apply to you this year.

b) How many lines did you highlight? ______

c) Survey 5 class members. How many lines did each student highlight?

______ ______ ______ ______ ______

d) Compare the results. Can you come to any conclusion? Explain why or why not.

e) Estimate and record the tax deductions for each line that you highlighted on page 3. Enter your taxable income on line 260.

For information about types of income and tax deductions, search the General Income Tax and Benefit Guide. Go to **www.mcgrawhill.ca/books/workplace12** and follow the links.

Chapter 4

☑ Check Your Understanding

1. a) Marco worked full-time during the summer. His family moved to a different city in October. What information must he provide to his former employer?

b) Explain why.

2. a) Completing most of the T1 General Tax form was

- ☐ easier than I thought it would be
- ☐ about what I thought it would be
- ☐ harder than I thought it would be

Check 1 answer.

b) Discuss your answer to part a) with several classmates.

Date ____________

4.3 Tax Deductions and Tax Credits

Focus: working with forms, filing income tax, reducing tax, number sense

Warm Up	
1. If Ivanka saves $50 per week, she will save $______ in 1 year.	**2. a)** I will be 65 years of age in ____ years. **b)** The year will be ______!
3. If you save $50 per week for the number of years in #2a), you will save $________.	**4. a)** What is 3% of $100? ____ **b)** What is 3% of $1000? ____ **c)** What is 3% of $2000? ____ **d)** What is 3% of $3000? ____
5. Calculate: **a)** 15% of $100 $______ **b)** 15% of $1000 $______ **c)** 15% of $10 000 $______ **d)** 15% of $20 000 $______	**6.** Gavin's gross pay is $780 per week. His employer deducts $292.50 to pay income tax, CPP, EI, and health insurance. **a)** What is Gavin's net pay? ________ **b)** What percent of Gavin's gross pay is his net pay? ______

What Are Tax Credits?

Go to pages 45–50 to write a definition for **tax credit** in your own words.

Expenses are treated in different ways when you file an income tax return.

- The full amount of a tax deduction is subtracted from income to determine taxable income. Child care expenses, moving expenses, and union dues are examples.
- Only a percent of the total amount of a **tax credit** can be used to reduce the amount of tax that you owe. The government gives tax credits to reduce taxes and to encourage certain types of activity or investment. Tuition fees, medical expenses, and charitable donations are examples.

978-0-07-090894-9

Date ______________________

1. Kristi had a total income of $48 540 last year.
   - She contributed $2000 to a registered retirement pension plan (RRSP).
   - She contributed $3500 to a pension plan through work.
   - She paid $700 in union dues.
   - The total of her child care expenses was $4000.

   a) Get a copy of page 3 of the T1 General form. Insert Kristi's amounts on the appropriate lines of page 3.

   b) Calculate the total tax deductions from Kristi's income.

   ____

   c) What line does this amount go on? ________

   d) Calculate Kristi's net income and her taxable income. Fill in the appropriate lines.

   e) Will Kristi pay income tax on the amount from part b)? YES NO Explain.

   ____

   ____

Tax Credits

	Receipt # 0001
Out of the Cold Program BN / Registration # 2345678	
Date donation received: **October 20, 20XX**	Donated by: **Kristi B Jones** (First name, initial, last name)
Eligible amount of gift for tax purposes: $75.00	Address: **123 Main St. Anytown, ON N5A 6S5**
	Date receipt issued: **December 20, 20XX**
	Location issued: **Anytown, ON**
	Authorised signature: ______________

2. You need receipts in order to claim a tax credit.

   a) What receipt is shown here? ______________________

   b) List the key information on this receipt.

   ____

   ____

   ____

Chapter 4

Date ____________________

For the current Schedule 1 form, go to **www.mcgrawhill.ca/books/workplace12** and follow the links.

Your Turn

In order to claim tax credits, you need to complete **Schedule 1**. This form is used to calculate federal tax. Get a copy of the most recent Schedule 1 form. Use it to answer the following questions.

3. How many steps are involved in completing Schedule 1? ________

4. **a)** Highlight the federal non-refundable tax credits that apply to you.

What tax credit is every Canadian entitled to claim?

b) Record values for the highlighted items. Use estimates when needed. Then, complete Step 1. What is the total amount of federal non-refundable tax credits? ________

c) Use a different colour to highlight tax credits that may apply to you within a couple of years. Explain your choices.

____

Go to pages 45–50 to write definitions for **Schedule 1** and **ON428** in your own words.

5. Complete Step 2. Then, complete Step 3 to determine your net federal tax.

Chapter 4

Get a copy of the most recent Ontario Tax form called **ON428**. This form is used to calculate provincial tax in Ontario. Use it to answer the following questions.

For the current Ontario Tax form, go to **www.mcgrawhill.ca/books/workplace12** and follow the links.

6. How many steps are involved in completing the Ontario Tax form? ________

7. **a)** Read the steps. The steps are similar to those for completing Schedule 1. For each step, highlight the items that apply to you.

b) Record values for the Ontario non-refundable tax credits you highlighted. Use estimates when needed. Then, complete Step 1. What is the total amount of Ontario non-refundable tax credits? ________

978-0-07-090894-9

c) Use a different colour to highlight the items that may apply to you within a couple of years. Explain your choices.

d) Complete Step 2 and Step 3.

e) Complete any other steps that apply to your situation. Then, go to Step 7 and determine your total Ontario tax.

You will use this work to complete page 4 of the T1 General form in the next section.

☑ Check Your Understanding

1. What do you think is the answer to the customer's question? YES NO Explain why.

2. Kyoko has a receipt for a donation to the United Way and another for professional dues.

a) For tax purposes, how is each item classified?

b) Where would each item appear on a tax return?

Date

Skills Practice 7: Identifying Tax Deductions and Tax Credits

For forms and publications from the Canada Revenue Agency, go to **www.mcgrawhill.ca/books/workplace12** and follow the links.

- Go to the Forms and Publications link on the CRA website.
- Click on **Tax Packages** and then click on the most recent year's **General Income Tax and Benefit Package**.
- Click on **Ontario** and then click on the most recent year's **General Income Tax and Benefit Package**. Select the html version. Click on the link for **Deductions (Net income and Taxable income)**.

1. Is each of the following items a tax deduction? Choose YES or NO.

a) RRSP contribution ______	**b)** Rent payments ______
c) Union dues ______	**d)** Charitable donation ______
e) Child care expenses ______	**f)** Support payments ______

2. List 2 other items that qualify as tax deductions.

a) ______ **b)** ______

- Click on the link for **Federal non-refundable tax credits (Schedule 1)**. Use the information to help answer the following questions.

3. Is each of the following items a tax credit? Choose YES or NO.

a) CPP contribution ______	**b)** Rent payments ______
c) Caregiver amount ______	**d)** EI premiums ______
e) Charitable donation ______	**f)** Medical expenses ______

4. List 2 other items that qualify as tax credits.

a) ______ **b)** ______

5. Do research and list 4 items that qualify as *provincial* tax credits.

a) ______ **b)** ______

c) ______ **d)** ______

Chapter 4

 978-0-07-090894-9

Tech Tip: Using an Online Income Tax Calculator

Use the CRA payroll deductions calculator to help calculate taxes.

- Go to the CRA payroll deductions online calculator.
- Select **Ontario** and then select **Weekly (52 pay periods a year)**.
- Click on **Salary / Bonus / Retroactive / Pension calculation**.
- Click on **Determine Gross Income** and enter $600.
- Click **OK**. Then, click **Calculate**.

For the CRA payroll deductions online calculator, go to **www.mcgrawhill.ca/books/workplace12** and follow the links.

1. Use the information to complete part a) of the table. Round all answers to the nearest dollar.

Gross Weekly Income	Taxable Income	Claim Code	Total Tax Deducted	Gross Annual Income	Total Annual Tax Deducted
a) $600	$600	1			
b)					
c)					
d)					

- Click **Back** and then click **Determine taxable income**.
- Enter $50 for Contributions to a registered retirement savings plan.
- Click **OK**. Then, click **Calculate**.

2. Use the information to complete part b) of the table.

3. A contribution to a registered retirement savings plan is a tax deduction / tax credit. (Circle one.)

- Click **Back**.
- From the pull-down menus for Total claim amount for federal TD1 and for Total claim amount for provincial TD1, select **Claim Code 3** for each. Then, click **calculate**.

4. Use the information to complete part c) of the table.

5. Give an example of an item that would move someone from Claim Code 1 to Claim Code 3.

____

6. Complete part d) of the table using the information for your current situation.

Date ______________________

4.4 Completing a Simple Tax Return

Focus: working with forms, filing income tax, number sense

Warm Up	
1. Which form do you use to calculate federal tax credits? ______________	**2.** What is the basic personal amount for the federal tax credit this year? ______________
3. Name 2 items that are allowable deductions from income. ______________ ______________	**4.** Which form do you use to calculate Ontario non-refundable tax credits? ______________
5. Estimate and then calculate 15% of $15 343.	**6.** Name 2 items that qualify for federal non-refundable tax credits. ______________ ______________

Chapter 4

Tax Preparation Resources

- There are many computer-based tax preparation programs.
- Some companies will let you try out their software for free.

1. a) Research the cost and features of any 2 computer-based tax programs. Complete the information requested in the charts.

For tax preparation software, go to **www.mcgrawhill.ca/books/workplace12** and follow the links.

Program	**Cost**
Features ______________ ______________ ______________ ______________	

 978-0-07-090894-9

Date ______________________

Program	Cost
Features	

b) Which program do you prefer? Explain why.

____

____

2. a) Check out the CRA website. Then, compare the resources for tax preparation.

	Help Provided	Cost
• CRA resources		
• Tax preparation software		

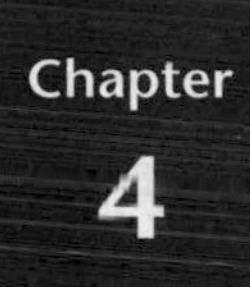

b) Which tax preparation resource would you recommend? Explain your choice.

____

____

For resources on the Canada Revenue Agency website, go to **www.mcgrawhill.ca/books/workplace12** and follow the links.

3. a) Use the T1 General form on the next page to complete your tax return. Use the data on the tax forms you completed in section 4.3. Using estimates will give you an idea of whether there is a refund or a balance owing on your tax return.

b) Does your work on the T1 General Form show a refund or a balance owing? (Circle one.)

What is the amount? __________

Date

Refund or balance owing

4

Net federal tax: enter the amount from line 55 of Schedule 1 (**attach** Schedule 1, even if the result is "0")	420	
CPP contributions payable on self-employment and other earnings (**attach** Schedule 8)	421+	
Social benefits repayment (enter the amount from line 235)	422+	
Provincial or territorial tax (**attach** Form 428, even if the result is "0")	428+	
Add lines 420 to 428. This is your **total payable.**	435=	•

Total income tax deducted (see the guide)	437	•
Refundable Quebec abatement	440+	•
CPP overpayment (enter your excess contributions)	448+	•
Employment Insurance overpayment (enter your excess contributions)	450+	•
Refundable medical expense supplement (use federal worksheet)	452+	•
Working Income Tax Benefit (WITB) (**attach** Schedule 6)	453+	•
Refund of investment tax credit (**attach** Form T2038(IND))	454+	•
Part XII.2 trust tax credit (box 38 on all T3 slips)	456+	•
Employee and partner GST/HST rebate (**attach** Form GST370)	457+	•
Tax **paid** by instalments	476+	•
Provincial or territorial credits (**attach** Form 479 if it applies)	479+	•
Add lines 437 to 479. These are your **total credits.**	482=	▶ –

Line 435 minus line 482 =

If the result is negative, you have a **refund**. If the result is positive, you have a **balance owing**.

Enter the amount below on whichever line applies.

Generally, we do not charge or refund a difference of $2 or less.

Refund 484 ________ •   **Balance owing** (see line 485 in the guide) 485 ________ •

Amount enclosed 486 ________ •

Attach to page 1 a **cheque** or **money order** payable to the Receiver General. Your payment is due no later than April 30, 2010.

Direct deposit – Start or change (see line 484 in the guide)

You do not have to complete this area every year. Do not complete it this year if your direct deposit information has not changed. **Refund, GST/HST credit, WITB advance payments, and any other deemed overpayment of tax** – To start direct deposit or to change account information only, **attach** a "void" cheque or complete lines 460, 461, and 462.

Notes: To deposit your **CCTB** payments (including certain related provincial or territorial payments) into the **same** account, also tick box 463. To deposit your **UCCB** payments into the **same** account, also tick box 491.

Branch number	Institution number	Account number	CCTB	UCCB
460 ________ (5 digits)	461 ________ (3 digits)	462 ________ (maximum 12 digits)	463 ☐	491 ☐

Ontario **Ontario Opportunities Fund**

You can help reduce Ontario's debt by completing this area to donate some or all of your 2009 refund to the Ontario Opportunities Fund. Please see the provincial pages for details.

Amount from line 484 above			1
Your donation to the Ontario Opportunities Fund	465–		•2
Net refund (line 1 minus line 2)	466=		•3

I certify that the information given on this return and in any documents attached is correct, complete, and fully discloses all my income.

Sign here ________

It is a serious offence to make a false return.

Telephone – – Date

490 **For professional tax preparers only**

Name:

Address:

Telephone: – –

4. a) Choose tax preparation software and use it to complete your tax return.

- Print your tax return.
- Sign it and date it.

b) Give 1 advantage and 1 disadvantage of using software to complete your tax return.

978-0-07-090894-9

Date

Income Tax Preparation Services

5. a) Research businesses and services that prepare income tax returns. Look for an example of each type of service shown in the table. Then, complete the table.

Service	Features	Cost
• Tax preparation service		
• Accountant		
• Bookkeeper		
• Volunteer service in the community		

b) Which service would you recommend for completing a simple tax return? Why?

For information about the Community Volunteer Income Tax Program, go to **www.mcgrawhill.ca/books/workplace12** and follow the links.

6. In 2008, 62% of tax returns were filed electronically in Canada. What trend do you predict for future years? Explain.

Chapter 4

☑ Check Your Understanding

1. Raoul finds this ad for a tax preparation service. List 2 questions he should ask before having them complete a tax return on his behalf.

Date

Skills Practice 8: Completing a Tax Return

- Use paper and pencil or tax preparation software to complete tax returns for #1 and #2.
- If you use software, you will likely need to enter your personal information to get started. This information includes your name, address, date of birth, and social insurance number.

1. a) Complete a tax return for Melanie.
- Melanie is 19 and single.
- She worked full-time during the summer and goes to high school.
- She lives with her parents and has a child.
- This is her tax information.

Total income: $12 000
Income tax deducted: $2200
CPP contributions: $650
EI premiums: $275
Child care expenses: $1500
Medical expenses: $225
Apply for the GST/HST credit.

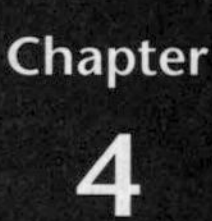

b) Does Melanie have a refund or a balance owing?

____

What is the amount? _______

 978-0-07-090894-9

2. a) Complete a tax return for Jordan.
- Jordan is 20, single, and a full-time employee.
- He lives with his parents and has no children.
- This is his tax information.

Total income: $20 000	Tuition fees: $750
Income tax deducted: $1850	Charitable donations: $125
CPP contributions: $800	Apply for the GST/HST credit.
EI premiums: $350	

b) Does Jordan have a refund or a balance owing?

What is the amount?

c) Jordan decides to contribute to an RRSP to reduce his taxes. Determine the impact of making a contribution of
- $500
- $1000
- $2000

(Input the RRSP allowable limit at $2000.)

d) Compare the amounts of tax payable in each case. What advice would you give Jordan about the best level of contribution to an RRSP?

e) Give 1 advantage and 1 disadvantage of making contributions to an RRSP.

3. a) How are the tax returns for Melanie and Jordan similar? How are they different?

b) If you were Melanie or Jordan, would you use a tax preparation service? YES NO Explain why.

4.5 Self-Employed?

Focus: filing income tax, record keeping, hiring a professional

Warm Up	
1. a) Hydro costs $135 per month. Estimate the annual total cost. ______ **b)** Estimate the sales tax on a $1400 washer and dryer set. ______	**2.** A news report says, "Over 90% of all new businesses go bankrupt within 5 years." Express this probability as a **a)** fraction ______ **b)** decimal ______
3. Estimate the weekly earnings for someone earning $20 000 per year. ______	**4.** How many times in 1 year would you pay a bill that is due every 3 months? ______

Benefits of Being Your Own Boss

- It is hard work to be self-employed, but you can claim expenses related to your business to reduce taxable income.
- Most people who are self-employed hire a professional to help them with planning, record keeping, and filing tax returns.

Chapter 4

1. Jen is a self-employed hairstylist. Her shop is part of the ground floor of her house. She uses a bookkeeper to help her manage the business.

a) Jen's business takes up about 25% of the living space of her home. Therefore, she can claim $\frac{1}{4}$ of some house expenses as business expenses. Check off the house expenses that you think she can claim.

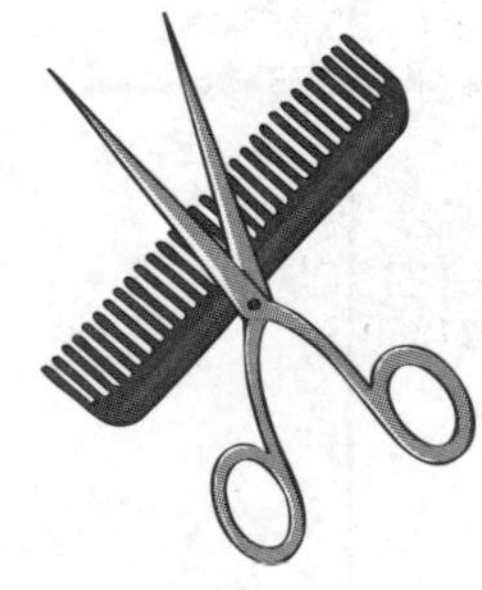

☐ groceries	☐ electricity	☐ heating
☐ telephone	☐ alarm system	☐ Internet access
☐ water	☐ cable TV	☐ property taxes
☐ home insurance	☐ clothes	☐ meals out

978-0-07-090894-9

Date

Jen collected the following data about her house expenses.

- The gas bill comes every month. The gas bills for the first 3 months of the year were $177, $247, and $163.
- The electricity bill comes every other month. February's bill was $320.
- The water bill comes quarterly. The bill due in March was $355.
- There are 2 phone lines in Jen's house. One line is for the shop. Her monthly phone bill is about $90.
- The alarm system bill is directly withdrawn from Jen's account every month. The bill for last month was $42.
- Home insurance is $55 per month.
- The property taxes are paid semi-annually. The annual bill is $2490.

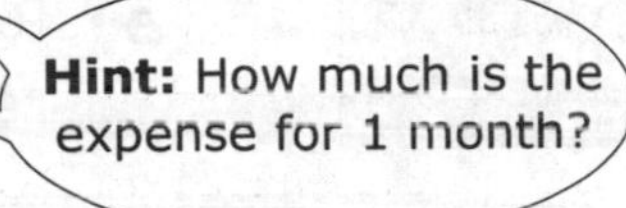

b) Set up a spreadsheet to record these expenses for 1 year. You will need to estimate the expenses for the rest of the year.
- Total each row so Jen will know her monthly expenses.
- Total each column for a total of the annual expense for each item.
- Title the spreadsheet **20**____. Use a row for each month.

Refer to **Tech Tip: Using a Spreadsheet** on page 64 for help with entering a formula.

You might use the following headings.

A	B	C	D	E	F	G	H	I
	Gas	**Electricity**	**Water**	**Phone**	**Alarm**	**Home Insurance**	**Property Tax**	**Total**
Jan								

2. Jen brainstormed a list of expenses that are 100% related to her business.

- furniture
- hairstyling chair
- appointment book
- scissors
- combs
- hairspray, gel, and mousse
- hair colour
- broom
- advertising
- washer and dryer
- towels
- shampoo
- smocks
- cash register
- electric shears
- curling irons
- hair dryer
- business cards
- cleaning supplies
- curlers

Use Jen's list to set up a second page on the spreadsheet from #1.
- The spreadsheet should allow Jen to record her business expenses for 1 year.
- Title the page Business Expenses.

3. Eventually items wear out and need to be replaced. The washer and dryer are 13 years old. Jen plans to replace them in 1 year.

a) Research the cost of a washer and dryer from a local retailer.

Appliance	Brand and Model	Price	Tax	Total Cost
• Washer				
• Dryer				

b) How much should Jen save per week so that she can pay cash for the washer and dryer in 1 year?

4. Jen's bookkeeper suggested that the business pay a mileage allowance whenever she drives her car for business reasons.

- Last week, Jen made deposits to her bank twice. The bank is 4.7 km from her house.
- Also, last week, Jen drove to an office supply store and to a wholesale store where she bought cleaning supplies. This trip was 17.3 km.

Chapter 4

a) Calculate the amount that should be reimbursed to Jen's business if the mileage allowance is 52¢/km.

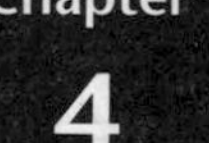

Hint: You need to enter 2 formulas.
- Enter a formula to calculate the amount per trip.
- Enter another formula to determine the total amount.

b) Set up a third page on the spreadsheet. Use it to record the following:
- date of travel
- reason for travel
- distance
- reimbursement amount

c) Enter the data from #4 into the spreadsheet. Use the spreadsheet to confirm your answer to part a).

 978-0-07-090894-9

- Jen deposits all of her income into 1 bank account.
- She pays all of her bills with 1 credit card.
- She is responsible for collecting and remitting HST.
- She has no payroll deductions.

5. Jen's schedule varies from day to day. Therefore, her weekly income can vary from week to week. Her average monthly income is between $2000 and $3000. She complains that when she files her annual tax return she always has to pay. Her bookkeeper determined that Jen's taxable income last year was about $19 000.

For the CRA payroll deductions online calculator, go to **www.mcgrawhill.ca/books/workplace12** and follow the links.

a) Go to the CRA payroll deductions online calculator. Use the calculator to determine the amount that would be deducted from Jen's weekly income if she were a regular employee. Since she is self-employed,
- do not deduct EI
- double the amount for CPP

Self-employed people also have to pay the employer's portion of CPP.

What is the amount? ______________

b) Based on the answer to part a), what suggestion could you make since Jen is concerned about her tax bill at the end of every year? ______________

____

- Jen needs to keep accurate business records that show her annual income and business expenses.
- She will use her records to complete a statement of business activities.
- Then, she can use the T1 form to file her business taxes as part of her personal income tax return.

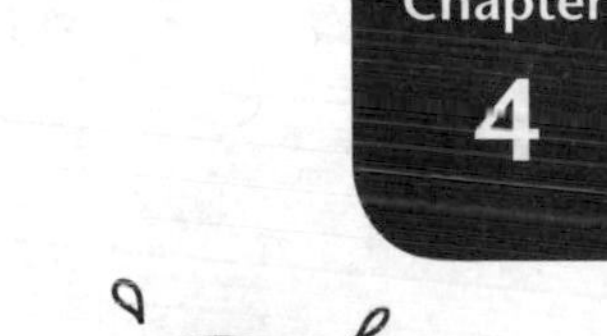

☑ Check Your Understanding

1. Jen can either keep records and file her own tax return or hire someone to do these tasks. What are the advantages of hiring a bookkeeper or an accountant to file a tax return for a self-employed person?

____

____

Chapter 4 Review

Match the description in column A with the correct term in column B.

A	B
1. used to summarize an employee's annual earnings and deductions	**a)** tax credit
2. used to determine the amount of federal tax payable	**b)** T1 General
3. used to determine the amount of federal and provincial tax to deduct from an employee's pay	**c)** tax deduction
4. used to determine the amount of Ontario tax payable	**d)** TD1
5. reduces the amount of tax payable	**e)** T4
6. subtracted from income to determine taxable income	**f)** ON428

7. a) Calculate Emil's approximate annual gross income if he earns about $575 per week.

b) Approximately 22% of gross income is deducted from Emil's pay. Calculate his approximate weekly net income.

8. How can keeping receipts for expenses help lower your income tax?

978-0-07-090894-9

Use the T4 to answer #9.

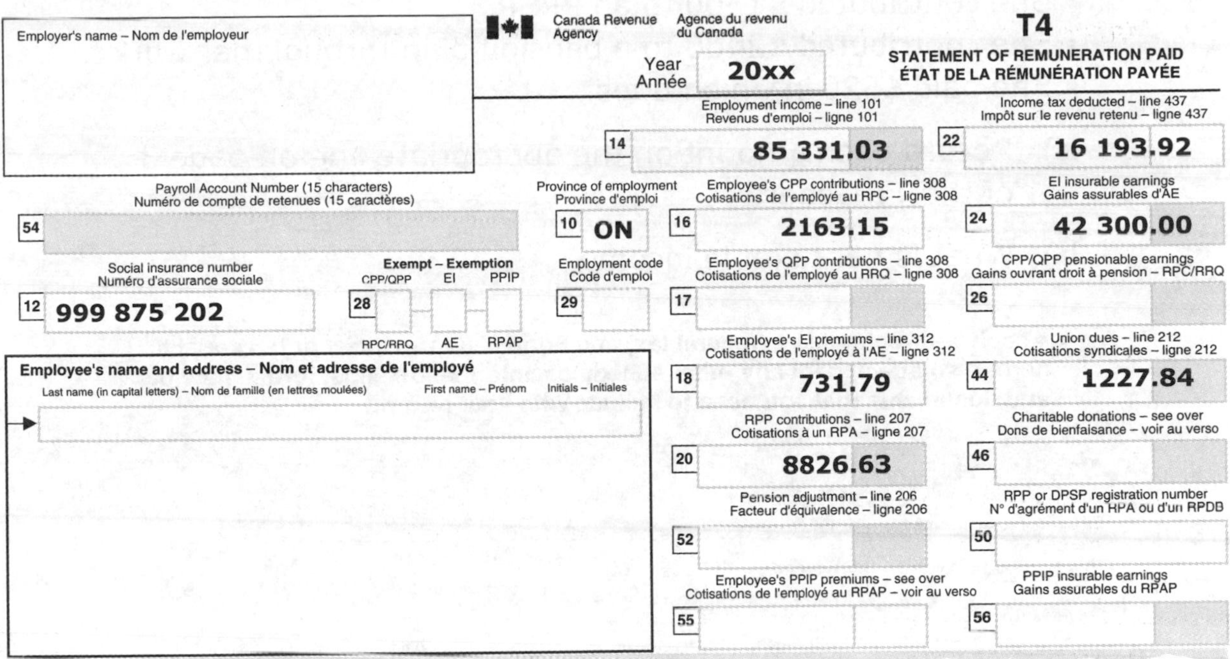
Canada Revenue Agency — Agence du revenu du Canada

T4
STATEMENT OF REMUNERATION PAID
ÉTAT DE LA RÉMUNÉRATION PAYÉE

Employer's name – Nom de l'employeur

Year / Année: 20xx

Box	Description	Amount
14	Employment income – line 101 / Revenus d'emploi – ligne 101	85 331.03
22	Income tax deducted – line 437 / Impôt sur le revenu retenu – ligne 437	16 193.92
54	Payroll Account Number (15 characters) / Numéro de compte de retenues (15 caractères)	
10	Province of employment / Province d'emploi	ON
16	Employee's CPP contributions – line 308 / Cotisations de l'employé au RPC – ligne 308	2163.15
24	EI insurable earnings / Gains assurables d'AE	42 300.00
12	Social insurance number / Numéro d'assurance sociale	999 875 202
28	Exempt – Exemption: CPP/QPP, EI, PPIP / RPC/RRQ, AE, RPAP	
29	Employment code / Code d'emploi	
17	Employee's QPP contributions – line 308 / Cotisations de l'employé au RRQ – ligne 308	
26	CPP/QPP pensionable earnings / Gains ouvrant droit à pension – RPC/RRQ	
18	Employee's EI premiums – line 312 / Cotisations de l'employé à l'AE – ligne 312	731.79
44	Union dues – line 212 / Cotisations syndicales – ligne 212	1227.84
20	RPP contributions – line 207 / Cotisations à un RPA – ligne 207	8826.63
46	Charitable donations – see over / Dons de bienfaisance – voir au verso	
52	Pension adjustment – line 206 / Facteur d'équivalence – ligne 206	
50	RPP or DPSP registration number / N° d'agrément d'un RPA ou d'un RPDB	
55	Employee's PPIP premiums – see over / Cotisations de l'employé au RPAP – voir au verso	
56	PPIP insurable earnings / Gains assurables du RPAP	

Employee's name and address – Nom et adresse de l'employé
Last name (in capital letters) – Nom de famille (en lettres moulées) | First name – Prénom | Initials – Initiales

9. Fill in each value using the T4.

a) Employment income ______	**b)** Province of employment ______
c) Income tax deducted ______	**d)** EI ______

10. List 2 tax advantages and 2 disadvantages of being self-employed compared to being an employee.

______

______

______

______

11. Your friend is in business for himself. His business starts to improve. What could he do to reduce his taxes?

______

______

Date

12. Zoe had a total income of $29 505 last year.

- She contributed $1500 to an RRSP.
- She contributed $2400 to a pension plan through her work.
- She paid $520 in union dues.

a) Record each amount on the appropriate line on page 3 of the T1 General.

b) What is her taxable income? ____________

Attach your Schedule 1 (federal tax) and Form 428 (provincial or territorial tax) here. Also attach here any other schedules, information slips, forms, receipts, and documents that you need to include with your return. 3

Net income

Description	Line	Amount		Line	Amount
Enter your **total income** from line 150.				150	
Pension adjustment (box 52 on all T4 slips and box 34 on all T4A slips)	206				
Registered pension plan deduction (box 20 on all T4 slips and box 32 on all T4A slips)	207				
RRSP deduction (see Schedule 7 and **attach** receipts)	208 +				
Saskatchewan Pension Plan deduction (maximum $600)	209 +				
Deduction for elected split-pension amount (see the guide and **attach** Form T1032)	210 +				
Annual union, professional, or like dues (box 44 on all T4 slips, and receipts)	212 +				
Universal Child Care Benefit repayment (box 12 on all RC62 slips)	213 +				
Child care expenses (**attach** Form T778)	214 +				
Disability supports deduction	215 +				
Business investment loss Gross 228 ______ Allowable deduction	217 +				
Moving expenses	219 +				
Support payments made Total 230 ______ Allowable deduction	220 +				
Carrying charges and interest expenses (**attach** Schedule 4)	221 +				
Deduction for CPP or QPP contributions on self-employment and other earnings (**attach** Schedule 8)	222 +		•		
Exploration and development expenses (**attach** Form T1229)	224 +				
Other employment expenses	229 +				
Clergy residence deduction	231 +				
Other deductions Specify:	232 +				
Add lines 207 to 224, 229, 231, and 232.	233 =		►	–	
Line 150 minus line 233 (if negative, enter "0"). This is your **net income before adjustments.**				234 =	
Social benefits repayment (if you reported income on line 113, 119, or 146, see line 235 in the guide) Use the federal worksheet to calculate your repayment.				235 –	•
Line 234 minus line 235 (if negative, enter "0"). If you have a spouse or common-law partner, see line 236 in the guide. This is your **net income.**				236 =	

Taxable income

Description	Line	Amount		Line	Amount
Canadian Forces personnel and police deduction (box 43 on all T4 slips)	244				
Employee home relocation loan deduction (box 37 on all T4 slips)	248 +				
Security options deductions	249 +				
Other payments deduction (if you reported income on line 147, see line 250 in the guide)	250 +				
Limited partnership losses of other years	251 +				
Non-capital losses of other years	252 +				
Net capital losses of other years	253 +				
Capital gains deduction	254 +				
Northern residents deductions (**attach** Form T2222)	255 +				
Additional deductions Specify:	256 +				
Add lines 244 to 256.	257 =		►	–	
Line 236 minus line 257 (if negative, enter "0") This is your **taxable income.**				260 =	

Use your taxable income to calculate your federal tax on Schedule 1 and your provincial or territorial tax on Form 428.

Chapter 4

978-0-07-090894-9

Date ____________________

Chapter 4 Practice Test

Match the description in column A with the correct term in column B.

A	B
1. used to summarize an employee's annual earnings and deductions ________	**a)** TD1
2. subtracted from income to determine taxable income ________	**b)** taxable income
3. used to determine the amount of federal tax payable ________	**c)** T4
4. used to determine the amount of federal and provincial tax to deduct from an employee's pay ________	**d)** T1 General
5. the amount that is left after all tax deductions ________	**e)** tax deduction
6. reduces the amount of tax payable ________	**f)** tax credit

Chapter 4

7. a) Calculate Danya's approximate annual gross income if she earns about $475 every 2 weeks.

b) Danya takes home approximately 92% of her gross income. Calculate her approximate bi-weekly net income.

8. What is the main focus of page 1 of the T1 General?

____

____

Date ______________________

Use the T4 to answer #9.

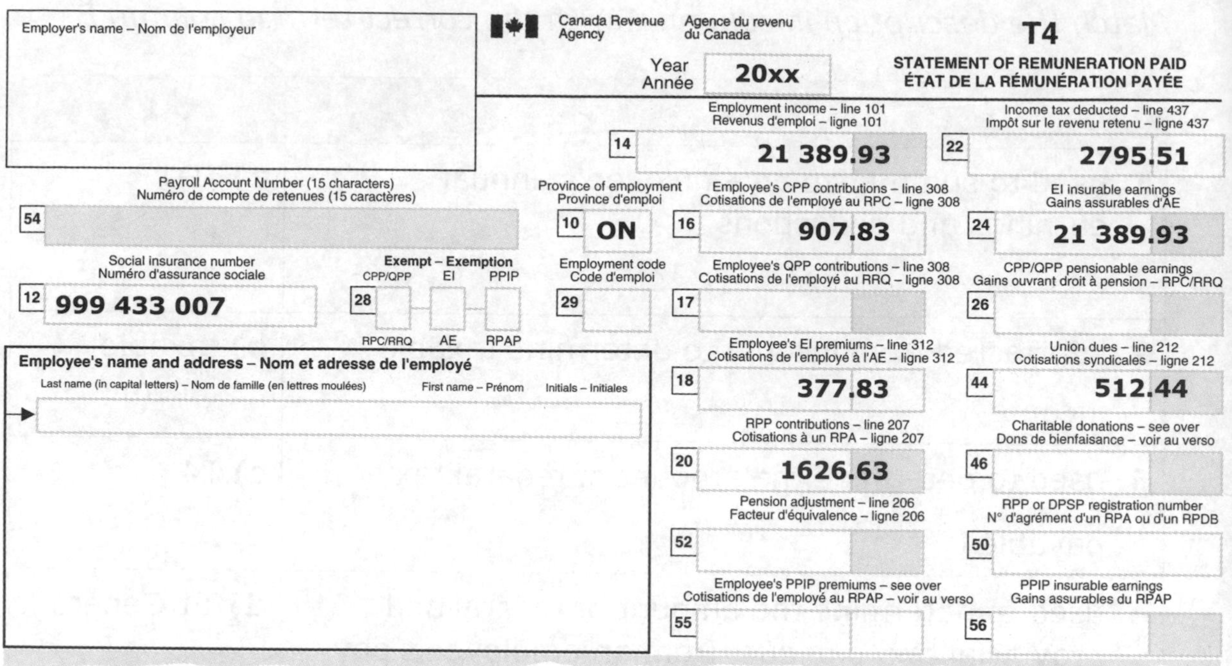

Employer's name – Nom de l'employeur

Canada Revenue Agency — Agence du revenu du Canada

T4

STATEMENT OF REMUNERATION PAID
ÉTAT DE LA RÉMUNÉRATION PAYÉE

Year / Année: **20xx**

Box	Description	Value
54	Payroll Account Number (15 characters) – Numéro de compte de retenues (15 caractères)	
12	Social insurance number – Numéro d'assurance sociale	999 433 007
28	Exempt – Exemption: CPP/QPP (RPC/RRQ), EI (AE), PPIP (RPAP)	
14	Employment income – line 101 / Revenus d'emploi – ligne 101	21 389.93
22	Income tax deducted – line 437 / Impôt sur le revenu retenu – ligne 437	2795.51
10	Province of employment / Province d'emploi	ON
16	Employee's CPP contributions – line 308 / Cotisations de l'employé au RPC – ligne 308	907.83
24	EI insurable earnings / Gains assurables d'AE	21 389.93
29	Employment code / Code d'emploi	
17	Employee's QPP contributions – line 308 / Cotisations de l'employé au RRQ – ligne 308	
26	CPP/QPP pensionable earnings / Gains ouvrant droit à pension – RPC/RRQ	
18	Employee's EI premiums – line 312 / Cotisations de l'employé à l'AE – ligne 312	377.83
44	Union dues – line 212 / Cotisations syndicales – ligne 212	512.44
20	RPP contributions – line 207 / Cotisations à un RPA – ligne 207	1626.63
46	Charitable donations – see over / Dons de bienfaisance – voir au verso	
52	Pension adjustment – line 206 / Facteur d'équivalence – ligne 206	
50	RPP or DPSP registration number / N° d'agrément d'un RPA ou d'un RPDB	
55	Employee's PPIP premiums – see over / Cotisations de l'employé au RPAP – voir au verso	
56	PPIP insurable earnings / Gains assurables du RPAP	

Employee's name and address – Nom et adresse de l'employé
Last name (in capital letters) – Nom de famille (en lettres moulées) | First name – Prénom | Initials – Initiales

9. Fill in each value using the T4.

a) Employment income ________	**b)** Union dues ________
c) Income tax deducted ________	**d)** Employee's CPP ________

Chapter 4

10. Explain why an employee holding 2 part-time jobs may wish to have 1 employer deduct extra income tax.

____

____

11. Eve has a receipt for tuition fees and one for moving expenses.

a) For tax purposes, how is each item classified?

____

____

b) Explain where each item would appear on a tax return.

____

____

978-0-07-090894-9

Date

12. DeMar had a total income of $66 520.55 last year.

- He contributed $2500 to an RRSP.
- His moving expenses totalled $2883.91.
- He paid $643.88 in union dues.
- He paid $3600 in child care expenses.

a) Record each amount on the appropriate line on page 3 of the T1 General.

b) What is his taxable income? ________

Attach your Schedule 1 (federal tax) and Form 428 (provincial or territorial tax) here. Also attach here any other schedules, information slips, forms, receipts, and documents that you need to include with your return. 3

Net income

Enter your **total income** from line 150.		150
Pension adjustment (box 52 on all T4 slips and box 34 on all T4A slips) 206		
Registered pension plan deduction (box 20 on all T4 slips and box 32 on all T4A slips)	207	
RRSP deduction (see Schedule 7 and **attach** receipts)	208+	
Saskatchewan Pension Plan deduction (maximum $600)	209+	
Deduction for elected split-pension amount (see the guide and **attach** Form T1032)	210+	
Annual union, professional, or like dues (box 44 on all T4 slips, and receipts)	212+	
Universal Child Care Benefit repayment (box 12 on all RC62 slips)	213+	
Child care expenses (**attach** Form T778)	214+	
Disability supports deduction	215+	
Business investment loss Gross 228 Allowable deduction	217+	
Moving expenses	219+	
Support payments made Total 230 Allowable deduction	220+	
Carrying charges and interest expenses (**attach** Schedule 4)	221+	
Deduction for CPP or QPP contributions on self-employment and other earnings (**attach** Schedule 8)	222+	
Exploration and development expenses (**attach** Form T1229)	224+	
Other employment expenses	229+	
Clergy residence deduction	231+	
Other deductions Specify:	232+	
Add lines 207 to 224, 229, 231, and 232.	233=	▶ –
Line 150 minus line 233 (if negative, enter "0"). This is your **net income before adjustments**.		234=
Social benefits repayment (if you reported income on line 113, 119, or 146, see line 235 in the guide) Use the federal worksheet to calculate your repayment.		235–
Line 234 minus line 235 (if negative, enter "0"). If you have a spouse or common-law partner, see line 236 in the guide. This is your **net income**.		236=

Taxable income

Canadian Forces personnel and police deduction (box 43 on all T4 slips)	244	
Employee home relocation loan deduction (box 37 on all T4 slips)	248+	
Security options deductions	249+	
Other payments deduction (if you reported income on line 147, see line 250 in the guide)	250+	
Limited partnership losses of other years	251+	
Non-capital losses of other years	252+	
Net capital losses of other years	253+	
Capital gains deduction	254+	
Northern residents deductions (**attach** Form T2222)	255+	
Additional deductions Specify:	256+	
Add lines 244 to 256.	257=	▶ –
Line 236 minus line 257 (if negative, enter "0") This is your **taxable income**.		260=

Use your taxable income to calculate your federal tax on Schedule 1 and your provincial or territorial tax on Form 428.

Chapter 4

Date ______________________

Task: Tax Planning

Aamira is 23, is single, and lives on her own. She holds 2 part-time jobs.

- Monday to Friday, she is a waitress in a restaurant. She usually works from 7 a.m. to 1 p.m. for the breakfast and lunch shift.
- Friday and Saturday, Aamira is a waitress in a busy bar. She usually works nights from 6 p.m. until closing.

Chapter 4

1. a) At the restaurant, Aamira earns the regular minimum wage.

What is this current wage? $________ per hour

b) How many hours does Aamira work at the restaurant during a regular week? ____________

c) Aamira is paid bi-weekly. Calculate her gross income for 1 pay period.

d) Aamira averages $40 per day in tips. Calculate her approximate annual total income from the restaurant if she works 50 weeks per year.

978-0-07-090894-9

Date

5 Owning a Home

1. Did her parents really buy their house for $47?

2. What does two-eighty mean?

3. a) By how much did her parents' house increase in value?

   b) By what percent did her parents' house increase in value?

4. Imagine that the young couple's house goes up in the same way as the parents' did. What can they expect it to be worth in 20 years?

Chapter 5

Date ______

5.1 Home Search

Focus: research housing prices

Warm Up	
1. What is $189K?	**2. a)** Round $179 900 to the nearest thousand dollars. ______ **b)** Express the answer using the notation in #1. ______
3. How many weeks are in **a)** 1 year? ______ **b)** 2 years? ______ **c)** 5 years? ______	**4.** How many months are in **a)** 5 years? ______ **b)** 10 years? ______ **c)** 20 years? ______
5. Someone with a net income of $720 per week earns either $______ or $______ per month.	**6.** What is 5% of $100 000?

Comparing Homes for Sale

1. Brainstorm the types of housing that people can buy in your community.

Chapter 5

978-0-07-090894-9

Date ____________________

2. a) On what streets or in what neighbourhoods in your community would you most like to live? Explain why.

____

____

b) On what streets or in what neighbourhoods in your community would you not like to live? Explain why.

____

____

3. **Real estate** refers to land and all buildings on the land. Houses are real estate. Real estate websites, magazines, and other publications often use abbreviations.

Go to pages 45–50 to write a definition for **real estate** in your own words.

a) Write the meaning of each abbreviation below.

b) Research other abbreviations used in real estate. You can use the Internet or local real estate publications. Write three more abbreviations along with their meanings.

For information about real estate abbreviations, go to **www.mcgrawhill.ca/books/workplace12** and follow the links.

Abbreviation	Meaning
C/A	
Cvac	
Sqft	
4BR	
3+1BR	

Chapter 5

Date

4. Write an advertisement that would attract buyers to a house with the following features. Use abbreviations.

• *north end neighbourhood*	• *storey and a half*
• *4 bedrooms: 2 upstairs, 1 on main floor, 1 in basement*	• *main floor bath with toilet, sink, tub, and shower*
• *downstairs bath with toilet and sink*	• *lot size 57 feet by 180 feet, fenced backyard*
• *central air conditioning*	• *paved driveway*
• *new roof installed this year*	• *$229 900*

5. a) Use real estate publications or the Internet to research the cost of housing in your community plus two others.

b) Complete the table by choosing a listing for each category. Record the main features of each listing. Be sure to specify the type of home.

For real estate websites, go to **www.mcgrawhill.ca/books/workplace12** and follow the links.

Price			
Less than $100K			
$100K to $200K			

Chapter 5

978-0-07-090894-9

Price			
$200K to $300K			
$300K to $500K			
Over $500K			

☑ Check Your Understanding

1. Select a home that you would like to purchase. You will use this home later in the chapter. Use the space below to attach a copy of the listing for the home.

Tech Tip: Using the TVM Solver to Calculate Mortgage Payments

Example

a) Kara is buying her first home for $255 000. Kara plans to make a 5% down payment and mortgage the rest. Her bank offers a 4.69% interest rate for a 5-year fixed rate mortgage based on an amortization period of 25 years. How much of a mortgage does Kara need?

Calculate the down payment.

$255 000 × 5% = $__________

```
255000*.05
         12750.00
255000-12750
        242250.00
```

Subtract the down payment. $255 000 − $__________ = $__________

Kara needs a mortgage for $__________.

b) Use a graphing calculator to determine Kara's monthly mortgage payment.
Since these calculations involve money, press **MODE**, ↓→→→, **ENTER** to set all calculations to 2 decimal places.
Press **APPS**, **ENTER**, **ENTER** to access the TVM solver.

- N is the number of payments, so N = ______.
- I% is the interest rate, so I% = ______.
- PV stands for ____________________. This is the amount borrowed, so PV = __________.
- PMT stands for Payment. This is the value we wish to calculate, so let PMT = 0 for now.
- FV is the ____________________ of the mortgage after all of the payments are made, so FV = 0.
- P/Y is for ____________________. Since Kara is making monthly payments, set P/Y = 12.
- C/Y is the number of times the interest is compounded in one year. All fixed rate mortgages in Canada have interest compounded twice per year, so C/Y = 2.

Chapter 5

978-0-07-090894-9

- The last line deals with when payments are due. The first payment is due at the END of the first month, so **END** needs to be highlighted.

After you set all of the variables, the program on the calculator does the work. Scroll up to PMT and press **ALPHA**, **ENTER**, which directs the calculator to SOLVE for the Payment.

- PMT = $ ____________.

Notice that the answer is negative! The TVM solver distinguishes between money received (+) and money given (−). The negative value makes sense since each payment is money that Kara gives up.

1. Use the TVM solver to determine each monthly mortgage payment.

a) $140 000 amortized over 20 years at 4.89%

N: ________, **I%:** ________, **PV:** ________, **PMT:** ____________,
FV: ________, **P/Y:** ________, **C/Y:** ________, **PMT: END BEGIN**

b) $368 000 amortized over 25 years at 4.25%

N: ________, **I%:** ________, **PV:** ________, **PMT:** ____________,
FV: ________, **P/Y:** ________, **C/Y:** ________, **PMT: END BEGIN**

c) $195 500 amortized over 25 years at 5.49%

N: ________, **I%:** ________, **PV:** ________, **PMT:** ____________,
FV: ________, **P/Y:** ________, **C/Y:** ________, **PMT: END BEGIN**

Date

5.2 Buying a Home

Focus: technology, number sense

Warm Up

1. What is 10% of $200 000?	**2.** What is 5% of $200 000?
3. What is the difference between a bungalow and a two-storey house?	**4.** Approximately what is 5% of $199 000?
5. How many monthly payments are made in **a)** 2 years? **b)** 3 years? **c)** 5 years?	**6.** How many pays do you usually receive in one year if you are paid **a)** weekly? **b)** monthly? **c)** bi-weekly?
7. If you deposit $100 per month, how much will you deposit in **a)** 1 year? **b)** 2 years?	**8.** How old will you be in 25 years?

Chapter 5

Paying for a Home

For most people, buying a home is the single biggest financial decision that they will ever make.

- Buying a home usually involves getting a **mortgage**, which is a loan used to buy property. It is repaid in regular payments over a set period of time.
- It can take as long as 25 to 30 years to pay off a mortgage. This is called the **amortization period**.
- Since interest rates are unlikely to remain the same for 25 years, most mortgages are broken down into 5-year **terms**. Term refers to the length of the current mortgage agreement. When the term expires, you can either pay the balance of the mortgage or sign a new mortgage agreement.

Go to pages 45–50 to write definitions for **mortgage**, **amortization period**, and **term** in your own words.

978-0-07-090894-9

Date

Types of Mortgages

- In a **fixed rate mortgage**, the interest rate is set for the term of the mortgage. That means the payments stay the same for the length of the term.
- In a **variable rate mortgage**, the interest can change every month. Interest rates can go up or down. This means the payments can change.

Go to pages 45–50 to write a definition for **fixed rate mortgage** and **variable rate mortgage** in your own words.

1. Give one advantage of each type of mortgage.

fixed rate

variable rate

2. a) What risk do you take with a variable rate mortgage?

b) What advice would you give someone who is considering a variable rate mortgage?

First Time Home Buyer

Before you can buy a home, you need to save for a **down payment**. This is the part of the home price that is not financed by a mortgage. First-time buyers need a down payment of 5%.

Go to pages 45–50 to write a definition for **down payment** in your own words.

3. List 2 advantages and 2 disadvantages of owning a home. Consider financial and non-financial factors.

Advantages of Buying	Disadvantages of Buying
a)	a)
b)	b)

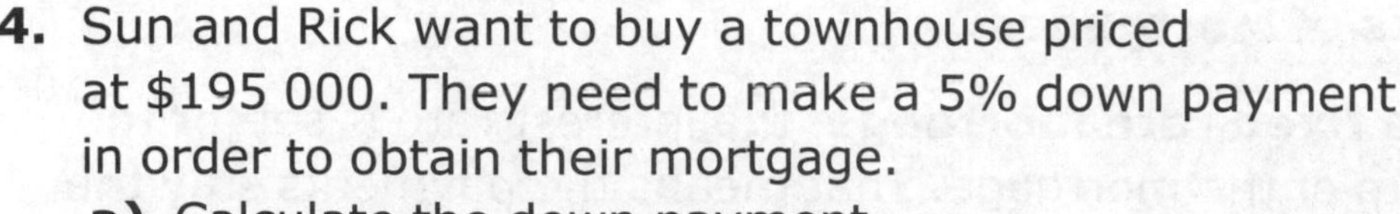

4. Sun and Rick want to buy a townhouse priced at $195 000. They need to make a 5% down payment in order to obtain their mortgage.
   a) Calculate the down payment.

   b) How much is the mortgage?

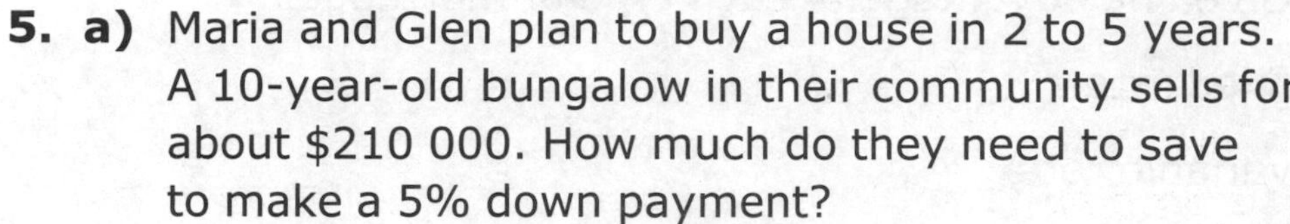

5. **a)** Maria and Glen plan to buy a house in 2 to 5 years. A 10-year-old bungalow in their community sells for about $210 000. How much do they need to save to make a 5% down payment?

   b) Maria and Glen have a combined net income of $54 000 per year. How much do they earn per month?

   c) They decide to save 10% of their monthly income. How long will it take them to save their down payment?

6. Peter sees a listing for a 3-bedroom bungalow on a small lot for $121 500.
   a) How much is a 5% down payment?

   b) Peter works as a line cook for $10.15/h and usually works 40 h/wk. What is his gross salary in a 4-pay month?

   c) Because he still lives with his parents, Peter can save 15% of his gross pay. How long will it take him to save the down payment for this house?

   d) His favourite aunt hears about his plans and gives him $2000 toward the down payment. How long will it take him to save the balance?

978-0-07-090894-9

How Much Can You Afford?

- According to some financial experts, you should not spend more than 32% of your gross monthly income on housing.
- Housing expenses include mortgage payments, property taxes, and heating expenses.
- For condo owners, the monthly condo fee is also included. This money covers shared expenses like snow removal, grass cutting, and building maintenance.

7. Nayara and Tom want to buy a condominium. Each month, they receive a combined gross income of $3175. The proposed monthly housing costs for the condo are $550 for the mortgage, $175 for property taxes, $125 for heating, and $125 for condo fees.

a) What is 32% of Nayara and Tom's gross monthly income?

b) Can they afford the condominium? Explain.

- According to the Canada Mortgage and Housing Corporation (CMHC), you should not spend more than 40% of your gross monthly income to repay debts.
- Debts include housing costs, and other things such as car loans and credit card payments.

8. Nayara and Tom make monthly car payments of $225. They also pay $150 on their credit card.

a) What is 40% of Nayara and Tom's gross monthly income?

b) Can they afford to pay the housing costs after paying for their other debts? Explain.

c) What advice would you give the couple if they want to buy the condominium?

Date ______________________

9. **a)** In the Tech Tip on page 171, Kara ended up with a monthly payment of $__________.

   b) Since her amortization period is 25 years, she has agreed to make monthly payments for 25 years! That means she will make ________ monthly payments before she actually owns the house!

   c) The total that Kara will repay the bank is

   __________ × __________ = $__________.
   monthly payment × number of payments = total paid

   d) Add in Kara's down payment. She will end up paying $__________ for this home.

   e) Suggest two options Kara might use to help her pay back the mortgage more quickly.

   ____

   ____

   f) How would your ideas in part e) save Kara money?

   ____

   ____

10. For each mortgage in #1 of the Tech Tip on page 171, calculate:
    - the total amount repaid to the bank
    - the total interest paid over the life of the mortgage

Chapter 5

Fixed Rate Mortgage Amount	Monthly Payment	Number of Payments	Total Amount Repaid	Total Interest Paid
a) $140 000				
b) $368 000				
c) $195 000				

978-0-07-090894-9

11. Look at your answers for #10. Compare the total interest paid and the original mortgage amount.

____

____

____

☑ Check Your Understanding

1. In the previous section, you selected a home to purchase.

The purchase price of the home is $__________.

a) Calculate 5% of the purchase price as a down payment.

____

b) Calculate the amount of the mortgage.

____

c) Research mortgage interest rates. Today's best interest rate for a 5-year fixed rate mortgage is _____.

For information about mortgage interest rates, go to **www.mcgrawhill.ca/books/workplace12** and follow the links.

d) Use a TVM solver or an online calculator to determine your monthly mortgage payment. Assume a 25-year amortization period.

N: ________, **I%:** ________, **PV:** ________, **PMT:** ____________,
FV: ________, **P/Y:** ________, **C/Y:** ________, **PMT: END BEGIN**

e) If you pay this amount every month for 25 years, how much will you pay before you own the home?

____

Chapter 5

Date ______________________

5.3 The Cost of Owning a Home

Focus: budgeting, number sense

Warm Up

1. If Cal makes a monthly mortgage payment of about \$1000, he pays about \$ ________ in 1 year.	**2.** Explain the difference between bi-monthly and semi-monthly. ______________________ ______________________ ______________________
3. An employee paid bi-weekly is usually paid ________ times per year.	**4.** An investment with quarterly compounding earns interest ________ times per year.
5. All fixed rate mortgages in Canada have interest compounded ________ times per year.	**6.** What is the average of 100, 120, and 170?

What Does It Cost to Own a Home?

Mortgage payments are not the only expense when you own a home. There are other expenses to consider.

- Some expenses are regular. Some occur only once in a while.
- Some expenses are predictable and some can catch you by surprise.

Chapter 5

1. In a small group, brainstorm expenses that you would expect from owning a home. Do not include everyday living expenses like food or clothing.

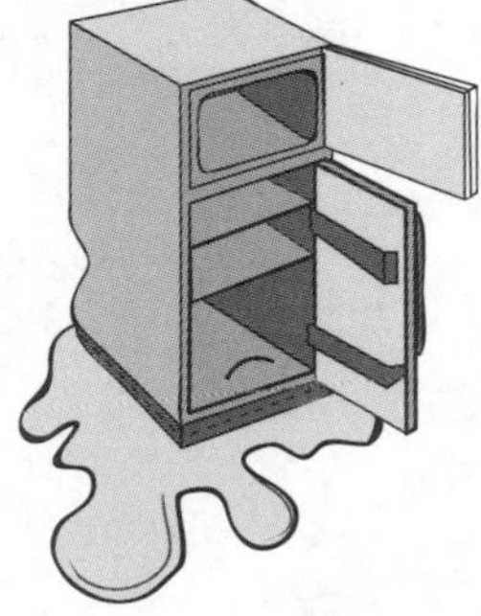

978-0-07-090894-9

Date

2. Talk to a homeowner. Develop a list of 10 home expenses. Find out the approximate cost of each in a typical year.

Home Expenses	Annual Cost

3. Gail is retired with a fixed income of $1900 per month. She lives in a 1-bedroom condominium.
   - Her mortgage payment is $618 per month.
   - The condo fees are $325 per month.
   - The hydro bill averages $150 every 2 months.
   - The quarterly water bill averages $180.

   a) Calculate Gail's fixed monthly housing expenses.

   b) Calculate Gail's average monthly expenses for **utilities.** Utilities refer to basic services such as electricity, gas, and water.

   c) On average, how much of her income is left each month?

Go to pages 45–50 to write a definition for **utilities** in your own words.

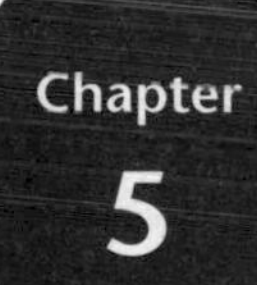

Date

4. Franca and Derek have owned their home for a year. They recorded their expenses on the spreadsheet below.

	A	B	C	D	E	F	G	H	I
1		**Mortgage**	**Property Tax**	**Security**	**Natural Gas**	**Electricity**	**Water**	**Cable/ Internet/ Phone**	**Total Month Expen**
2	**January**	1163.57		41.50	234.69			104.99	
3	**February**	1163.57	912.32	41.50	264.09	240.00		104.99	
4	**March**	1163.57		41.50	222.83		301.46	104.99	
5	**April**	1163.57		41.50	217.06	278.89		104.99	
6	**May**	1163.57	912.32	41.50	187.37			104.99	
7	**June**	1163.57		41.50	187.37	168.09	316.08	104.99	
8	**July**	1163.57		41.50	187.37			146.99	
9	**August**	1163.57	912.32	41.50		238.36		146.99	
10	**September**	1163.57		41.50	390.20		312.42	146.99	
11	**October**	1163.57		41.50	164.21	189.12		146.99	
12	**November**	1163.57	912.32	41.50	164.21			146.99	
13	**December**	1163.57		41.50	164.21	202.39	277.09	146.99	
14	**Total Annual Cost Per Expense**								

Chapter 5

Check that the total of column 1 is the same as the total of row 14.

a) Complete column I by adding all the values in each row.

b) Complete row 14 by adding all the values in each column.

c) In which month did Franca and Derek have the greatest home expenses? ________

d) What is their average monthly cost for electricity?

____

e) On average, how much do Derek and Franca spend on household expenses each month?

____

978-0-07-090894-9

Expect the Unexpected

Sometimes, expenses are unexpected. For example:
- A city sewer can back up, flooding your basement.
- An appliance can stop working.

5. Research the cost of replacing the following items, including taxes. Then, record information for 2 additional items of your choice.

a) microwave oven	**b)** fridge
c) garage door	**d)** dishwasher
e) 15 m^2 of carpet	**f)** furnace
g)	**h)**

☑ Check Your Understanding

1. a) List expenses that a homeowner has that a renter may not have.

b) List responsibilities that a homeowner has that a renter may not have.

c) List freedoms that a homeowner has that a renter may not have.

978-0-07-090894-9

Date ____________

Chapter 5 Review

The following advertisement appeared in a newspaper.

1. Round the price to the nearest thousand dollars. $__________

2. Explain 4+1 bedrooms.

____

____

3. a) After selling your current home for $293 500 and paying some bills, you make a down payment of $250 000. The mortgage on your new home is $349 900. The mortgage will be amortized over 25 years at a rate of 5.32%. Use a TVM solver or an online calculator to determine the monthly mortgage payment.

N: ______, **I%:** ______, **PV:** ______, **PMT:** ______,
FV: ______, **P/Y:** ______, **C/Y:** ______, **PMT: END BEGIN**

b) If you made monthly payments for 25 years, what is the total amount that you would repay the bank?

____

c) What is the total amount of interest that you would pay?

____

d) What is the total amount that you would pay for your home, including the down payment?

____

Chapter 5

 978-0-07-090894-9

Date

4. The spreadsheet shows last year's expenses for the home in #1.

a) Complete column G and row 14.

b) Which month had the greatest home expenses?

c) What was the average monthly cost for natural gas?

d) On average, how much was spent on household expenses each month?

	A	B	C	D	E	F	G
1		**Property Tax**	**Natural Gas**	**Electricity**	**Water**	**Cable/ Internet/ Phone**	**Total Monthly Expense**
2	**January**		272.89	340.22		146.99	
3	**February**	1050.00	303.28			146.99	
4	**March**		274.09	301.46	189.12	146.99	
5	**April**		232.13			146.99	
6	**May**	1050.00	197.30	338.36		146.99	
7	**June**		187.37			146.99	
8	**July**		177.37	368.79	264.21	146.99	
9	**August**	1050.00	164.21			146.99	
10	**September**		217.06	312.42		146.99	
11	**October**		244.49			132.47	
12	**November**	1050.00	290.25	416.68	277.09	132.47	
13	**December**		278.89	340.22		132.47	
14	**Total Annual Cost**						

Chapter 5

5. List 3 other expenses that you would expect to pay if you owned this home.

a)

b)

c)

Date ______________________

Chapter 5 Practice Test

1. a) The following abbreviations are found in real estate advertisements. Give the meaning of each.

Sqft ______________________

C/A ______________________

Condo ______________________

Kit ______________________

b) What is the difference between a 4BR house and a 3+1BR house?

____

____

2. For each price range, describe the type of accommodations, if any, that can be purchased in your community.

a) Under $100 000 ______________________

b) $200 000 to $300 000 ______________________

____

c) Over $400 000 ______________________

3. a) All fixed rate mortgages in Canada have interest compounded ______________________, that is, __________ times per year.

b) The Azirs have a $266 000 mortgage amortized over 25 years at 4.55% interest. Use a TVM solver or an online calculator to determine their monthly payment. __________

c) The Azirs will make __________ monthly payments before they finish paying for their home.

d) What total amount will the Azirs repay the bank? Assume that the interest rate stays the same.

______________ × ______________ = ______________

monthly payment   number of payments   total paid

e) How much interest will they pay over the life of the mortgage?

____

Chapter 5

978-0-07-090894-9

4. a) David has a 5% down payment on a semi-detached home for sale at \$314 000. What is the amount of his down payment?

b) What is the amount of the mortgage after making the down payment in part a)?

5. What are 5 expenses that you would expect to pay if you owned a condo? Identify each as a fixed expense or a variable expense.

a)

b)

c)

d)

e)

6. Marina lives in a 2-bedroom condominium overlooking a lake. Her expenses are as follows.

- The bi-weekly mortgage and property taxes are \$718.
- The condo fees are \$525 per month.
- The electricity bill averages \$320 bi-monthly.
- The quarterly water bill averages \$210.

a) Calculate Marina's fixed monthly expenses for housing.

b) Calculate Marina's average monthly expenses for utilities.

c) What is her average total monthly cost for housing?

7. What is 1 advantage and 1 disadvantage of owning a home? Consider financial or non-financial factors.
Advantage of buying:

Disadvantage of buying:

Date

Task: Buying Your Dream Home

Most people do not live their whole life in the place where they were born. Perhaps you have already moved once or more than once. Dream a little and select a Canadian community in which you would like to live.

To conduct a real estate search, go to **www.mcgrawhill.ca/books/workplace12** and follow the links.

1. a) Conduct a real estate search. Select a dream home, such as, a condominium, a duplex, or a detached house. Save the ad that describes your dream home.

b) Round the purchase price to the nearest thousand dollars. $________

c) State the annual property taxes, if given. If not given, use 1% of the value of the house and calculate the property taxes. $________

Your submission for this task will include
- an electronic folder of web pages or a collection of real estate ads
- a spreadsheet showing the full costs of the house

978-0-07-090894-9

Date ______________________

Measuring and Designing Glossary

Write the definition for each key term as you learn about it. Provide an example.

Key Terms		
capacity	net	surface area
composite shape	personal references	volume
exchange rate	scale drawing	

Term	Definition

Glossary

Date ______________________

Term	Definition

Glossary

 978-0-07-090894-9

Date

6 Measuring and Estimating

1. What error is the girl making?

2. What error is the boy making?

3. How long do you think the drive will take? Explain your answer.

Chapter 6

Date ______________________

6.1 Length

Focus: metric measure, Imperial measure, measurement references

Warm Up	
1. Solve *without* a calculator. **a)** 14 × 1 = ______ **b)** 14 × 10 = ______ **c)** 14 × 100 = ______	**2.** Solve *without* a calculator. **a)** 0.7 × 10 = ______ **b)** 0.7 × 100 = ______ **c)** 0.7 × 1000 = ______
3. Describe the pattern when multiplying by 10, 100, and 1000. ______________________ ______________________	
4. Count by 12s. ____, ____, ____, ____, ____ ____, ____, ____, ____, ____	**5.** Write 2 pairs of numbers that multiply to 12. ____ × ____ ____ × ____

Metric Length

1. Measure each line in the chart. Record the length in centimetres and in millimetres. The first one is done for you.

	Length in Centimetres	Length in Millimetre
a) ______________	4.3 cm	43 mm
b) __________		
c) ____________________		
d) ___________________		
e) ___		
f) ______________		
g) ________		
h) _______________		

Chapter 6

978-0-07-090894-9

2. Draw lines of the following lengths. Do not use a ruler. Instead, estimate each of the lengths.

Length	Estimation
a) 1 cm	
b) 5 cm	
c) 10 mm	
d) 5 mm	
e) 15 mm	

f) Measure each line in the chart. Label the actual measurement. See how close you were.

- Estimating the length of an item or distance is difficult without something to help you.
- Using a set of **personal references** can help you estimate certain lengths.
- A personal reference for 1 m might be the distance from the end of your nose to the tip of your longest finger when your arm is out-stretched. A personal reference for 1 cm might be the width of your cell phone's key.

Go to pages 187–188 to write a definition for **personal references** in your own words.

3. Collect 4 personal references that will help you estimate the common lengths in the chart. Describe your personal references in the chart.

Metric Length	Personal Metric Reference
1 cm	
10 cm	
1 m	
2 m	

4. Go to #13 on page 194 and complete the column titled Metric Length.

Chapter 6

Date

5. a) Complete the "Units" column by stating the metric unit that you would use to measure each item.

Item	Unit	Estimate	Metric Measurement
length of classroom			
height of a light switch			
thickness of a loonie			
diameter of a penny			
width of classroom door			

b) Complete the "Estimate" column by estimating the metric measure of each item. Use the personal references you have gathered.

c) Complete the "Measurement" column by measuring each item using a ruler or measuring tape.

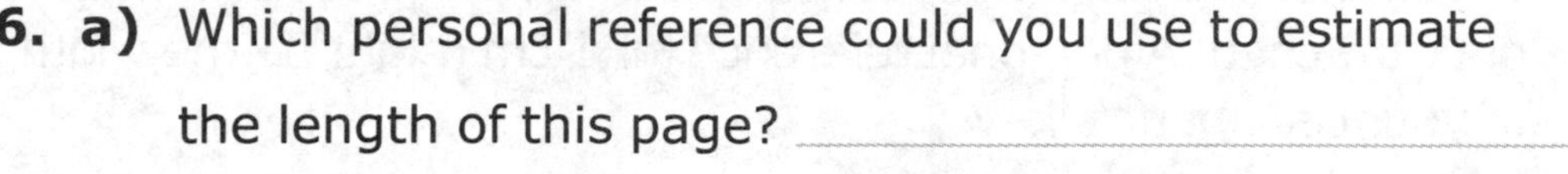

6. a) Which personal reference could you use to estimate the length of this page?

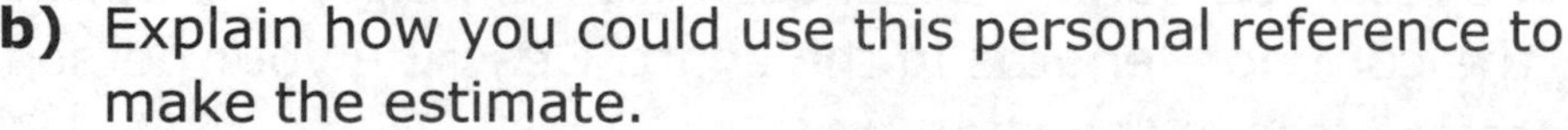

b) Explain how you could use this personal reference to make the estimate.

Imperial Length

7. a) What is half of a half?

b) What is half of your answer for part a)?

8. This diagram of an inch is divided into 16 equal parts. Identify each fraction shown with an arrow.

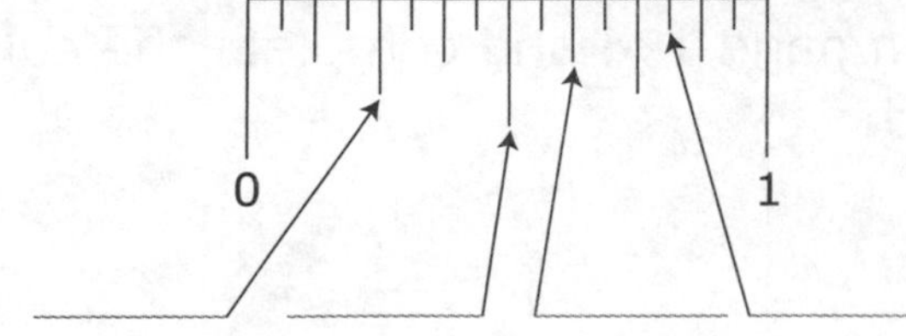

Chapter 6

 978-0-07-090894-9

Date

9. Measure each line. Record the length in inches or fractions of an inch.

a) ______________________________

b) _____________

c) ________________________________

d) ____

e) ____

f) ____________________

g) _______

h) ____________________________________

Length in Inches

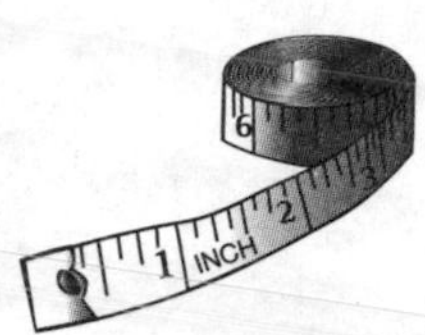

10. Draw lines of the following lengths. Do not use a ruler. Instead, estimate each of the lengths.

There are two short forms for inch: in. and ".

Length	Estimation
a) 1 inch	
b) 2 in.	
c) 3"	
d) $\frac{1}{2}$ inch	
e) $1\frac{1}{2}$ in.	

f) Measure each line in the chart. Label the actual measurement. See how close you were.

Chapter 6

11. a) How many inches are in 1 foot? ______

b) How many inches are in $\frac{1}{2}$ foot? ______

c) How many inches are in 2 feet? ______

d) How many inches are in 3 feet? ______

In the Imperial system:
- 12 inches is referred to as 1 ______
- 3 feet is referred to as 1 ______

- As with metric measurement, it's easier to estimate Imperial lengths using references.
- Good references use parts of the body or common things around you.
- The Imperial system was developed around personal references.

12. Collect 4 personal references that will help you estimate the following Imperial lengths.

Imperial Lengths	Personal Imperial Reference
1 inch	
1 foot	
2 feet	
3 feet	

13. What lengths could you use these body parts to estimate?

Personal Reference	Metric Length	Imperial Length
Your outstretched hand		
The length of your foot		
The length of your arm		
Your height		

 978-0-07-090894-9

Date

14. a) Complete the "Units" column with the Imperial unit that you would use to measure each item.

Item	Unit	Estimate	Imperial Measurement
Length of classroom			
Height of a light switch			
Thickness of a loonie			
Diameter of a penny			
Width of classroom door			

b) Complete the "Estimate" column by estimating the Imperial measure of each item. Use the personal references you have gathered.

c) Complete the "Imperial Measurement" column by measuring each item using a ruler or measuring tape.

15. a) Which personal references would you use to estimate the height of the classroom in Imperial measurement?

b) Explain how you would use that personal reference.

☑ Check Your Understanding

1. You are planning a special party and want to buy a tablecloth for a large table you have borrowed.

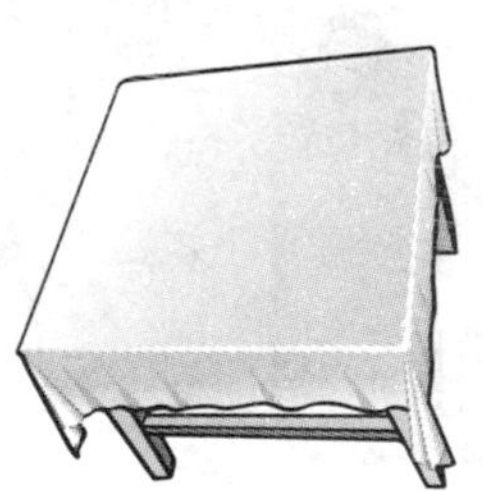

a) Explain which personal references you would use and how you would use them to measure the size of the cloth you need.

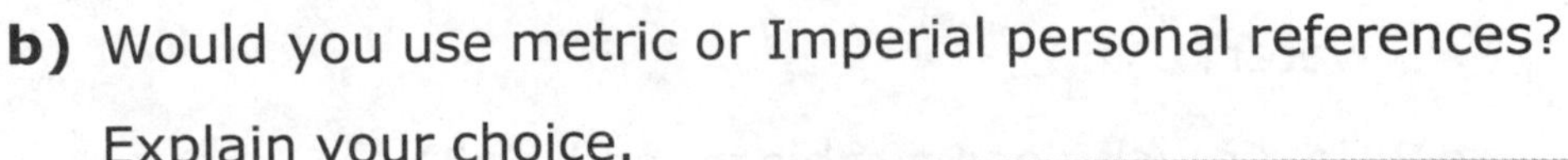

b) Would you use metric or Imperial personal references? Explain your choice.

Chapter 6

Date ______

6.2 Capacity

Focus: metric measure, Imperial measure, measurement references

Warm Up	
1. Solve *without* a calculator. **a)** 1500 ÷ 1 = ______ **b)** 1500 ÷ 100 = ______ **c)** 1500 ÷ 1000 = ______	**2.** Solve *without* a calculator. **a)** 355 ÷ 1 = ______ **b)** 591 ÷ 100 = ______ **c)** 473 ÷ 1000 = ______
3. Describe the pattern for dividing the same number by 10, 100, and then 1000. ______	
4. Solve *without* a calculator. **a)** 1.9 × 1000 = ______ **b)** 0.355 × 1000 = ______ **c)** 1500 ÷ 1000 = ______	**5.** List these Imperial units from smallest to largest: foot, inch, mile, yard ______, ______, ______, ______
6. a) There are ______ mL in 1 litre. **b)** There are ______ mL in $\frac{1}{2}$ litre.	**7.** Circle the better buy. 250 mL for $1.99 or 2 L for $9.99

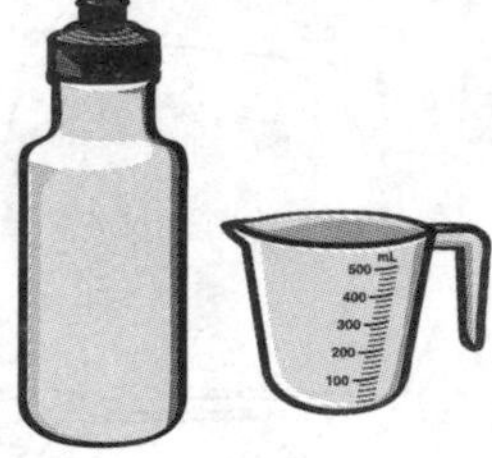

What Do You Already Know?

1. a) By what unit is gasoline sold in Canada? ______

b) By what unit is gasoline sold in the United States? ______

c) Which unit for selling gasoline is bigger? ______

d) What is the capacity of a small plastic bottle of water? ______

e) How much does a tablespoon hold? ______

Chapter 6

 978-0-07-090894-9

Metric Capacities

- The **capacity** of a container is the greatest amount that it can hold.
- You can estimate a capacity using a personal reference, just like you can estimate a length.

Go to pages 187–188 to write a definition for **capacity** in your own words.

2. Collect measurement references for the following metric capacities.

millilitre = mL
litre = L

Common Capacities	Reference
10 mL	
500 mL	
1 L	
2 L	

3. The chart in #2 provides some personal references. Use these references to estimate the following capacities. The last 4 rows are for containers of your choice.

Container	Approximate Metric Capacity
A typical coffee cup	
A small red plastic gasoline container	
A baby food jar	
A kitchen sink	

20 L

Date

4. Circle the most appropriate capacity.

Container	Most Appropriate Capacity			
a) A car's gas tank	500 mL	5 L	50 L	500 L
b) A small bottle of shampoo	30 mL	300 mL	3 L	30 L
c) A large drink from a fast food restaurant	0.5 mL	50 mL	1 L	2.5 L
d) A blue plastic bottle in a water dispenser	200 mL	2000 mL	20 L	2000 L

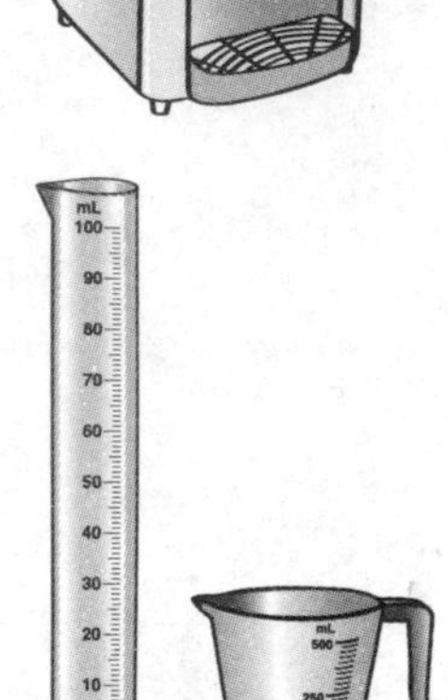

5. Look at the units on several graduated cylinders and metric measuring cups.

a) What units are used on the graduated cylinders? ______

b) What units are used on the measuring cups? ______

c) Are there any units on these items that you do not recognize? If so, list them.

______

______

6. Use a metric measuring cup or a graduated cylinder to measure out the following capacities. What personal reference could you use for each amount?

1 cc stands for 1 cubic centimetre. This is equivalent to 1 mL.

Capacity	Personal Reference
a) 10 mL	
b) 40 mL	
c) 75 mL	
d) 90 mL	
e) 150 mL	

Chapter 6

978-0-07-090894-9

US Imperial Capacities

- There are two type of Imperial capacities: US and British.
- Both use the same names for units: ounce, pint, quart, and gallon.
- Some of the units represent different sizes. For example, the US fluid ounce is slightly larger than the British fluid ounce.
- In this book, all references to Imperial capacities will refer to US Imperial units because the United States shares a border with Canada and is a major trading partner.

7. One US pint is equal to 16 fluid ounces. Convert each US measurement to the unit given.

a) 1 US quart
= 2 pints

= ________ fluid ounces

b) 1 US gallon
= 4 quarts

= ________ pints

= ________ fluid ounces

8. a) Use measuring cups with Imperial measure to measure out the following capacities. What personal reference could you use for each amount?

The abbreviation for pint is "pt". The short form for fluid ounce is "fl oz".

Common Imperial Capacities	Approximate Metric Equivalent	Personal Reference
1 fluid ounce	30 mL	
8 fl oz	250 mL	
1 quart	1 litre	
1 gallon	4 litres	

The abbreviation for quart is "qt". The short form for gallon is "gal".

b) Approximate metric equivalents are included in the chart. How might these help you remember Imperial capacities?

____

____

Chapter 6

Date

9. The chart in #8 provides some personal references. Use these references to estimate the following Imperial capacities. The last 2 rows are for containers of your choice.

Container	Approximate Imperial Capacity
A typical coffee cup	
A small red plastic gasoline container	
A baby food jar	
A kitchen sink	

10. Circle the most appropriate capacity.

	Container	Most Appropriate Capacity			
a)	A car's gas tank	1 qt	1 gal	5 gal	15 gal
b)	A small bottle of shampoo	1 fl oz	8 fl oz	16 fl oz	2 qt
c)	A large drink from a fast food restaurant	6 fl oz	16 fl oz	16 qt	16 gal
d)	A blue plastic bottle in a water dispenser	1 qt	5 qt	1 gal	5 gal

11. a) A coffee shop sells coffee in four sizes of cups. Use the information in the chart to determine the cost per fluid ounce for each size of cup. Round your answers to the nearest cent per fluid ounce.

Size	Capacity	Cost Before Tax	Unit Cost (¢/fl oz)
Medium	10 fl oz	$1.28	
Large	14 fl oz	$1.45	
Extra large	20 fl oz	$1.59	

Chapter 6

978-0-07-090894-9

b) Based on your answer for part a), which cup of coffee is the better buy? ______________________

c) Why would you choose a size other than the one that is the better buy? Explain your answer.

____

____

☑ Check Your Understanding

1. While watching an American television station, Jordan hears an ad for a grocery store. The store sells a gallon of milk for $2.99. Without considering currency exchange, what is the milk's approximate price per litre?

2. a) List 4 containers in your classroom.

Container	Estimate of Metric Capacity	Estimate of Imperial Capacity

b) Use your personal references to estimate the metric capacity of each container.

c) Use your personal references to estimate the Imperial capacity of each container.

3. a) Select one of your items from #2. Measure the actual metric and Imperial capacity of the container.

____

b) Are you better at estimating metric or Imperial capacity? ______________________

Chapter 6

Date ____________________

6.3 Estimating Large Numbers

Focus: estimating large numbers, developing strategies

Warm Up	
1. Round the following numbers to the nearest 10. **a)** 49 ______ **b)** 52 ______ **c)** 17 ______ **d)** 35 ______	**2.** Add the rounded answers from #1.
3. Add the numbers from #1.	**4.** Calculate the difference between your answers for #2 and #3. ____________________
5. Estimate how much a person will earn in 8 hours, if they make $11.90 per hour.	**6.** Round the amounts to the nearest dollar. **a)** $1.10 ______ **b)** 99¢ ______ **c)** $8.88 ______ **d)** $97.25 ______
7. Add the rounded answers from #6.	**8. a)** How else could you round the numbers in #6? ____________________ **b)** Recalculate the total using new values.

Make an Educated Guess

- How can you determine the number of fans at a basketball game, or the number of students at a dance?
- In many cases, the ability to estimate is more useful than the ability to calculate an exact answer. It's close enough to know that there were *about* 2000 fans at the game.
- Estimation also works well with time. For example, a flight scheduled to depart at 10:37 and arrive at 12:46 means that you'll be in the air for a bit more than 2 hours. Rarely is it important to calculate the length of the flight as 2 hours and 9 minutes.

1. a) Estimate the number of people in this picture. ______

   b) Describe the strategy you used to answer part a).

   c) Compare strategies with 2 of your classmates. What strategy did they use?

Chapter 6

Date ____________

2. a) Pick a square in the picture. How many people are in the square? ______

Animal populations are often estimated using this strategy.

b) How many squares are in the picture? ______

c) Assume that each square has about the same number of people in it. About how many people are in the picture? ______

d) State 1 advantage of using this method of estimating the number of people in the picture.

____

____

e) State 1 disadvantage of using this method of estimating the number of people in the picture.

____

____

Chapter 6

978-0-07-090894-9

3. Mei wants to build a rectangular patio in her backyard. The patio will be built in the centre of 4 trees, which form a rectangle. Mei is using square patio stones that measure 12″ by 12″.

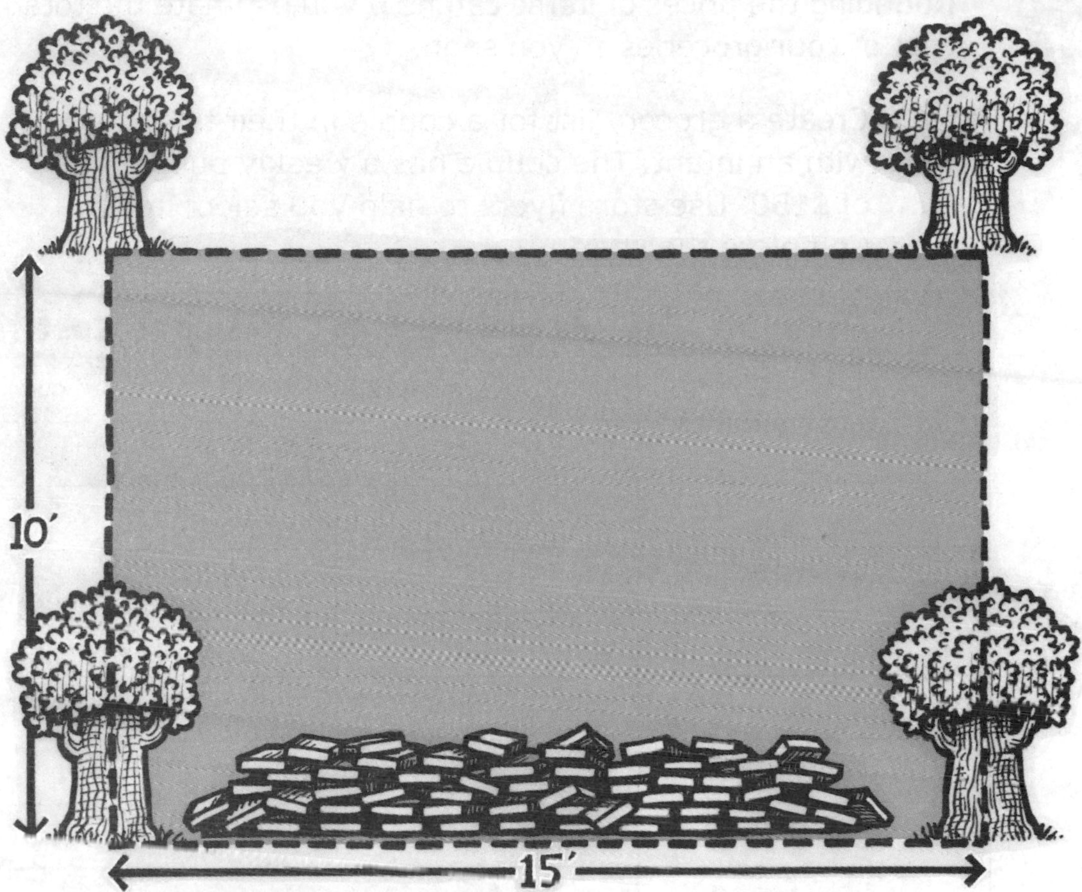

a) Draw a sketch of the patio Mei wants to build.

b) Calculate how many patio stones Mei would need to cover the patio.

c) Estimate how many patio stones there are in the picture. ________

d) Describe a strategy you could use to estimate the number of patio stones in the pile.

____

____

Chapter 6

Date

- When going grocery shopping, it is important to have a budget.
- When you shop, it is difficult to add the actual prices unless you have a calculator with you.
- Rounding the prices of items can help you estimate the total cost of your groceries as you shop.

4. a) Create a grocery list for a couple in their twenties with an infant. The couple has a weekly budget of $150. Use store flyers to help you select items. Complete the chart.

Item	Actual Cost	Rounded Cost
Estimated Total Cost		

Chapter 6

978-0-07-090894-9

b) What different strategies did you and your friends use for estimating the amount of this bill? Which ones worked best?

______

______

______

______

5. A website says that the driving distance between Gloucester (a suburb of Ottawa) and Orlando, Florida is 1439 miles. Driving time is approximately 24 hours. Estimate the following items.

a) How many times would you need to stop for fuel? ______

How long would each stop last? ______

b) What other stops would you need to make?

______

Estimate the total time needed for these stops. ______

c) So, the total time for the trip would not be 24 hours. It would be closer to ______ hours.

How many nights would you sleep over? ______

d) If you leave Gloucester at 6:00 A.M. on a Saturday morning, what day and approximately what time would you arrive in Orlando?

______

☑ Check Your Understanding

1. One square kilometre of a provincial park contains 12 deer. The park has an area of about 85 square kilometres. Describe how you could estimate the deer population of the park.

______

______

______

Chapter 6

Skills Practice 9: Converting Between Imperial Measures

There are 12 inches in 1 foot.
You can use proportional reasoning to help you convert feet to inches.

$$\frac{12\text{ in.}}{1\text{ ft}} = \frac{\_\_\_\text{ in.}}{6\text{ft}} \qquad \frac{12\text{ in.}}{1\text{ ft}} \overset{\times 6}{=} \frac{\_\_\_\text{ in.}}{6\text{ ft}}$$

You can also count by 12s.

1 ft = 12 in.
2 ft = 24 in.
3 ft = 36 in.
4 ft = 48 in.
5 ft = 60 in.
6 ft = 72 in.

1. Solve.

a) 4 ft = _____ in. **b)** 3 ft = _____ in.

c) 5' = _____" **d)** 1' = _____"

Convert 6 ft 3 in. to inches.
1 ft = 12 in., so 6 ft = 72 in.
6 ft 3 in. = 72 in. + 3 in.
= 75 in.

2. Convert each measurement to inches.

a) 1 ft 7 in. = _____ inches

b) 4 ft 11 in. = _____ inches

c) 10' 6" = _____ inches

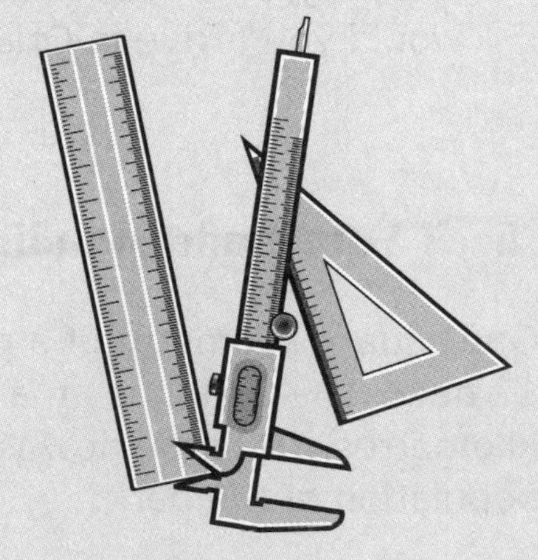

Chapter 6

 978-0-07-090894-9

Date ______________________

Convert 32 in. to feet and inches.

32 = 24 + 8

= 2 ft 8 in.

There are 24 inches in 2 feet.
There are 36 inches in 3 feet.
So 32 inches is 2 foot something.

3. Convert each measure to feet and inches.

a) 27 in. = ______ ft ______ in.

b) 70 in. = ______ ft ______ in.

Convert fractions of an inch to lowest terms.

Most tape measures and rulers divide each inch into sixteenths. Label the fractions shown.

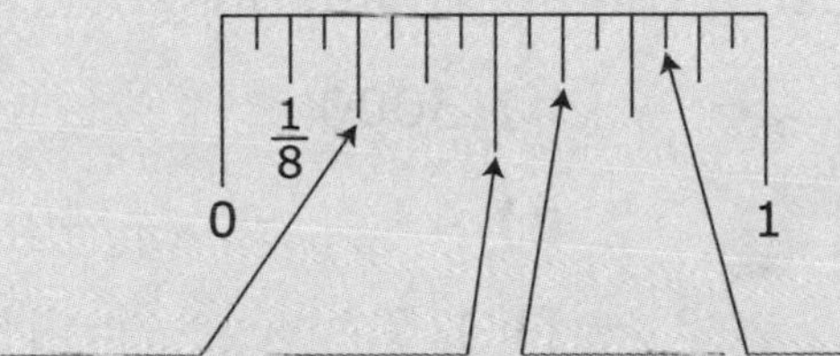

4. Small measurements can be measured as a fraction of an inch. Write these fractions in lowest terms.

a) $\frac{4}{16}$" = ______ **b)** $\frac{10}{16}$" = ______ **c)** $\frac{14}{16}$" = ______

Chapter 6

Skills Practice 10: Converting Between Metric Measures

1. a) Arrange the following metric units from shortest to longest.

kilometre *centimetre* *metre* *millimetre*

____

b) Write the common abbreviation for each unit.

______ ______ ______ ______

2. Fill in the blanks.

a) There are 10 ______________________ in 1 cm.

b) 1 m equals 100 ______________________.

c) 1 km equals ______________________ m.

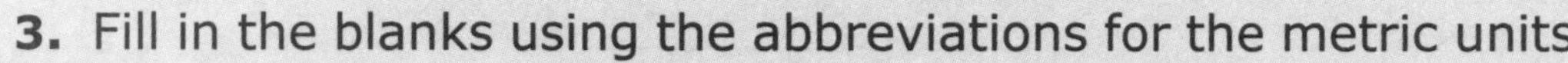

3. Fill in the blanks using the abbreviations for the metric units.

a) 2 m = 200 ______ **b)** 3000 ______ = 3 km

c) 400 cm = 4 ______ **d)** 4 ______ = 40 mm

e) 10 cm = 100 ______ **f)** 1.5 ______ = 1500 m

g) 260 mm = 26 ______ **h)** 260 mm = 0.26 ______

You can use proportional reasoning to help you convert centimetres to metres.

$$\frac{400 \text{ cm}}{? \text{ m}} = \frac{100 \text{ cm}}{1 \text{ m}}$$

$\div 4$

$$\frac{400 \text{ cm}}{? \text{ m}} = \frac{100 \text{ cm}}{1 \text{ m}}$$

$4 \div 4 = 1$

100 cm = 1 m

400 cm = 4 m

4. Convert each measure to the units shown.

a) 500 cm = ______ m **b)** 500 m = ______ km

c) 9 cm = ______ mm **d)** 9 m = ______ cm

e) 1.5 m = ______ cm **f)** 1.5 km = ______ m

5. Circle the larger measure.

a) 450 m or 45 km

b) 1 m or 120 cm

c) 300 cm or 0.5 km

d) 70 mm or 0.7 cm

 978-0-07-090894-9

Date ____________

6.4 Converting Units

Focus: metric measure, Imperial measure, proportional reasoning

Warm Up	
1. How many cents are in 1 dollar? ______	**2.** How many minutes are in 1 hour? ______
3. How many years are in 1 decade? ______	**4.** What is **a)** half of 12? ______ **b)** $\frac{1}{4}$ of 12? ______
5. State 3 metric units for measuring length. ______	**6.** State 3 Imperial units for measuring length. ______
7. How many nickels are in $2? ______	**8.** How many months are in $2\frac{1}{2}$ years? ______

What Units Do You Usually Use?

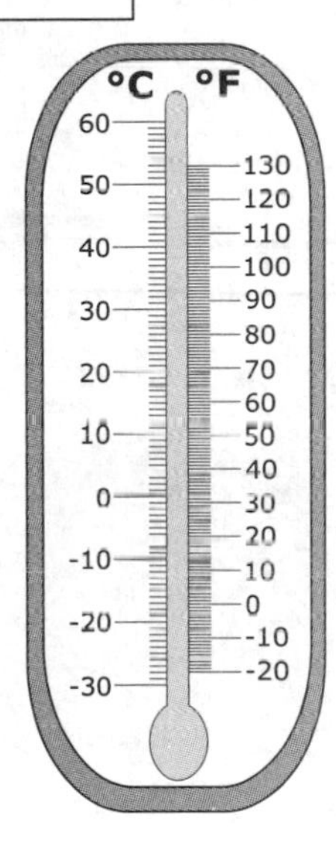

- Sometimes it is necessary to convert a measurement to a different unit.
- For example, you may measure the length of a room in inches but a store sells trim by the foot. You may need to mix litres and millilitres to get the right mix of gas and oil for your grass trimmer.

1. Fill in the blanks to complete the statement, "I tend to measure..." The first one is done for you.

a) the outside temperature in degrees Celsius

b) the oven temperature in degrees ______

c) my weight in ______

d) my height in ______

e) driving distances in ______

f) lengths in my home in ______

g) liquids in the kitchen in ______

h) weights in the kitchen in ______

Chapter 6

Date ______________________

Converting Between Metric Units

2. Write the metric units from shortest to longest.

centimetre kilometre metre millimetre

____

3. Often, if you know how to convert between 2 units, you are able to use what you know to convert between multiples of those units.

a) 1 m = ________ cm 2 m = ________ cm

b) 1 cm = ________ mm 3.5 cm = ________ mm

c) 1 km = ________ m 0.5 km = ________ m

d) Show or explain how you can use proportions to make these conversions.

____

____

____

For a review of how to convert from 1 metric unit to another, see **Skills Practice 10: Converting Between Metric Measures** on page 210.

4. Measure the following 3 items. State the measurement in 2 different metric units. Add 2 more items of your choice to the bottom of the chart.

Item	Length in Metric Units
a) the length of this book	______ ______ or ______ ______
b) the height of the classroom door	______ ______ or ______ ______
c) the thickness of a loonie	______ ______ or ______ ______
d) ______________	______ ______ or ______ ______
e) ______________	______ ______ or ______ ______

Chapter 6

 978-0-07-090894-9

5. Write the metric units from lightest to heaviest.

milligram   kilogram   gram

____

6. Fill in each box.

a) 1 kg = ______ g   2 kg = ______ g

b) 1 g = ______ mg   500 g = ______ mg

You would usually talk about "weighing" something. Mathematicians and scientists refer to "measuring its mass."

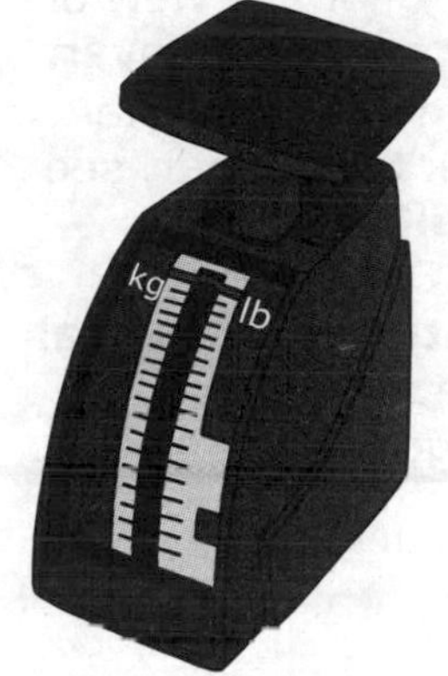

7. Weigh the following 2 items. State the weight in 2 different metric units. Add 2 more items of your choice to the bottom of the chart.

Item	Weight in Metric Units
a) this book	______ ______ or ______ ______
b) a loonie	______ ______ or ______ ______
c) ______________	______ ______ or ______ ______
d) ______________	______ ______ or ______ ______

8. a) Which unit do you think is better to use when weighing this book? Explain your answer.

____

____

b) Show how you can use proportions to convert grams to kilograms.

Chapter 6

Date ______________________

Converting Between Imperial Measures

9. Write the Imperial units from shortest to longest.

foot   inch   mile   yard

____

10. Fill in the blanks. Use a tape measure or yard stick for reference.

a) 1 ft = ________ in.   2 ft = ________ in.

b) 1 yd = ________ ft   10 yd = ________ ft

For a review of how to convert from one Imperial unit to another, see **Skills Practice 9: Converting Between Imperial Measures** on page 208.

- Imperial lengths are often stated as a combination of feet and inches. Sometimes just inches are used.
- Twenty-two inches might be shown as 22" or 1' 10". People rarely refer to it as 1.833 ft.

11. Convert the units as indicated.

a) 18 inches = ________ ft ________ in.

b) 27 inches = ________ ft ________ in.

c) 48 inches = ________ ft ________ in.

d) 5 ft 4 in. = ________ in.

e) 6 ft = ________ in.

12. Measure the following 3 items. State the measurement in 2 different Imperial units. Add 2 more items of your choice to the bottom of the chart.

Item	Length in Imperial Units
a) my height	5 ft 11 in. or ______ in.
b) the height of the classroom door	______ ______ or ______ ______
c) the thickness of a loonie	______ ______ or ______ ______
d) ______________	______ ______ or ______ ______
e) ______________	______ ______ or ______ ______

Chapter 6

978-0-07-090894-9

13. List the following Imperial weights from lightest to heaviest.

pound ton ounce

____

- There are 16 ounces in 1 pound.
- There are 2000 pounds in 1 ton.
- The abbreviation for ounce or ounces is "oz".
- The abbreviation for pound or pounds is "lb".
- The abbreviation for ton is "T".

14. Fill in the blanks.

a) $\frac{1}{2}$ lb= ________ oz

b) $\frac{1}{4}$ lb = ________ oz

c) $\frac{3}{4}$ lb = ________ oz

d) 20 oz = ________ lb

e) 4000 lb = ________ T

☑ Check Your Understanding

1. The perimeter of your living room is 500 inches. You need to put baseboard around the perimeter of the room. Baseboard is sold by the foot. How many feet do you need to buy?

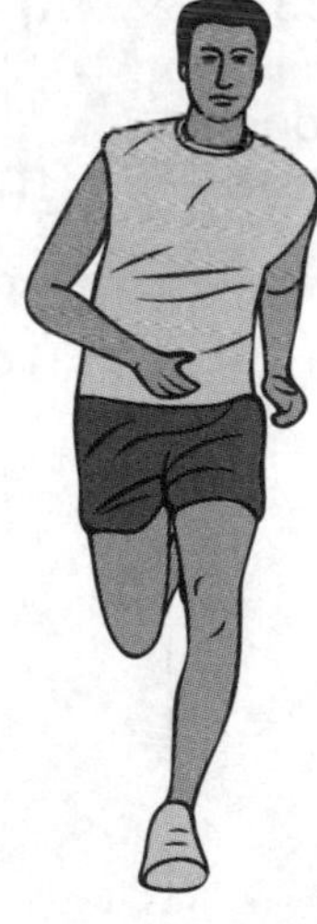

2. Mohammed has entered a 1500-metre race. How many kilometres will he run?

3. You are on holiday in the United States and buy a roast that weighs $2\frac{1}{2}$ pounds. How many ounces is that?

4. Kevin jokingly says that he is 5 ft 19 in. How tall is he?

Skills Practice 11: Using Ratio and Proportion to Convert Measurements

Equivalent Ratios

1. Jose is playing cards. He has 1 club and 3 diamonds. The ratio of clubs to diamonds is 1 to 3. This is commonly written 1:3.

a) Jose draws 4 more cards. One of the new cards is a club. To keep the ratio of clubs to diamonds the same, how many of the new cards must be diamonds?

$$\frac{\text{1 club}}{\text{3 diamonds}} = \frac{\text{2 clubs}}{\text{? diamonds}}$$

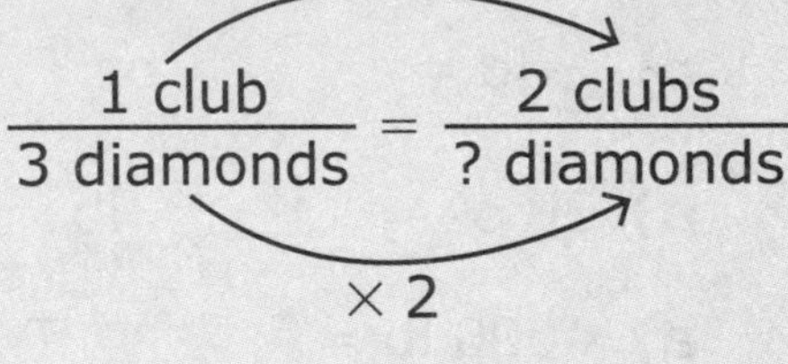

b) Write 2 equivalent ratios for the cards Jose has in his hand.

3 clubs:_____ diamonds

4 clubs:_____ diamonds

$1 CDN = $0.62 US
100¢ CDN = 62¢ US

Currency

Go to pages 187–188 to write the definition for **exchange rate**.

- The **exchange rate** between Canadian and American money varies from day to day.
- The exchange rate refers to the value of $1 CDN when you buy money from another country.

2. On November 7, 2007, the exchange rate hit a record high. $1 CDN was equal to about $1.10 US.

a) Sandi wrote a proportion to help her calculate how many US dollars she could have gotten for $2 CDN on that day.

$$\frac{\text{1 CDN}}{\text{1.10 US}} = \frac{\text{2 CDN}}{\text{? US}}$$

Explain or show how Sandi could use her proportion to calculate how many US dollars she could have bought.

Chapter 6

978-0-07-090894-9

b) On that day, how many US dollars could Sandi have bought for $100 CDN?

c) On that day, how many US dollars could Sandi have bought for $200 CDN?

d) Sandi's friend from New York came to visit. She had $150 US. How many Canadian dollars could she have bought on that day?

Construction

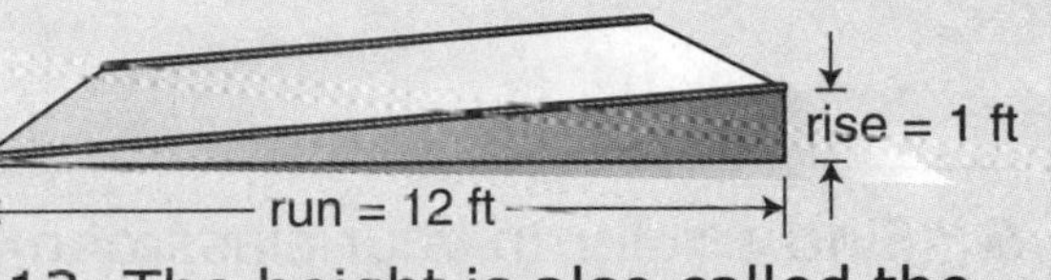

The ratio of the height to the horizontal length of a wheelchair ramp should not be greater than 1:12. The height is also called the "rise." The horizontal length is also called the "run."

4. Complete the chart for the rise or run of a wheelchair ramp with a 1:12 ratio.

$\frac{1}{12} = \frac{?}{24}$

Rise	Run
	24 feet
6 inches	
	6 metres
15 centimetres	
	15 feet
9.5 centimetres	

Chapter 6

Date ______________________

6.5 Converting Between Systems

Focus: unit conversion, proportional reasoning

Warm Up	
1. a) How many feet are in 1 yard? ________ **b)** How many square feet are in 1 square yard? ______________	**2.** Gas is sold in litres in Canada. What unit is used in the United States? ______________
3. What is your personal reference for 1 yard? ______________	**4.** What is your personal reference for 1 metre? ______________
5. Find a ruler in your classroom. How long is it? ________ cm ________ in.	**6.** A plane is scheduled to leave Pearson International Airport at 17:35. What time is that? ______________

Metric and Imperial Measurement

- The metric system is Canada's official measurement system. However, many people still use Imperial units for certain measurements.
- For example, lumber and wood trim are sold by the foot.
- In Canada, we buy gasoline by the litre. When we travel to the United States, we buy gasoline by the gallon.

Chapter 6

978-0-07-090894-9

Converting Length

1. Use a tape measure and create a set of approximate metric conversions for each Imperial length.

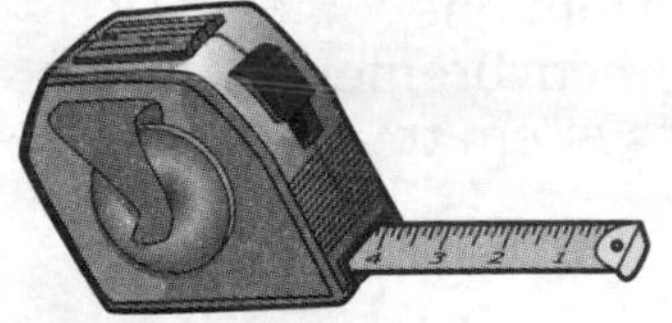

Imperial Length	Approximate Metric Conversion
1 in.	
6 in.	
1 ft	
3 ft	
6 ft	

2. Use a tape measure and create a set of approximate Imperial conversions for each metric length.

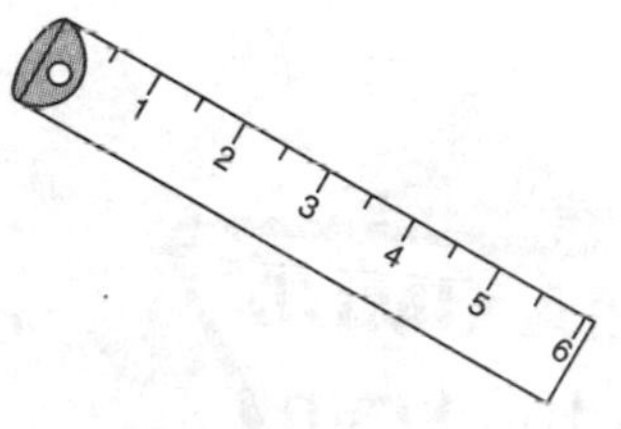

Metric Measure	Approximate Imperial Equivalent
1 mm	
1 cm	
10 cm	
50 cm	
3 m	

3. Work with a partner and measure each other's height.

My height: ______ cm or ______ ft ______ in.

My partner's height: ______ cm or ______ ft ______ in.

4. The bases in baseball are 90 feet apart. Approximately how many metres is this?

Chapter 6

Date ______

Go to page 291 for **Conversions Tables** that will help you convert from one measurement system to another.

Travelling in the United States

5. **a)** 1 mi = ______ km **b)** 1 km = ______ mi

6. Most 400-series highways in Ontario have a speed limit of 100 km/h. What is the speed limit in miles per hour?

______ mph

Go to **www.mcgrawhill.ca/books/workplace12** and follow the links to unit conversions.

7. The speed limit on parts of Interstate 79 in Pennsylvania is 70 mph. What is the speed limit in kilometres per hour?

______ km/h

8. An American travel website says the driving distance from Toronto to Orlando, Florida, is just under 1300 mi

a) Convert this distance to km

MAXIMUM 100 km/h

b) How many hours would it take you to drive from Toronto to Orlando, if your average speed was 100 km/h?

c) Is this a realistic estimate? Explain why or why not.

______

______

______

9. While you're in the United States, you hear that London, Ontario got 10 to 12 in. of snow.

a) Approximately how many centimetres is that?

b) What personal reference would you use for that height?

______

Chapter 6

978-0-07-090894-9

Go to **www.mcgrawhill.ca/books/workplace12** and follow the links to road trip planners. Select a city in the United States that you would like to visit. You will start your trip from your hometown.

10. a) 1 gal = ______ L **b)** 1 mi = ______ km

11. a) Pick an American city you would like to visit.

____

b) How far is your destination from your hometown?

______ km ______ mi

12. Assume that your car has a 50-L gas tank.

a) You will need to fill up along your route. Find a city along your route where you could stop to fill your gas tank. ______________

b) Research the price of gasoline in the city from part a). What is the price per gallon? ______

13. a) How much will it cost in American funds to fill the gas tank using the price in #12b)?

b) What is the current exchange rate between the US and the Canadian dollar?

$1 US = $ ______ CDN

c) Calculate the cost, in Canadian dollars, of filling the car.

Chapter 6

Weight Conversions

14. a) Use a scale or balance and create a set of approximate conversions for each weight.

Metric Weight	Imperial Weight
1 kg	______ lb
______ g	1 lb
______ g	1 oz

Go to **www.mcgrawhill.ca/books/workplace12** for links to exact conversions.

b) Check the following conversions from page 213, #6, for metric and page 215, below #13, for Imperial.

1 kg = ______ g   1 lb = ______ oz

15. You need 5 lb of fish for a favourite recipe. The supermarket sells fish by the kilogram. How many kilograms of fish should you buy?

16. A backyard hammock made in Sweden is rated to carry up to 160 kg. How many pounds can the hammock safely hold?

17. A nurse says that a newborn baby weighs 3978 g.

a) How much does the baby weigh in kilograms?

b) What is its weight in pounds?

Chapter 6

 978-0-07-090894-9

Temperature Conversions

- In North America, both the Celsius and Fahrenheit systems are used.

  Temperature in Celsius = $\frac{5}{9}$ × (Temperature in °F − 32)

  Temperature in Fahrenheit = ($\frac{9}{5}$ × Temperature in °C) + 32

The abbreviation for degrees Celsius is °C. The short form for degrees Fahrenheit is °F.

18. Claire decides to take a winter vacation in Florida. She flies from Toronto to New Orleans.

a) When Claire leaves Toronto, the news reports that the temperature is −10 °C. She text messages her friend in New Orleans, who asks for the temperature in °F. Convert the temperature for Claire.

b) When Claire arrives in New Orleans, the pilot announces that the temperature is 85 °F. Convert this to °C.

19. Omar is making lasagna using a recipe from the Internet. The recipe says to bake the dish for $1\frac{1}{2}$ hours at 175 °C. Omar's oven shows temperatures in Fahrenheit. At what temperature, in degrees Fahrenheit, should the lasagna be baked?

☑ Check Your Understanding

1. Even though Canada officially uses the metric system, what Imperial measurements do you use? Give 3 examples.

Chapter 6

Date ______

6.6 Measurement Systems at Work and at Home

Focus: proportional reasoning, basic calculations, decision making

Warm Up	
1. Convert the metric measurements. **a)** 1 L = ______ mL **b)** 2 L = ______ mL	**2.** Solve. **a)** $\frac{1}{2} + \frac{1}{4} =$ ______ **b)** $\frac{1}{4} + \frac{1}{8} =$ ______
3. a) 1 m = ______ mm **b)** 2 m = ______ mm	**4. a)** 1 kg = ______ g **b)** 14 kg = ______ g
5. How many 4-hour periods are in 1 day?	**6. a)** What is the ratio of male to female students in your class right now? ______ : ______ **b)** State 2 equivalent ratios to your answer to part a).

Measure Up!

At work and in everyday life, you might work with measurements several times each day.

1. A brand of chainsaw requires a gasoline to oil ratio of 40:1.

a) Explain the meaning of a 40:1 ratio.

______

______

b) How much gasoline would you add to 10 mL of oil? ______

c) How much gasoline would you add to 20 mL of oil? ______

Chapter 6

978-0-07-090894-9

d) Your gas can holds 5 L. You plan on adding the oil at home, then driving to a gas station to add the gasoline. How much gasoline and how much oil will you need?

e) What could happen if the mixture of gasoline and oil is incorrect?

Cooking for a Crowd

2. Jared works for a catering service. He is preparing breakfast for 100 people. To make 10 pancakes, Jared needs to mix 1 cup of water with 2 cups of pancake mix.

a) How much water and mix will Jared need for 20 pancakes?

water ______ mix ______

b) How much water and mix will he need for 30 pancakes?

water ______ mix ______

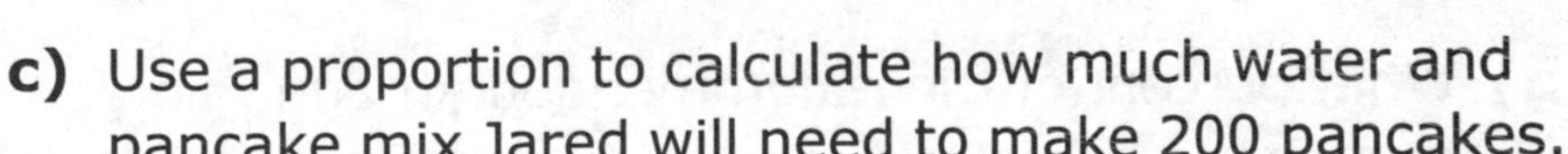

c) Use a proportion to calculate how much water and pancake mix Jared will need to make 200 pancakes.

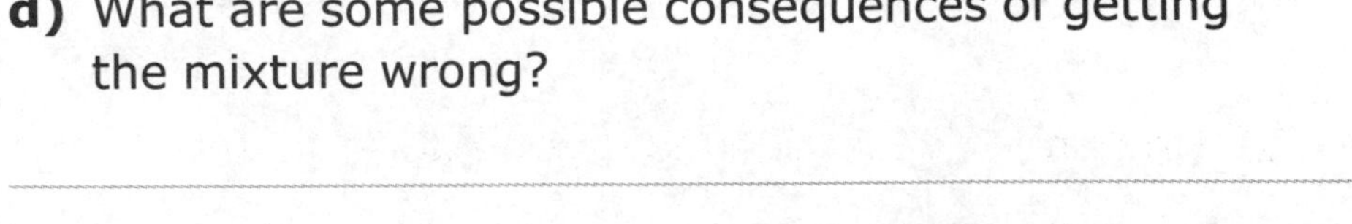

d) What are some possible consequences of getting the mixture wrong?

Chapter 6

Watching Your Health

3. Most nutritionists recommend that you drink plenty of water. One authority suggests calculating your daily water requirement in this way:

______________ ÷ 2 = ______________

your weight in pounds   daily ounces of water

a) How much do you weigh? ______ lb

b) Determine your daily water requirement in ounces.

c) Convert your answer from part b) to millilitres.

d) If you followed the recommendation above, how much water would you drink in 1 week? ______

e) Monitor your water consumption for 1 week.

S	M	T	W	T	F	S

f) What was your total water consumption for the week? ______

g) What percent of the recommended amount did you drink?

h) Research the health benefits of drinking water.

____

____

i) Sheryl has a 3-year-old daughter who weighs 34 lbs. How many millilitres of water should her daughter drink each day?

Chapter 6

 978-0-07-090894-9

Handling Medication

4. Brandon is taking care of his siblings, Crystal and Evan. Crystal is 3 years old and weighs 42 lb. Evan is 16 months old and weighs 22 lb. Below is a dosage chart for children's acetaminophen.

Weight (lb)	Age (years)	Single Oral Dose
Under 24	Under 2	As directed by a doctor
24–35	2–3	1 teaspoon = 5 mL
36–47	4–5	$1\frac{1}{2}$ teaspoons = 7.5 mL
48–59	6, 7, 8	2 teaspoons = 10 mL
60–71	9–10	$2\frac{1}{2}$ teaspoons = 12.5 mL
72–95	11	3 teaspoons = 15 mL

A single dose may be repeated every 4 hours, as needed. It is hazardous to exceed 5 doses of acetaminophen per day.

a) Brandon gave Crystal 1 kitchen tablespoonful, which looked like about $1\frac{1}{2}$ teaspoonsful. He gave Evan 1 kitchen teaspoonful. What would you have done?

b) What are some possible consequences of improper administration of medicine?

c) Brandon gave each child the medicine at 6 A.M. At what other times of the day could he administer the medicine?

✔ Check Your Understanding

1. Explain why measuring accurately is important.

Chap

Date ____________

Chapter 6 Review

1. Measure each line. Write the length in centimetres and in millimetres.

a) ____________________

b) ________

c) ______________________

d) __________________________

e) ___

Length in Centimetres	Length in Millimetres

2. Convert the length of each line in #1 to inches. Do not use a ruler.

a)	b)	c)	d)	e)

3. Measure the length of each line in #1 to the nearest fraction of an inch.

a)	b)	c)	d)	e)

4. a) Estimate the number of bricks in this wall. ______

b) Explain how you determined your estimate.

____

____

Chapter 6

978-0-07-090894-9

5. Fill in the blanks.

a) 1 L = _______ mL **b)** 1 pt = _______ fl oz

c) 1 qt = _______ pt **d)** 1 gal = _______ qt

6. Use >, <, or = to make the following statements true.

> means "greater than"
< means "less than"

a) I litre _______ 1 gallon **b)** 1 mL _______ 1 oz

c) 1 L _______ 1 qt **d)** 500 millilitre _______ 1 pint

7. Fill in each blank with a number that gives an approximation for the unit conversion.

a) One metre is approximately _____ feet.

b) One gallon is approximately _____ litre(s).

c) One inch is approximately _____ centimetre(s).

d) One foot is approximately _____ centimetre(s).

e) One litre is approximately _____ ounce(s).

8. A pickup truck has a 70-litre gas tank.

a) What is the capacity of the gas tank, in gallons?

b) A gas station in Niagara Falls, New York, sells gasoline for $2.67 US per gallon. Calculate the cost to fill the truck's gas tank.

c) Use the exchange rate you researched on page 221. What is the cost of filling the tank, in Canadian dollars?

d) A gas station in Niagara Falls, Ontario, sells gasoline for 98¢ per litre. Which gas station sells gas for the better price?

Date ______________________

Chapter 6 Practice Test

1. Measure each line to the nearest fraction of an inch.

a) ____________________________________

b) ______________________

c) ______

d) ____

e) __

Length in Inches

2. Convert the length of each line in #1 to centimetres. Do not use a ruler.

a)	b)	c)	d)	e)

3. Remeasure each line in #1. Show each length to the nearest 0.1 cm.

a)	b)	c)	d)	e)

4. Use the symbols >, <, or = to make the following statements true.

> means "greater than"
< means "less than"

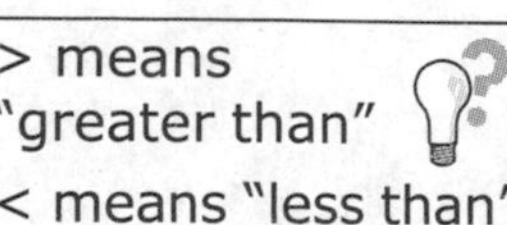

a) 1 gal _____ 1 qt

b) 1 qt _____ 1 L

c) 15 mL _____ 1 fl oz

d) 500 mL _____ 1 qt

5. Fill in the blanks.

a) 2 litres = _____ millilitres **b)** 1 pt = _____ oz

c) 1 qt = _____ pt **d)** 1 gallon = _____ quarts

Chapter 6

Date

6. a) Estimate the number of tiles in this shower stall.

b) Explain how you made your estimate.

7. Fill in each blank with a number that gives an approximation for the unit conversion.

a) One yard is approximately ____ metre(s).

b) One gallon is approximately ____ litre(s).

c) One foot is approximately ____ centimetre(s).

d) One metre is approximately ____ feet.

e) One litre is approximately ____ quart(s).

8. a) A motorcycle has a 20-L gas tank. How many gallons is this?

b) A gas station in Port Huron, Michigan, sells gas for $2.94 per gallon. Calculate the cost to fill the motorcycle's gas tank in US dollars.

c) Use the exchange rate you researched on page 221. What is the cost of filling the tank, in Canadian dollars?

d) A gas station in Sarnia, Ontario, sells gas for 96¢/L. Which city has lower priced gasoline?

Chap

Date

Task: Plan A Shopping Trip

- A Canadian who stays in the United States for a 48-hour period is allowed to bring $400 CDN worth of goods back into Canada.
- This amount includes any taxes paid on the items in the United States.
- You are going to plan a 2-day shopping trip to the United States.
- Before leaving, you will identify the price in Canada of what you want to buy.
- Then you will check the price in the United States.
- You will calculate where you can get the better buy.

Go to **www.mcgrawhill.ca/books/workplace12** and follow the links to Canadian and American retailers. What is the price of each item in Canada? in the United States?

1. Go to **www.mcgrawhill.ca/books/workplace12** and follow the links to road trip planners. Select a city in the United States that you would like to visit. ________

2. a) List 5 items you would like to buy while on your trip.

____

b) Research the cost of these items from Canadian stores near where you currently live. Note any important information about each item, such as the model number and the capacity of any container.

c) Select 1 or more retailers in the United States. What is the price of each item in US dollars?

978-0-07-090894-9

Date

7 Measurement and Design

Chapter 7

1. An old saying goes, "Measure twice, cut once." Explain what you think the saying means.

2. What do you think the woman means by, "There goes our budget"?

3. If you had a budget of $2000, what home renovation project would you like to do?

Date

7.1 2-D Scale Drawings

Focus: measuring, scale, proportional reasoning, problem solving

Chapter 7

Warm Up

1. What fraction of a metre is **a)** 50 cm? ______ **b)** 25 cm? ______ **c)** 75 cm? ______	**2.** What fraction of a foot is **a)** 6 inches? ______ **b)** 3 inches? ______ **c)** 9 inches? ______
3. How many 50-cm sections are in **a)** 2 m? ______ **b)** 3 m? ______ **c)** 4.5 m? ______	**4.** How many 6-in. sections are in **a)** 18 in.? ______ **b)** 9 ft? ______ **c)** $11\frac{1}{2}$ ft? ______
5. A road map uses a scale of 1 cm : 7 km. What is the actual distance between 2 towns that are 6 cm apart on the map? ______ ______	**6.** A particular yarn for a knit sweater yields 4 rows per inch. How many rows do you need to make an arm that is 15 in. long? ______ ______

Using Scale Drawings

- A dressmaker works from a pattern.
- A landscaper works from a drawing.
- An electrician works from a blueprint.
- A truck driver works from a map.

All of these people need to know how to read a scale drawing.

A **scale drawing** is a reduced or enlarged picture of an object.

Go to pages 187–188 to write the definition for **scale drawing** in your own words.

978-0-07-090894-9

Date

1. A bathroom floor is 8 ft long by 5 ft wide.

a) In the top-left corner of the grid above, create a scale diagram of the bathroom floor using a scale of 1 square to 1 ft. Label it Drawing A.

b) In the top-right corner of the grid above, create a scale diagram of the bathroom floor using a scale of 1 square to 2 ft. Label it Drawing B.

c) In the bottom-left corner of the grid above, create a scale diagram of the bathroom floor using a scale of 1 square to 6 in. Label it Drawing C.

d) A bathtub is 5' × 3'. Draw a bathtub to scale in each bathroom. Use this symbol to show the tub:

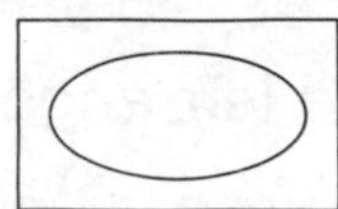

e) Which scale drawing do you prefer working with? Explain why.

Date ______

Chapter 7

2. a) Measure the length and the width of this book in centimetres. Round to the nearest centimetre.

length = ______ cm width = ______ cm

b) Draw a scale diagram of this book using a scale of 1 square to 3 cm.

c) Measure the diameter of 1 of the holes in the book. Round to the nearest centimetre. ______

d) Rounding to the nearest centimetre, measure the distance

- of 1 hole from the left edge of the book ______
- of the top hole from the top of the book ______
- between the top hole and the middle hole ______
- from the bottom of the book to the bottom hole ______

e) Draw all 3 holes to scale on your diagram above.

978-0-07-090894-9

Chapter 7

3. a) One wall in a family room measures 12 ft long and 8 ft high. Make a scale diagram using the scale 1 square to 6 in.

You have artwork to hang.

- Two prints are each 36" high × 24" wide.
- Two plaques are each 12" high × 18" wide.
- One photo is 21" high × 15" wide.

b) Calculate the number of squares needed to draw each piece of art to scale.

Print: ______ squares × ______ squares = ______

Plaque: ______ squares × ______ squares = ______

Photo: ______ squares × ______ squares = ______

c) Draw each piece of art on the diagram. You can cut out paper templates to help you decide where to hang the pieces.

d) How can your knowledge of proportional reasoning help you plan where to put the pictures?

____

____

Date ____________________

4. When you move, you get new closets and storage areas. Designing a closet to organise your belongings is an inexpensive solution to storage challenges.

a) A closet is 3 m long and 2.4 m high. Choose an appropriate scale and draw a scale diagram of the closet as if you were looking into it.

Scale: 1 square to ____________.

b) Design the interior of the closet with the following features:

- At least 1 rod for hanging pants.
- At least 1 rod for hanging shirts.
- Drawers or baskets for socks, underwear, etc.
- Compartments or a rack for sports equipment.
- Shelves for sweaters, books, etc.

c) Add 1 other item of your choice to your closet design.

 978-0-07-090894-9

5. a) Measure the length and the width of your classroom. Use whichever units you prefer.

   length = ________ width = ________

   b) Count the number of squares along each side of a piece of grid paper: ______ squares × ______ squares.

   c) Choose a scale that allows your scale diagram to take up most of the page.

   Scale: 1 square to ____________.

   d) Draw a scale diagram of the floor of the classroom as seen from above.

   e) Mark the location of doors and windows on the diagram.

Check pages 286–289 at the back of this book for grid paper.

6. Your class is considering rearranging the furniture in the classroom.

   a) Use another piece of grid paper to make scale templates of the big items in your classroom (desks, cabinets, white board, etc.).

   b) Arrange and rearrange the templates on the diagram from #5 until you have a design you like. Do not attach the templates to the diagram.

   c) Show your design to someone else. Do they have suggestions for improving it? Once you have decided on a final layout, attach the templates to the diagram.

☑ Check Your Understanding

1. Repeat #5 and #6 using an area of personal interest, such as
   - another classroom, a computer lab, or a weight room
   - a flower bed, a courtyard, or a parking area
   - a bedroom, a garden, a kitchen, or a bathroom

2. What other situations might use a scale drawing?

____

____

Chapter 7

Skills Practice 12: The 3–4–5 Method of Checking for a 90° Angle

A triangle with a 90° angle has a special property.

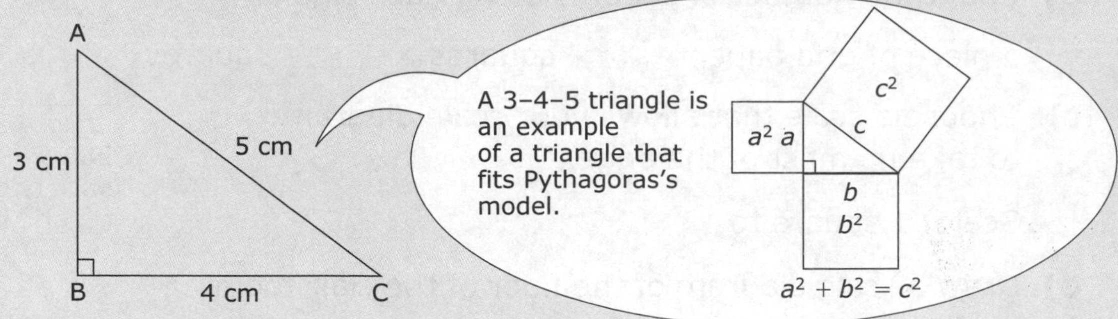

AB is 3 cm. $3^2 = 9$

BC is 4 cm. $4^2 = 16$ } $9 + 16 = 25$

AC is 5 cm. $5^2 = 25$

- When the sum of the areas of the squares on the short sides equals the area of the square on the long side, the triangle has a 90° angle.

1. Which of these triangles has a 90° angle? How do you know?

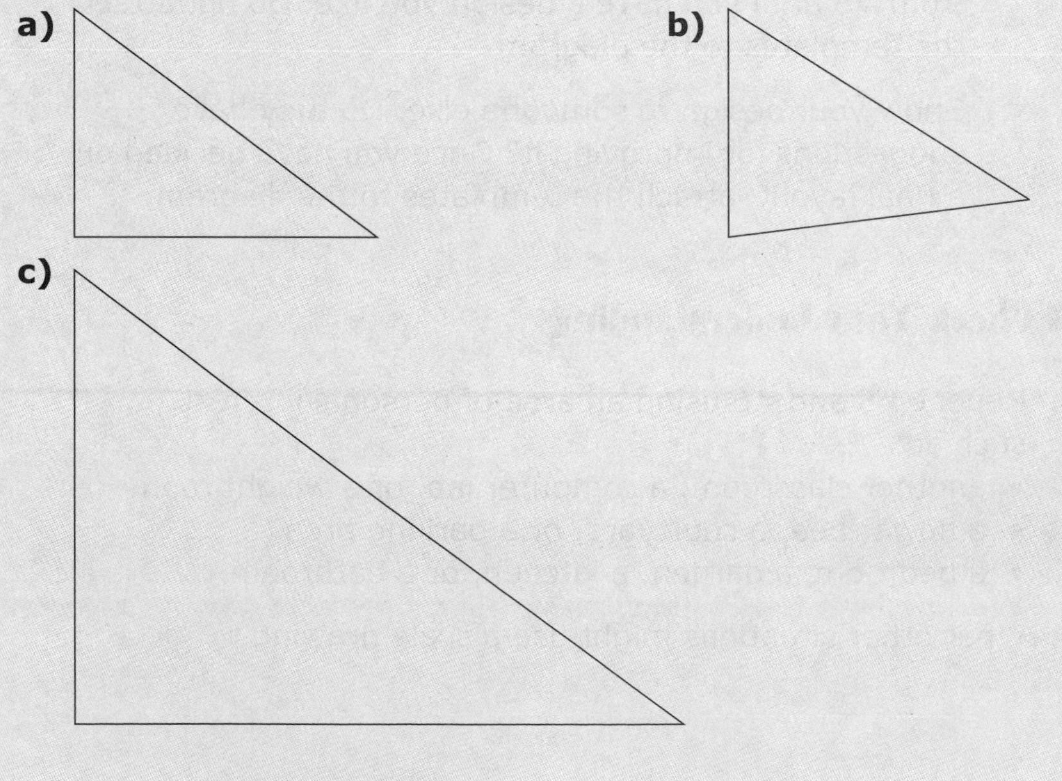

 978-0-07-090894-9

Skills Practice 13: Start Square and You'll Finish Square

When installing floor tile, it is a good idea to start in the centre of the room and move outward toward the walls. It is important that your tiles flow perfectly horizontally and vertically from the centre. Below is a diagram of an empty room.

1. Measure the length of each of the 2 longer walls and mark the midpoint of each wall. Draw a light line between these 2 points.
2. Repeat step 1 using the 2 shorter walls.
3. The intersection of these 2 lines is the centre of the room. Use the steps below to check if the 2 lines meet at exactly 90°.
   a) Carefully measure 3 cm from the centre along the vertical line. Mark this location on the line.
   b) Measure 4 cm from the centre along the horizontal line. Mark this location on the line.
   c) Measure the distance between these 2 marks. ____________

Skills Practice 12: The 3–4–5 Method of Checking for a 90° Angle on page 240 will help you with this.

4. Is your measurement in #3c) exactly 5 cm? If so, then you did #1 and #2 correctly so the lines meet at 90°. If the distance is not exactly 5 cm, your lines are not "square," meaning that they do not meet at exactly 90°. Redo steps 1 to 3.

5. Why is it important to start laying tiles at the centre of the room using a 90° angle?

6. Check if the corners of your classroom are square.

a) Measure 3 ft along the wall from 1 side of a corner. Mark the location.

b) Measure 4 ft along the wall from the other side of the same corner. Mark the location.

c) If the corner is square and you have measured carefully, what distance should there be between the 2 marks? ______

d) Check it.

e) If you don't get the measurement you expect, redo parts a), b), and c). Is the corner square? YES NO
Explain how you know.

 978-0-07-090894-9

Date ____________________

7.2 Perimeter and Area Applications

Focus: scale, measurement, problem solving

Chapter 7

Warm Up

1. Define perimeter. ______________________ ______________________ ______________________	**2.** Define area. ______________________ ______________________ ______________________
3. a) If the dimensions of a garden are given in feet, then the unit for expressing perimeter is ____________. **b)** The abbreviation for this unit of measure is ______.	**4. a)** If the dimensions of a playground are given in metres, then the unit for expressing area is ____________ ____________. **b)** The abbreviation for this unit of measure is ______.
5. Calculate $3^2 + 4^2$.	**6.** Calculate 5^2.
7. Fill in the missing dimensions. 6 ft 3 ft ______ ______	**8.** Fill in the missing dimensions. 7 m ______ ______ ______
9. a) Determine the perimeter of the rectangle in #7. **b)** Determine the area of the rectangle in #7.	**10. a)** Determine the perimeter of the square in #8. **b)** Determine the area of the square in #8.

Date

Applying Scale Diagrams

Chapter 7

1. A bathroom floor is 8 ft long by 5 ft wide.

You worked with this bathroom in #1 on page 235.

a) On the grid below, draw a scale diagram of the bathroom using a scale of 1 square to 6 inches.

For an interactive bathroom planner, go to **www.mcgrawhill.ca/books/workplace12** and follow the links.

b) A bathtub is 5' × 3'. Draw a bathtub to scale. Use this symbol to draw the tub:

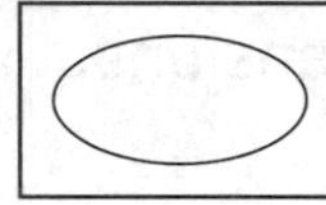

c) Mark a 2-ft wide door on your diagram.

d) Baseboard trim rests on the floor and is nailed to the base of the walls. Use a coloured pencil to show where there is baseboard in your diagram. How much baseboard do you need for the bathroom?

e) How many 8-foot lengths will you need? ______

 978-0-07-090894-9

f) If one 8-foot length costs $14.99, calculate the before-tax cost of all of the baseboard.

g) Calculate the cost of the baseboard, including tax.

h) Some bathrooms have vinyl flooring. On the diagram on page 244, colour the area that will be covered. Calculate the area of the floor.

i) Some bathrooms have ceramic tile flooring. How many 6" × 6" tiles would you need for this area?

j) Tiles come in boxes of 12. How many boxes do you need?

k) If a box of tiles costs $17.99, calculate the before-tax cost of the tiles you need to cover the room.

l) How much would the tiles cost after tax?

Date

- Not all jobs or projects use just squares or rectangles.

2. a) Draw a diagonal line across the rectangle.

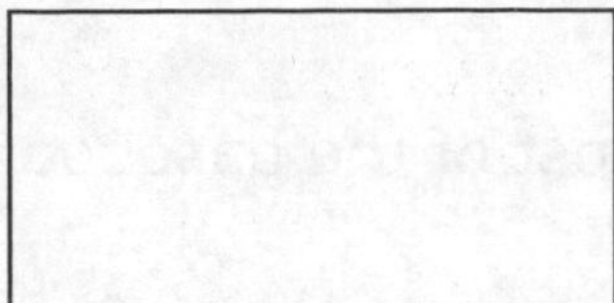

b) How does the area of each triangle relate to the area of the rectangle?

c) Determine the area of each of the following triangles.

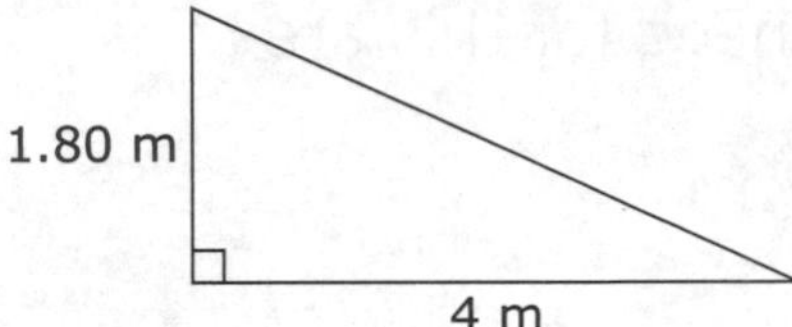

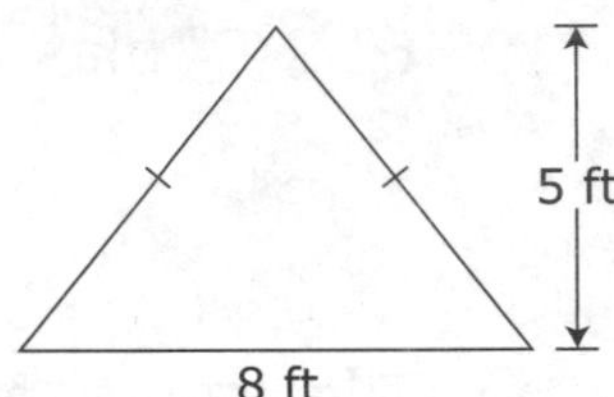

d) Calculate the area of the back of a garage that needs to be painted.

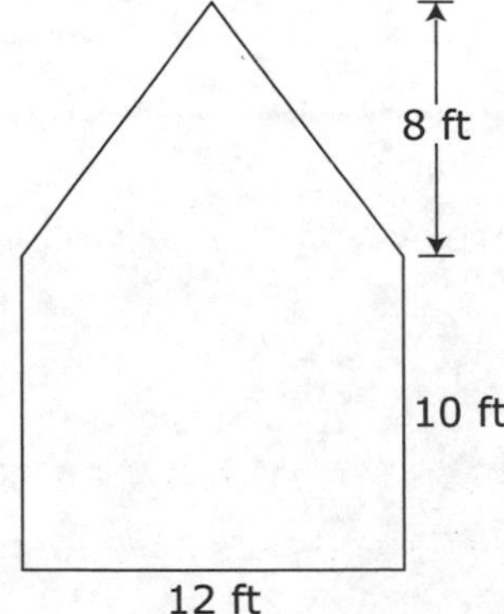

 978-0-07-090894-9

- Three friends have volunteered to paint their hockey team's logo at centre ice of the local rink.
- The outside edge of the circular crest must be 3 m from centre ice.
- The friends want to know the area of the ice that needs to be painted.

Estimating Circular Area

3. a) The distance between the centre of a circle and the outside edge is called the ______. Make a sketch of the circle on the grid below.

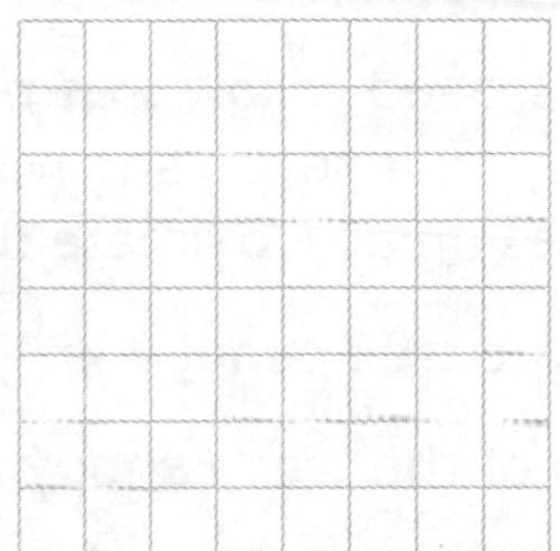

b) You can use the radius of a circle to help estimate the area of the circle. Draw 4 squares on the diagram above as shown below.

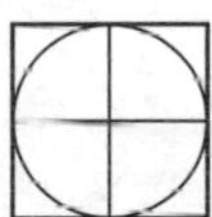

c) Calculate the area of each square.

d) Calculate r^2.

e) Calculate the area of the 4 squares.

f) Since the area of the circle is less than 4 times the radius squared, an estimate for the area of the circle to be painted is ______.

Chapter 7

Calculating Circular Area

- The exact area of a circle is π times the radius squared, or $A = \pi r^2$.
- Use 3.14 to approximate π.

4. Calculate the area of the ice that will need to be painted.

$A = \pi r^2$

$= \_\_\_\_ \times \_\_\_\_ \times \_\_\_\_$

$= \_\_\_\_$

Rounded to the nearest square unit, the area to be painted is __________.

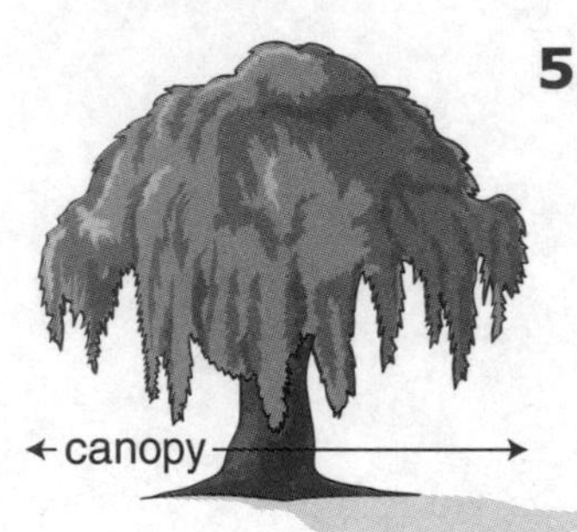

5. Suki is having a diseased willow tree removed. The grass beneath the canopy is dead, so she will put sod in its place. The tree canopy has an approximate diameter of 12 feet.

a) The radius of the tree canopy is ______ feet.

b) Make a sketch of the tree canopy as seen from above.

What is the scale of your diagram? ______________

c) Estimate the area of the sod that Suki needs to buy.

d) Calculate the area of the sod needed. Round your answer up to the nearest square foot.

 978-0-07-090894-9

Date ____________________

☑ Check Your Understanding

1. A city landscaper wants to put 3 flower beds in a rectangular grass area.

a) The rectangle is 75 ft wide and 30 ft long. Draw a scale diagram of the rectangle on the grid below.

What is the scale of your diagram? ____________

b) Each circular flower bed has a radius of 12 ft. Draw the flower beds to scale on the diagram.

c) Calculate the area of each flower bed.

d) Calculate the total area of the 3 flower beds.

e) Calculate the area of the rectangle that is covered by grass.

Date ____________

7.3 Estimating the Cost of a Project

Focus: rounding, proportional reasoning, problem solving

Chapter 7

Warm Up	
1. Round to the nearest dollar. **a)** \$18.99 ______ **b)** \$11.29 ______ **c)** \$47.88 ______	**2.** Round to the nearest \$10. **a)** \$18.99 ______ **b)** \$11.29 ______ **c)** \$47.88 ______
3. Without a calculator, add the rounded values in #1.	**4.** Without a calculator, add the rounded values in #2.
5. What is 10% of the rounded value in #3? ______	**6.** What is 10% of the rounded value in #4? ______
7. What is half of the value in #5? ______	**8.** What is half of the value in #6? ______

How Much Will It Cost?

- Estimating the cost of a project can help you decide if you will go ahead with it.
- To estimate the cost, you need to estimate the quantity of the materials needed.
- Rounding prices and estimating taxes also help you make a reasonable estimate for the total cost of a job.

1. Estimate the following values.

a) 70 fence boards at \$3.99 each.

b) The tax on the 70 fence boards in part a).

c) The perimeter of four $9\frac{1}{2}''$ by $11\frac{1}{2}''$ picture frames.

d) The area of the glass needed for the 4 frames in part c).

978-0-07-090894-9

2. Three cedar trees currently sit near the corner of a property. The owners want to create a garden around the trees. Then, they will add more cedars of the same size to fill the garden. The scale of the diagram is 1 square to 1 foot.

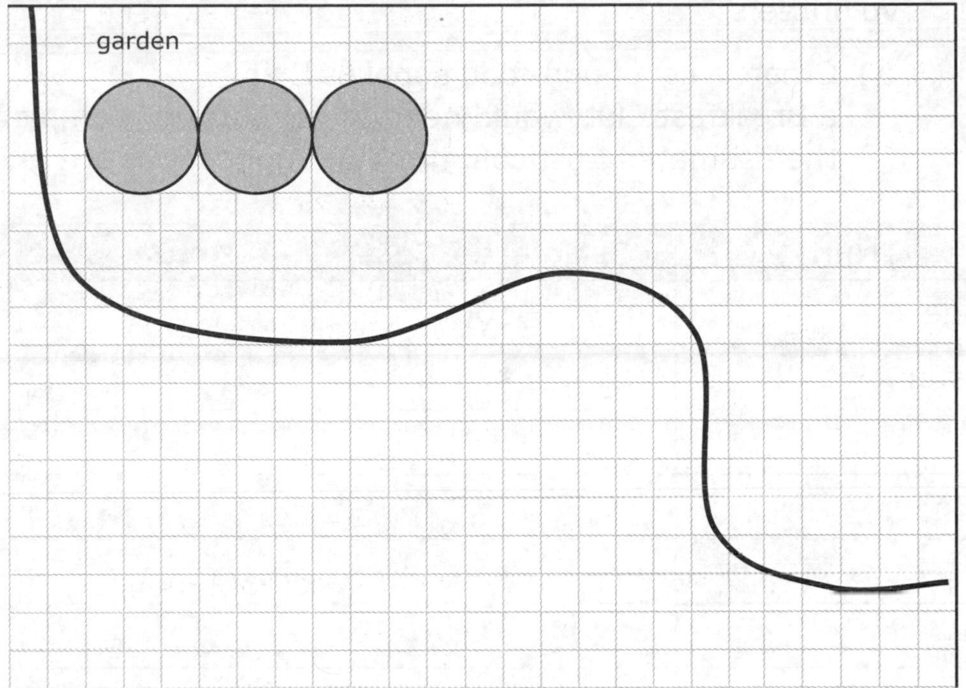

a) Draw the additional cedars to fill the garden on the diagram.

b) How many cedars did you add? ______

c) A local nursery is selling cedars for $47.99 each. Without using a calculator, estimate the cost of the additional cedars before tax.

d) Estimate the tax on the cedars.

e) What is your estimate of the total cost?

f) Calculate the exact total cost and compare this to your estimate.

Chapter 7

3. Some schools run a Breakfast Club for students in the morning. Students are welcome to come for a free breakfast. Many students come because they enjoy eating with friends. The program is run by volunteers.

a) Create a list of non-food supplies that a Breakfast Club would need to get started. Complete the Estimated Cost column. Two suggestions are given.

Item	Estimated Cost	Actual Cost
Fridge	$100	
Toaster	$20	
Totals		

b) Used appliances and materials are available free or for sale in most communities. Research the availability of free items or the cost of buying the items in part a). Complete the Actual Cost column.

Go to **www.mcgrawhill.ca/books/workplace12** and follow the links for online sources of inexpensive items.

978-0-07-090894-9

Date ______________________

c) Create a list of food items that the Breakfast Club would need to keep in stock.

Chapter 7

d) Survey another class in the school to determine the number of students who would attend a Breakfast Club. Express the result as a fraction. ______

e) Based on the population of your school, use the result in part d) to estimate how many students would attend the Breakfast Club.

f) Use flyers from grocery stores to create a shopping list with an estimated cost based on the number of students attending the Breakfast Club.

g) Students liked the Breakfast Club so much that the number of students attending increased by 25% during the first month. Which costs will increase by 25%?

____

____

h) Which costs will not increase?

____

____

4. A hotel needs to clean the drapes of a large window in its front entrance.

- The drapes hang from a rod at the top of the window to the floor below.
- The rod is 10 ft above the floor.
- The window is 6' 10" wide.
- The material for the drapes is twice the width of the window.

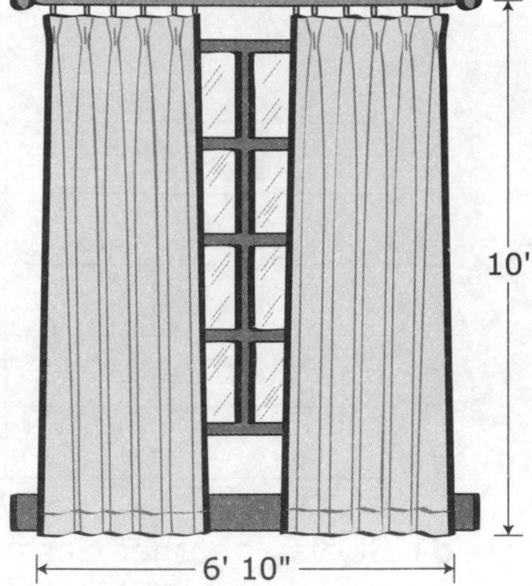

a) Estimate the area of the drapes.

b) Calculate the area of the drapes.

c) Dry cleaners charge by the square yard to clean drapes. Create a number of estimates you could submit to the hotel management based on the following costs.

Cost Per Square Yard	Estimated Cost	Estimated After-Tax Cost
Clean It Right $4.99		
Hotel Cleaning $5.23		
Drapes for Us $6.50		
Window Coverings Inc. $7.18		

 978-0-07-090894-9

- The hotel manager checks the reputations of the various companies.
- He also checks online to see about any specials.
- Drapes for Us has a monthly special. If you get 1 set of drapes cleaned at the regular price, you can have a 2nd set of drapes cleaned at 50% off.

Clean one set of drapes, Get 50% off the second set.

This month only.

50% *off*

5. The hotel restaurant has a set of drapes the same size as those in the hotel entrance.

a) If the manager does the 2 sets at the same time, estimate the cost of cleaning the second set.

b) Estimate the cost of cleaning both sets.

c) Calculate the cost of cleaning both sets.

☑ Check Your Understanding

1. Why might someone wish to consider a number of estimates before making a decision on a project?

2. What might happen if an estimate for material is

a) too small?

b) too large?

Date

Chapter 7

Skills Practice 14: Calculating Surface Area

Go to pages 187–188 to write the definition for **surface area** in your own words.

Surface area is the number of square units needed to cover the outside of an object.

Rectangular Prisms

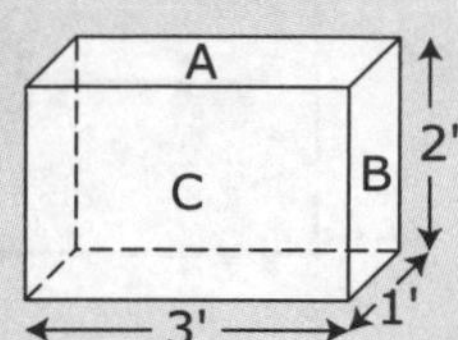

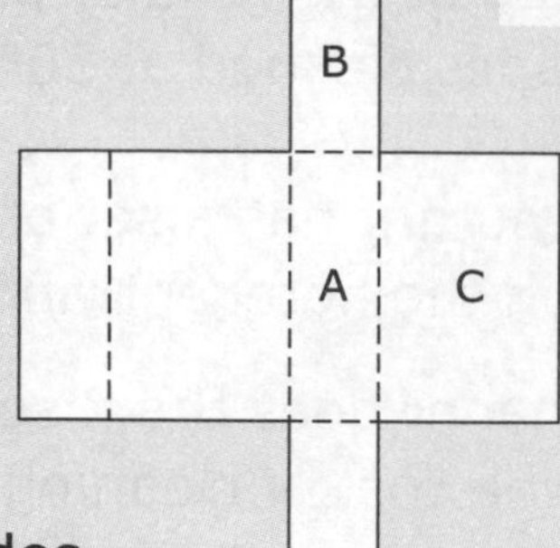

In all rectangular prisms, the 6 sides are made up of 3 pairs of rectangles.

2-D Shape	Area $A = l \times w$	Number of Matching Faces	Total Area
A. Top/Bottom	$3 \times 1 = 3$	2	$3 \times 2 = 6$ ft^2
B. Left/Right	____ × ____		____ × ____ = ____ ft^2
C. Front/Back	____ × ____		____ × ____ = ____ ft^2
		Total Surface Area	

1. A cereal box has dimensions 22 cm, 14 cm, and 5 cm.

a) Sketch a net of the cereal box.

b) Calculate the total surface area of the box.

2-D Shape	Area	Number of Matching Faces	Total Area
		Total Surface Area	

 978-0-07-090894-9

2. Find the surface area of the following rectangular prisms.

a)

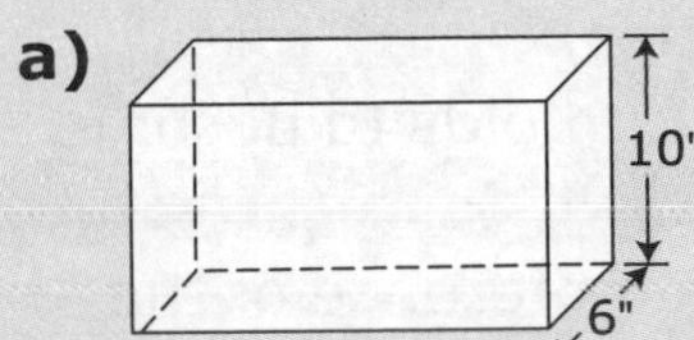

b)

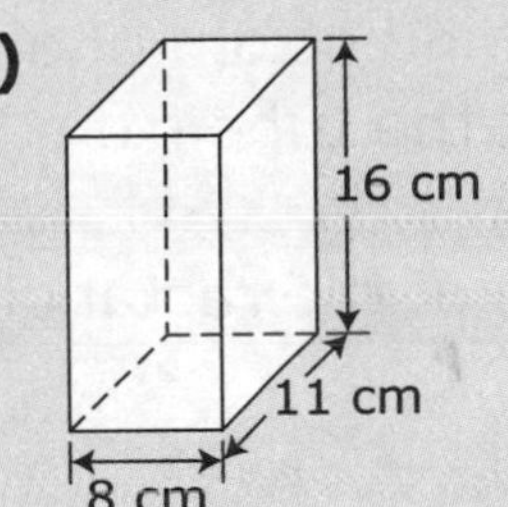

Triangular Prisms

In triangular prisms, the triangles are matching sides.

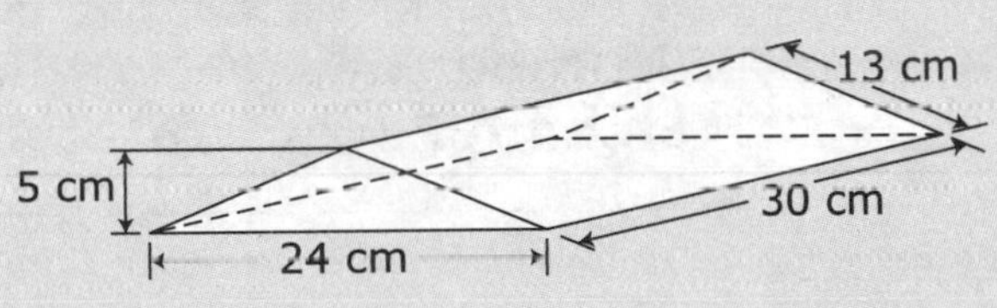

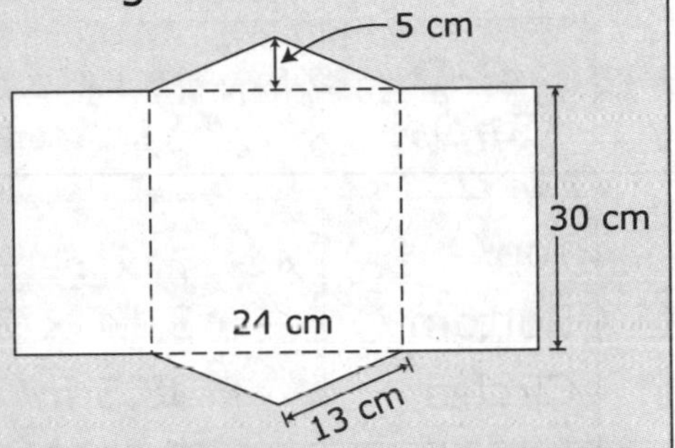

2-D Shape	Area	Number of Matching Faces	Total Area
Front/Back Triangles	$A = (\text{base} \times \text{height}) \div 2$ $= 24 \times 5 \div 2$ $= 60\text{ cm}^2$		
Left/Right Rectangles	$A = l \times w$ = ______		
Bottom Rectangle	$A = l \times w$ = ______		
		Total Surface Area	

3. Calculate the surface area of the following triangular prism.

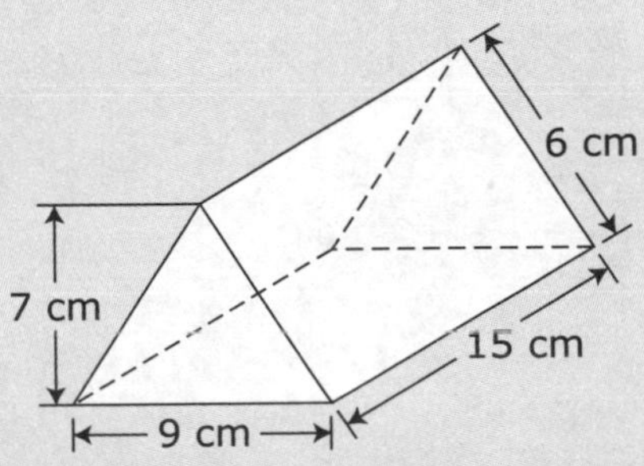

Chapter 7

Cylinders

- The top and bottom of a cylinder are circles.
- If you cut the tube from top to bottom, it unfolds to become a rectangle.
- The width of the rectangle equals the circumference of the circle.

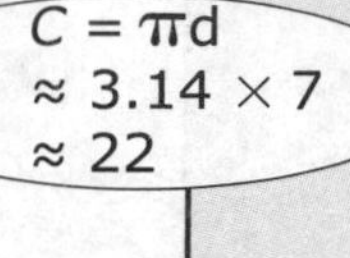

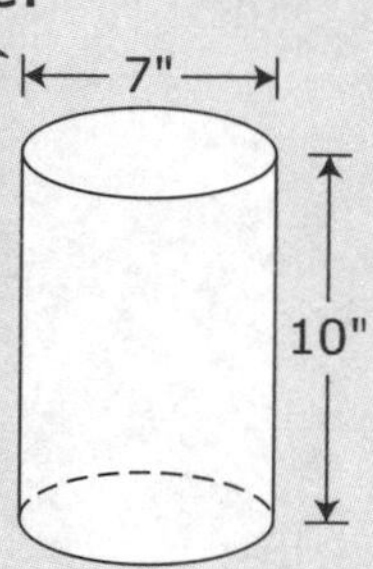

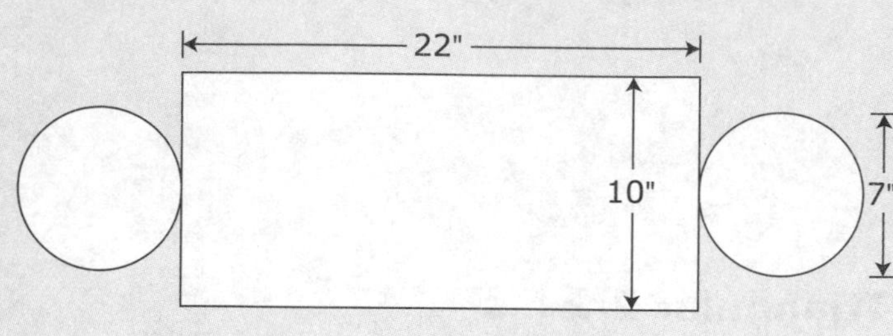

2-D Shape	Area	Number of Matching Faces	Total Area
Top/ Bottom Circles	$A = \pi \times r^2$ $\approx 3.14 \times 3.5 \times 3.5$ $\approx 38.5\text{ in}^2$		
Rectangle	$A = l \times w$ = _____		
	Total Surface Area		

4. Find the surface area of the following cylinders.

a)

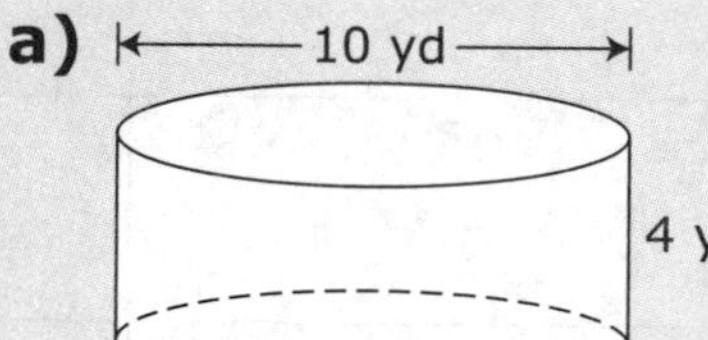

b)

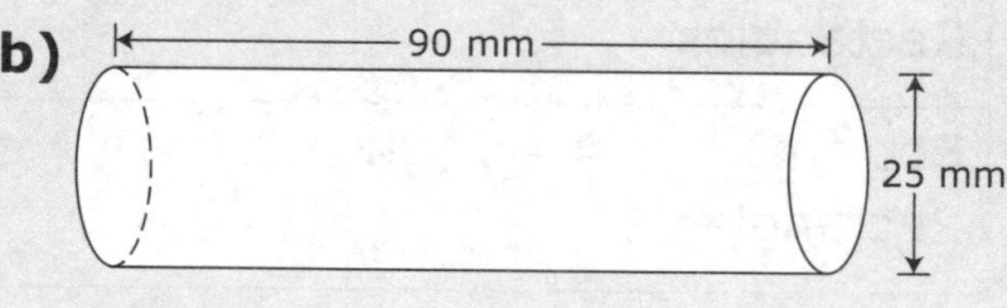

978-0-07-090894-9

Date

7.4 3-D Scale Models

Focus: measuring, rounding, proportional reasoning, problem solving

Chapter 7

Warm Up	
1. What is the highest number that can be rolled with 1 die?	**2.** Explain why your answer to #1 is correct.
3. A die has side lengths of 1.5 cm. What is the area of 1 face of the die?	**4.** What is the total area of all of the faces of the die?
5. What object can be made if you fold along the dotted lines?	**6.** Make a sketch of the object in #5.

Nets

- A **net** is a flat, 2-dimensional model representing a 3-dimensional object.
- A net is what an object would look like if it were *unfolded*.
- In #5 above, the drawing is a net of a cube.

Go to pages 187–188 to write the definition for **net** in your own words.

Date

Chapter 7

1. a) Get a die. Draw the dots of 3 faces you can see at a time on the cube below.

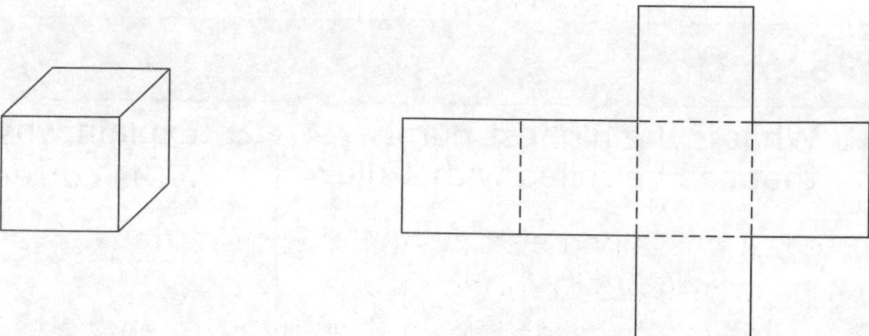

b) Pick up the die. Identify the number of dots on 1 face, and then the number on the opposite face. Draw the same dots on the net above.

c) Choose a 2nd face. How many dots are on the opposite face? Draw the dots on the net above.

d) What do you notice about the numbers of dots on opposite sides of a die?

2. a) The bottom of a toy car says, "1 : 70." What does this mean?

b) The toy has a length of approximately 6.5 cm. What is the approximate length of an actual vehicle of that make? Give your answer in metres.

c) The toy has a width of approximately 2.6 cm. What is the approximate width of an actual vehicle of that make? Give your answer in metres.

978-0-07-090894-9

d) The toy has a height of approximately 2.4 cm. What is the approximate height of an actual vehicle of that make? Give your answer in metres.

e) If modelling clay or a similar material is available, create a 3-D model of the toy car. Otherwise, use paper or cardboard to create a box that the toy car could fit in. You may wish to sketch the net of your box below.

3. a) Find a rectangular, 3-dimensional object in your classroom.

Object: ____________

b) Measure the 3 dimensions of the object.

length = ______ width = ______ height = ______

c) Select a scale for making a model. 1 : ______

d) Calculate the dimensions of the model.

length = ______ width = ______ height = ______

e) Create the model.

4. The company you work with makes candies. For the holidays, they are making mini mints with a diameter of 1". The container is a tube in the shape of a triangular prism. The dimensions are shown in the diagram.

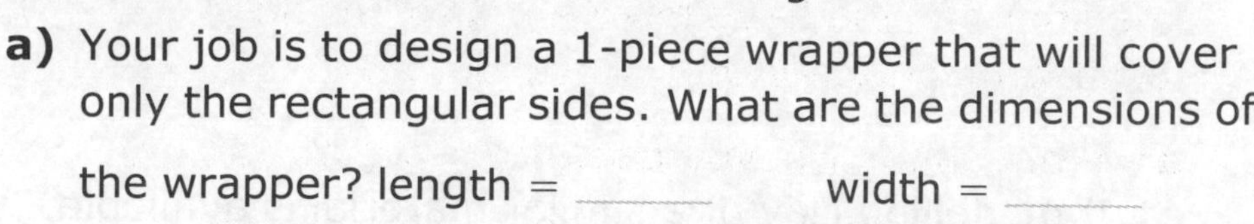

a) Your job is to design a 1-piece wrapper that will cover only the rectangular sides. What are the dimensions of the wrapper? length = ______ width = ______

b) Design a wrapper, to scale, for the candy box.

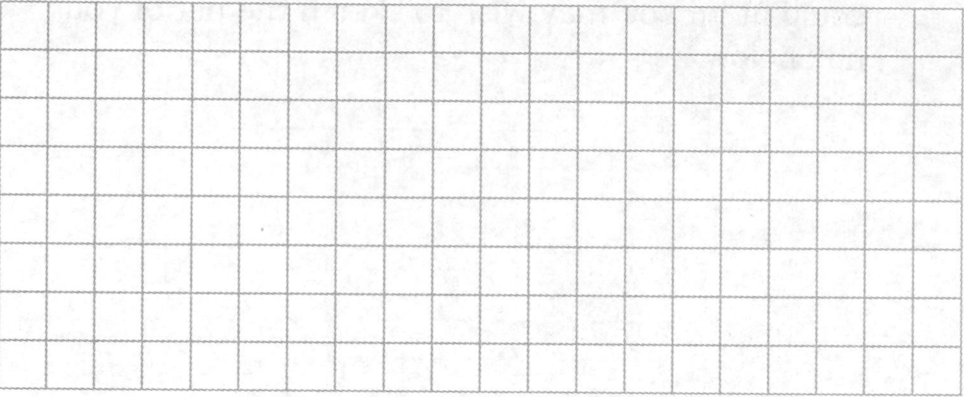

c) How many candies will fit in the box? ______
Explain your answer.

____

5. A type of chip used for card playing is 3 cm in diameter and 3 mm thick.

a) Make a reasonably accurate sketch of 1 chip.

b) Work in groups to build cylindrical tubes that will hold 20, 50, or 100 chips.

c) Calculate the total surface area of any 1 tube.

2-D Shape	Area	Number Needed	Total Area
		Total Surface Area	

 978-0-07-090894-9

d) What would be the length of a tube that held 75 chips?

6. A golf ball has a diameter of approximately 43 mm. Imagine that you have been hired to design a cardboard container that will hold 4 balls.

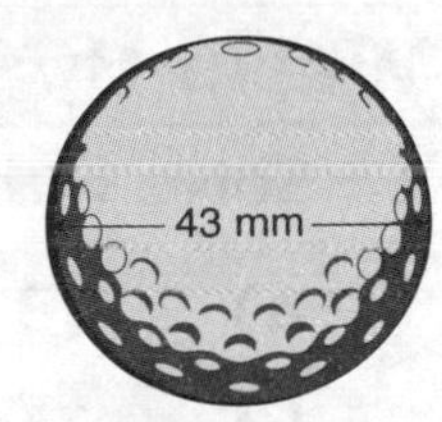

a) What shape will you choose for the container?

b) Make a sketch of the container. Include dimensions on your sketch.

c) Calculate the total surface area of the container.

2-D Shape	Area	Number Needed	Total Area
		Total Surface Area	

d) Create an accurate 3-D model of your container.

☑ Check Your Understanding

1. Create a 3-D scale model of something of personal interest to you. It could be
   - a guitar or a skateboard
   - a piece of furniture like your favourite chair or a bookcase
   - a package that holds a cell phone or an item of clothing
   - something larger, like your bedroom or a planter box

Chapter 7

7.5 Capacity and Volume Applications

Focus: unit conversion, rounding, proportional reasoning, problem solving

Warm Up

1. Solve without a calculator. **a)** $2 \times 3 \times 5 =$ ______ **b)** $4 \times 4 \times 10 =$ ______	**2. a)** Show what 10^3 means. **b)** Therefore, $10^3 =$ ______.
3. a) 1 L = ______ mL **b)** 500 mL = ______ L	**4. a)** 1 gallon = ______ quarts **b)** 1 quart = ______ fluid ounces

5. List the following measures from least to greatest.

1 oz, 250 mL, 1 gallon, 2 L, 1 quart, 16 ounces, 500 mL

______, ______, ______, ______, ______, ______, ______

Go to pages 187–188 to write the definitions for **capacity** and **volume** in your own words. Give an example of each.

Capacity and Volume

- **Capacity** is the amount of liquid a container can hold.
- **Volume** is the amount of space an object takes up.
- While the 2 terms do not mean the same thing, many people use the word volume when they are talking about an object's capacity.

1. In Canada, the label on most containers holding liquid gives their capacity in litres or millilitres. Estimate the metric capacity of the items below.

A. ______________ B. ______________

C. ______________ D. ______________

 978-0-07-090894-9

Chapter 7

2. In the United States, many containers holding liquids state their capacity in ounces, quarts, or gallons. What is the Imperial capacity of the items in #1?

A. ______________ **B.** ______________

C. ______________ **D.** ______________

Painting

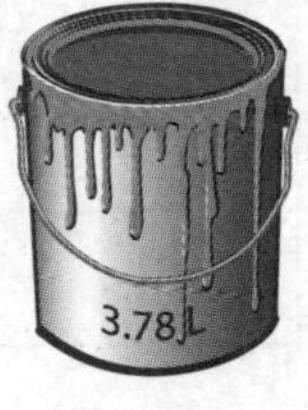

3. One of the first things that many people do when they move into a new home is paint. A typical large can of interior paint bought in a Canadian store has a capacity of 3.78 L.

a) Why do you think the container holds such an odd amount? Why not 3.5 L or 4 L?

Look at section 6.5.

____

b) Most paint manufacturers claim that 1 L of paint covers 10.5 m^2 or 110 ft^2. You can round the numbers to make this easier to remember:

"1 ________ of paint will cover about ________ m^2, which is about ________ ft^2."

4. Steve wants to paint the TV room in his basement. It is a big room, measuring 31 ft by 12 ft. The walls are 8 feet high.

a) Calculate the surface area of the ceiling.

b) Steve wants to put 2 coats of paint on the ceiling. Use your answer in #3b) to estimate the number of cans of paint Steve will need.

c) The walls will be a different colour than the ceiling. Calculate the surface area of the walls.

d) Estimate the number of cans of paint Steve will need in order to apply 2 coats of paint to the walls. ________

Chapter 7

- Steve needs about ______ cans of paint for the ceiling.
- He needs about ______ cans of paint for the walls.

e) Research the price of a good quality interior latex paint. Calculate the total cost.

Area Painted	Brand of Paint	Price Per 3.78-L Can	Number of Cans	Cost of Paint
Ceiling				
Walls				
			Subtotal	
			Tax	
			Total	

Entertaining

5. Esther found a recipe for Mexican Bean Dip online.

a) She is making the dip for a family reunion that 30 people will attend. How much of each ingredient will she need?

Ingredient	Amount
Cheddar cheese	
Sour cream	
Cream cheese	
Refried beans	
Salsa	
Cumin	

b) What did you multiply each ingredient by? ____________

Why? ____

____

 978-0-07-090894-9

c) When Esther goes shopping, she will likely find the ingredients sold in metric units. Use the conversion table on page 291 or do an Internet search for *unit converter*. Find one that will allow you to convert between Imperial and metric capacities.

Volume might be used instead of *capacity*.

Ingredient	Imperial Measure (from part a)	Exact Metric Conversion	Appropriately Rounded Metric Measure
Cheddar cheese			
Sour cream			
Cream cheese			
Refried beans			
Salsa			
Cumin			

d) There are 2 sizes of sour cream at the grocery store. The 500-mL tub is $1.89. The 1-L tub is $2.99. Which tub do you suggest she buy?

e) Salsa also comes in 2 sizes. The 350-mL jar is $1.99. The 700-mL jar is $4.49. Which jar should she buy? Explain your reasoning.

f) Get a local grocery flyer and make a shopping list for Esther. Estimate the total cost of making the dip for 30 people.

6. **a)** How many 2-cm cubes would you need to build a model of the volume of a brick with dimensions 8 cm × 2 cm × 2 cm?

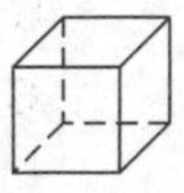

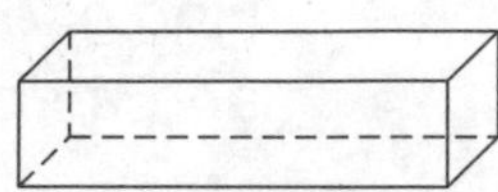

b) Use 2-cm linking cubes to build the brick.

How many did you use? ______

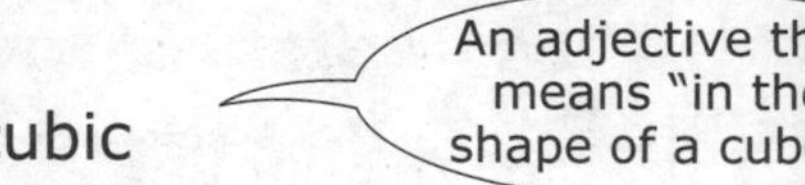

c) The volume of the brick is ______ cubic centimetres.

d) Using the same thinking, how many cubic inches are in a cubic foot? ______
Explain your answer and/or make a sketch below.

7. **a)** Use materials in the classroom to build a cubic foot.
b) How many cubic feet would you need to build a cubic yard? ______
c) Explain your answer to part b). ______

______

Landscaping

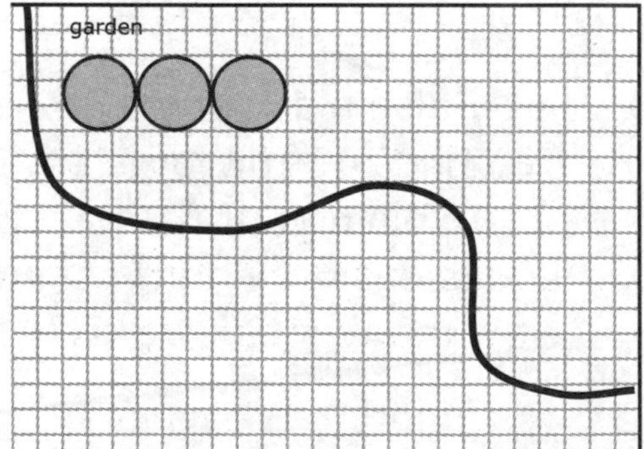

8. In section 7.3, you worked on a project involving the planting of cedar trees.

a) Sketch in the cedars that you decided on earlier.

b) Recall the scale of the diagram. Each square on the diagram represents an area of ______ in the garden.

c) Estimate the area of the garden. ______

d) Compare estimates with other students. Discuss the strategies that you used. Do you need to revise your estimate?

 978-0-07-090894-9

Date

- The owners of the property are laying garden fabric on the ground to prevent weeds from growing.

   e) Estimate the area of the garden that will be covered with fabric.

   f) Garden fabric is sold in rolls that cover 50 ft^2. How many rolls will the owners need to buy?

- The owners will cover the fabric with 4 inches of mulch.

   g) If you know the approximate area of the garden that needs mulch, how can you determine the amount of mulch needed?

   h) What fraction of a foot is 4 inches?

   i) Estimate the volume of mulch needed in cubic feet.

   j) Mulch is often sold by the cubic yard. Convert your answer from part i) to yd^3.

   k) Research the cost of mulch from a local retailer. Calculate the total price, including tax.

☑ Check Your Understanding

1. Looks easy! Painting. Landscaping. Entertaining. How many steps were involved in

   a) painting the room?

   b) finishing the garden?

   c) making a dip?

2. Explain the difference between capacity and volume with respect to an in-ground pool made with 4-inch thick concrete walls.

Review the definitions on page 264.

Date

7.6 Composite Shapes and Figures

Focus: measuring, rounding, proportional reasoning, problem solving

Chapter 7

Warm Up	
1. Six inches is what fraction of a foot? ______	**2.** What is the approximate Imperial equivalent of 3.78 L? ______
3. How many square feet make up 1 square yard? ______	**4.** Which area is greater, 1 m^2 or 1 yd^2? ______
5. Round $87.99 to the nearest **a)** $1. ______ **b)** $10. ______ **c)** $100. ______	**6.** Calculate the tax on $87.99.

Go to pages 187–188 to write the definition for **composite shape** in your own words.

Determine the Area of a Composite Shape

- A **composite shape** is made of more than 1 shape. For example, the blueprint below consists of a rectangle and a square.

1. Felicia recently moved into a condo in downtown Ottawa. She wants to carpet her dining room and her living room. Below is a sketch of the area.

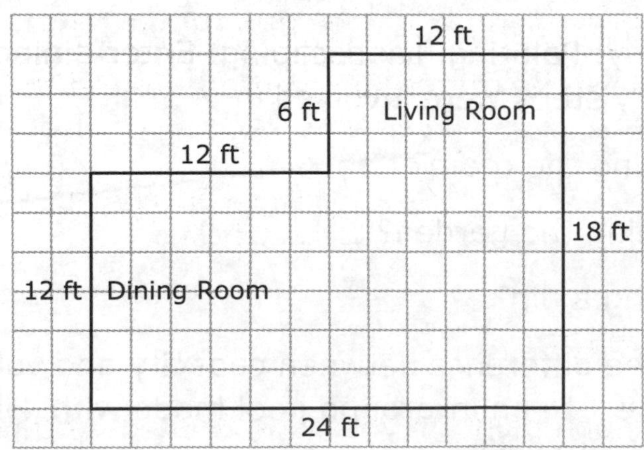

How can Felicia determine how much carpet is needed?

______

 978-0-07-090894-9

Chapter 7

2. Label the missing dimensions for each of the following composite shapes.

a)

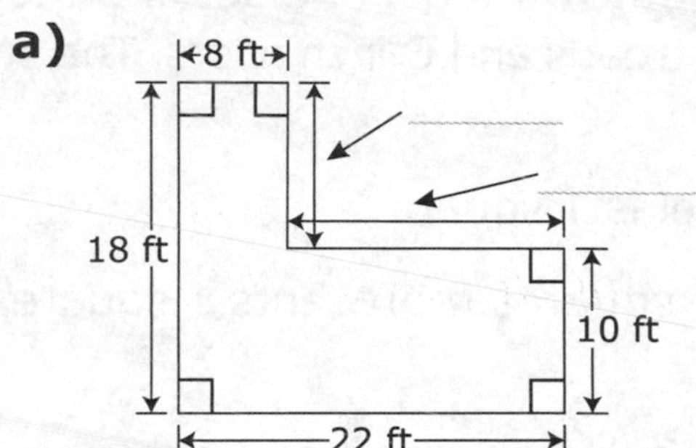

b)

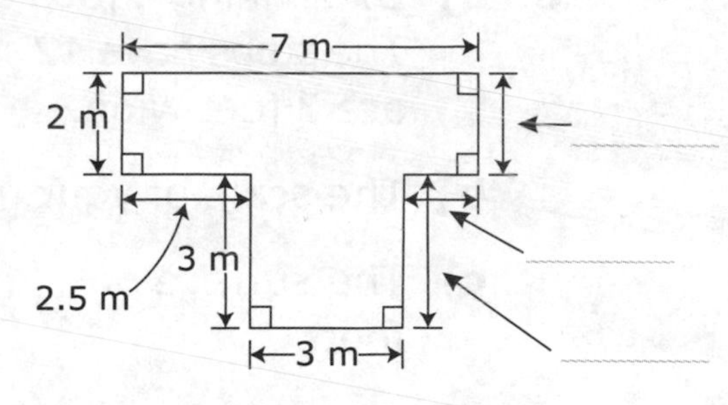

3. Divide the shapes above into groups of regular shapes.

4. Determine the area of each of the composite shapes in #2.

a)

b)

5. The key on a basketball court is in the shape of a rectangle. The free-throw area is in the shape of a semicircle. Often, these areas are painted so that they stand out from the rest of the court.

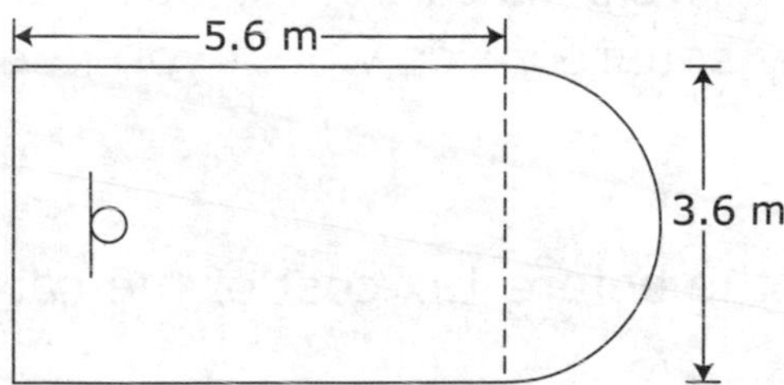

a) Recall the formula for the area of a circle.

b) Calculate the area to be painted. Round to 2 decimal places.

Key:

Free Throw Area:

Total Area:

c) How much paint do you need to paint both keys on the court with 2 coats?

Date ____________________

Composite Figures

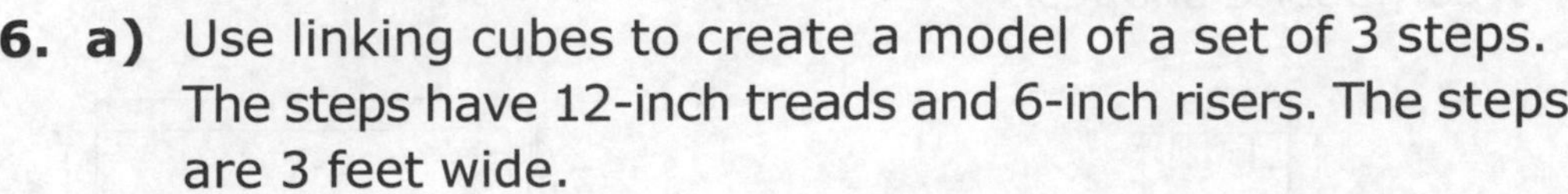

6. a) Use linking cubes to create a model of a set of 3 steps. The steps have 12-inch treads and 6-inch risers. The steps are 3 feet wide.

   b) The scale of your model is 1 square : ____________.

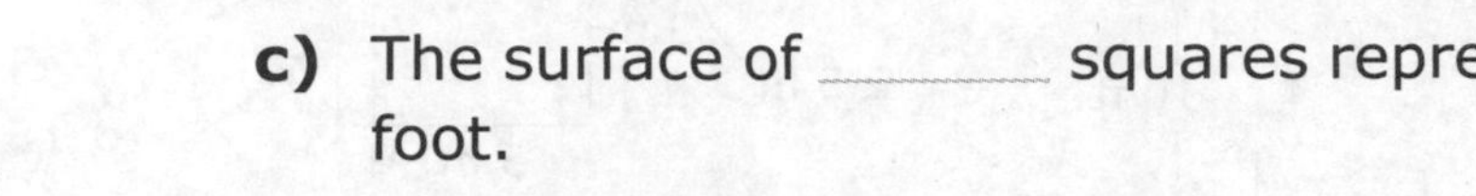

   c) The surface of ________ squares represents 1 square foot.

   d) The volume of ________ cubes represents 1 cubic foot.

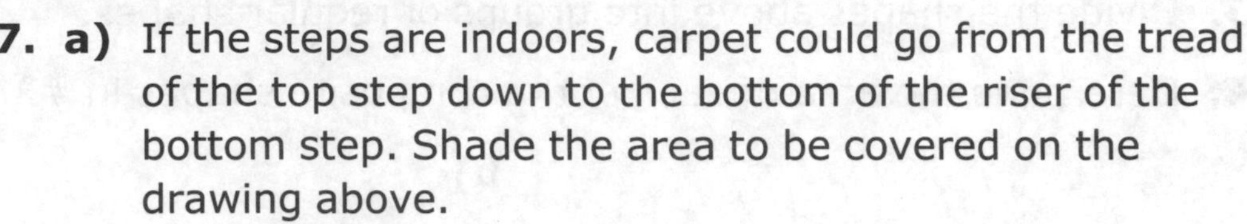

7. a) If the steps are indoors, carpet could go from the tread of the top step down to the bottom of the riser of the bottom step. Shade the area to be covered on the drawing above.

   b) Calculate the area of the carpet.

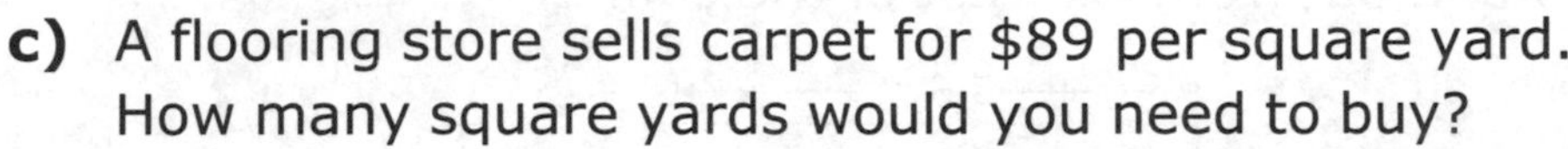

   c) A flooring store sells carpet for $89 per square yard. How many square yards would you need to buy?

   d) Calculate the before-tax cost of the carpet.

   e) Calculate the after-tax cost of the carpet.

8. If the steps are outdoors, they could be made of concrete that is poured into a wooden frame.

   a) Determine the volume of the steps.

978-0-07-090894-9

b) Concrete is often ordered in cubic yards. Convert your answer from part a) to cubic yards.

☑ Check Your Understanding

1. You have volunteered at a daycare to help build a wooden sandbox for the children.

   a) Design a composite rectangular shape. Include dimensions.

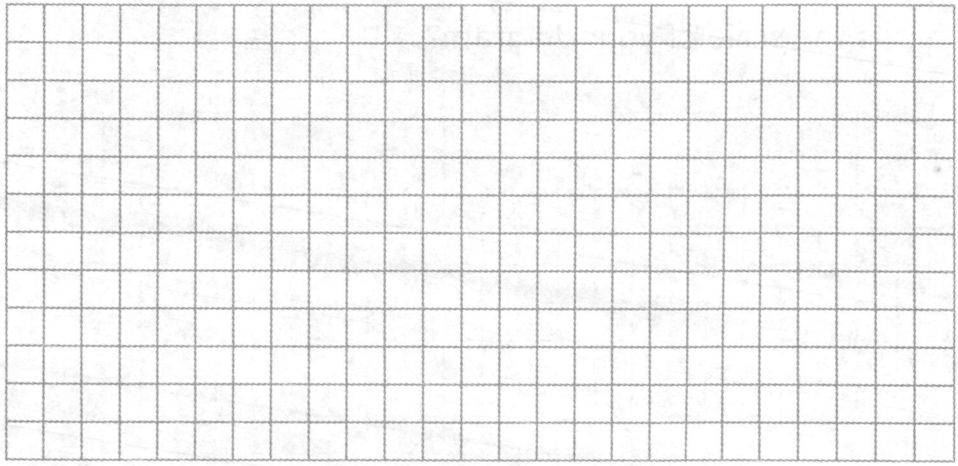

   b) How many feet/metres of wood do you need to build the walls?

   c) How many square feet/square metres of plywood do you need to build the floor of the sandbox?

   d) How high will the walls of the sandbox be? ________

   e) How many cubic yards/cubic metres of sand do you need to fill the sandbox?

Date

Chapter 7 Review

Chapter 7

1. a) The package of a model of a Lear jet says, "1 : 72." What does this mean?

b) Once built, the model of the jet is 15" long. What is the length of the jet?

2. a) Make a scale diagram of a wall measuring 3.6 m wide and 2.4 m high.

What is the scale of your diagram?

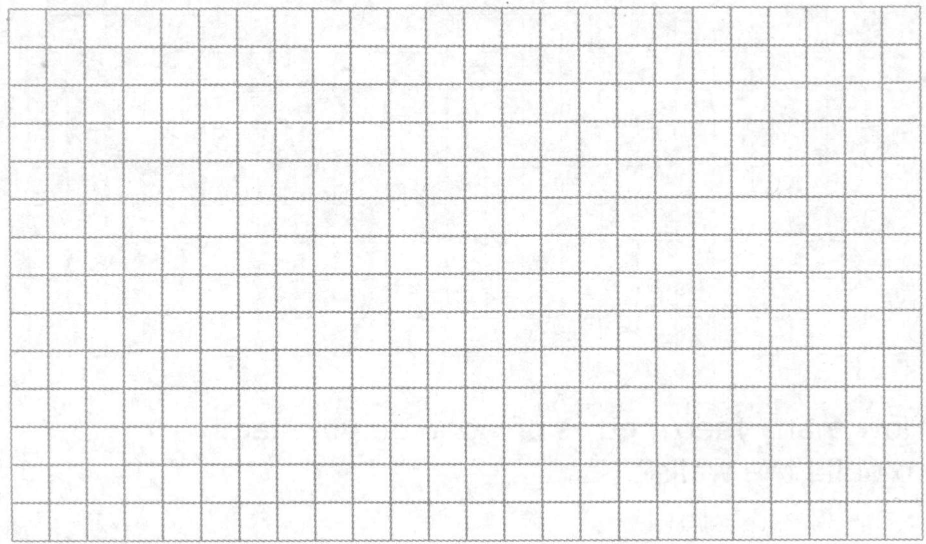

b) One litre of paint covers approximately 10 m^2. How many 1-L cans of paint do you need to put 2 coats of paint on the wall?

c) On the diagram of the wall above, sketch, to scale, the perimeter of an 80 cm by 60 cm piece of art.

978-0-07-090894-9

Chapter 7

3. a) This tent has nylon walls and a nylon floor. Calculate the approximate surface area of the tent.

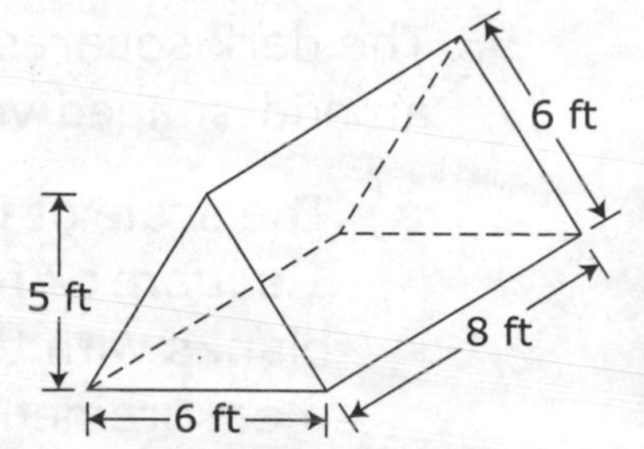

2-D Shape	Area	Number Needed	Total Area
		Total Surface Area	

b) Many campers hang a tarp above the tent to prevent rain from falling on it. What is the area of a circular tarp with a diameter of 10 ft?

c) The tarp has a sewn nylon edge around its perimeter to prevent fraying. What is the length of the material sewn around the edge of the tarp?

4. Bryan is replacing the vertical boards on two 8-ft sections of fence in his backyard. The boards he needs are $5\frac{3}{4}$" wide. He will leave a $\frac{1}{4}$" gap between the boards.

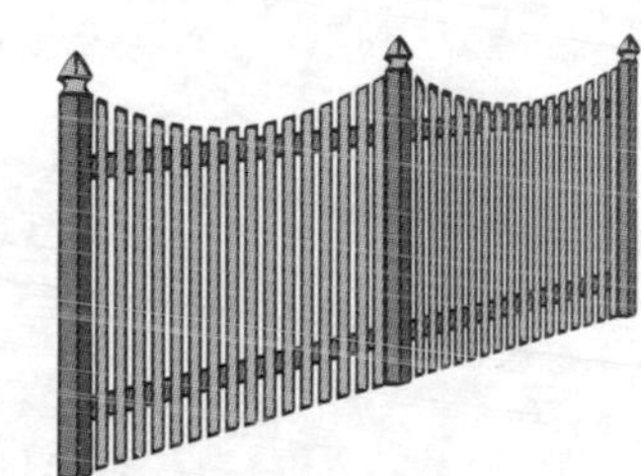

a) How many boards will Bryan need to buy?

b) Each board costs $3.19. What is the after-tax cost of the job?

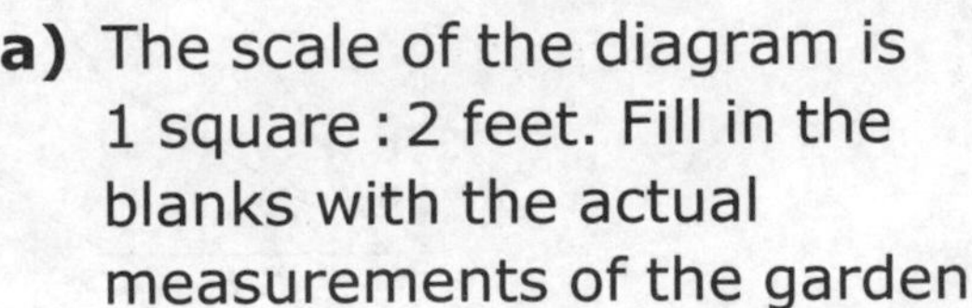

5. The dark squares in the plan show an odd-shaped vegetable garden.

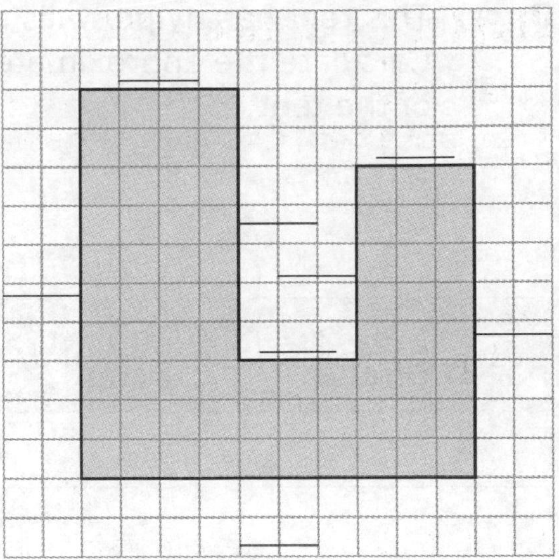

a) The scale of the diagram is 1 square : 2 feet. Fill in the blanks with the actual measurements of the garden.

b) On the diagram, divide the garden into a number of regular shapes.

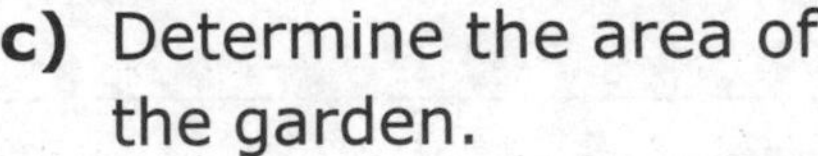

c) Determine the area of the garden.

d) You want to add a layer of peat moss 3 inches deep. Determine the volume of peat moss needed.

e) A 3.8-ft^3 bag of peat moss costs \$4.99. Calculate the total cost of the peat moss.

978-0-07-090894-9

Chapter 7 Practice Test

Chapter 7

1. a) The blueprints for an addition to a school are drawn with a scale of 1 : 48. Explain the meaning of "one to forty-eight."

b) A line 6 inches long on the drawing represents a wall of what length when the addition is built?

2. a) Make a scale diagram of a 110-yard long by 65-yard wide football field. Include the centre line. Put an end zone 10-yards long at each end of the field.

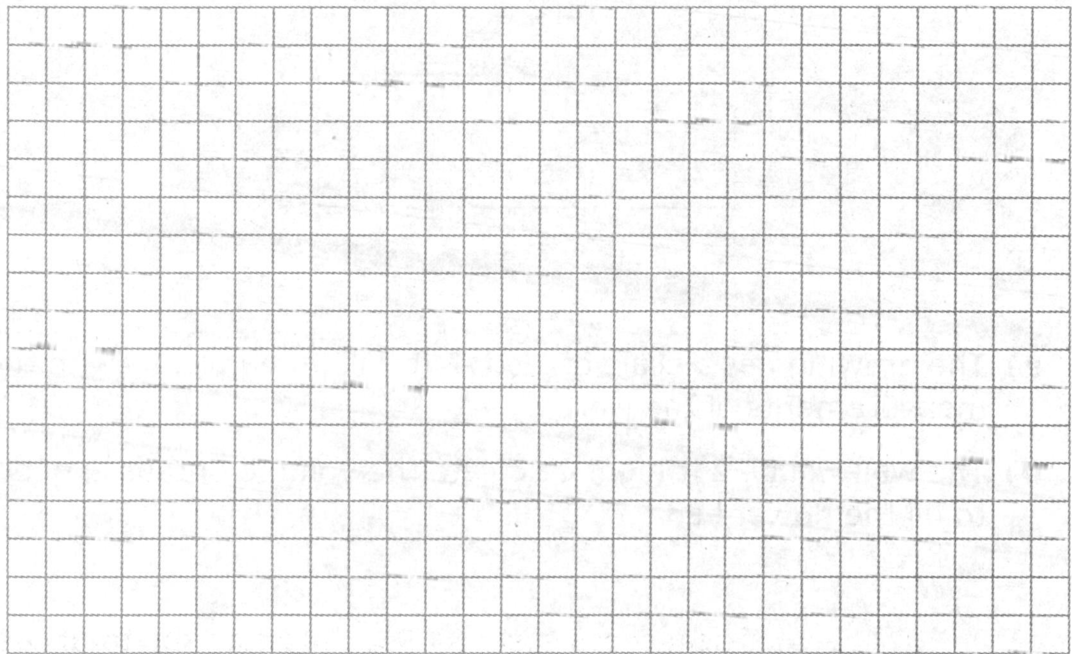

b) What is the total area of the field including the end zones?

c) The perimeter of the field needs the white border repainted. How many cans of white paint are needed if 1 can will make a line 35 yards long?

978-0-07-090894-9

Chapter 7

3. Determine the area of each of the following shapes.

a)

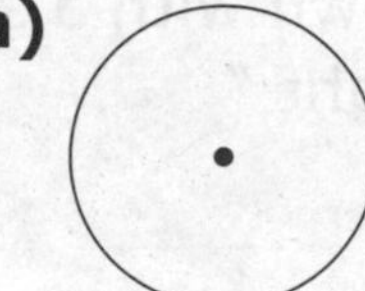

b)

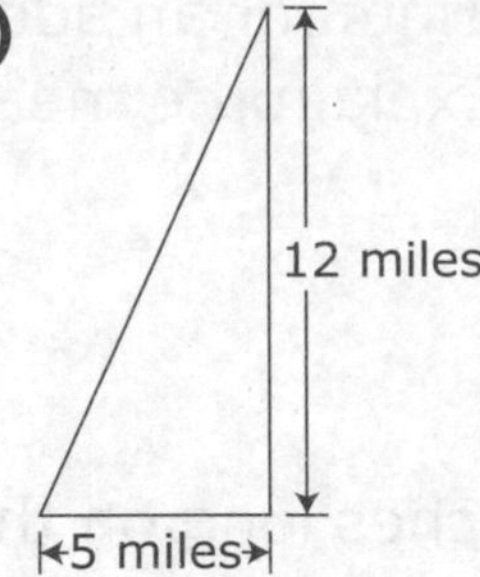

4. A landscaping company is building a retaining wall to enclose a raised flower bed.

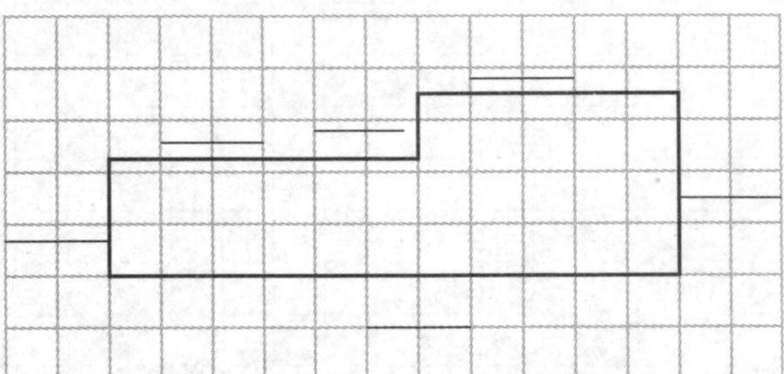

a) The drawing has a scale of 1 sq : 2 ft. Fill in the blanks with the measurements of the wall.

b) The wall will be 2 ft high. Calculate the volume of topsoil needed to fill the flower bed.

c) Convert your answer from part b) to cubic yards.

d) Marigolds will be planted around the perimeter of the flower bed at 6" intervals. How many marigolds will be needed?

 978-0-07-090894-9

5. Some shingles on 1 side of a house were damaged in a wind storm. A sketch of that side of the roof is below.

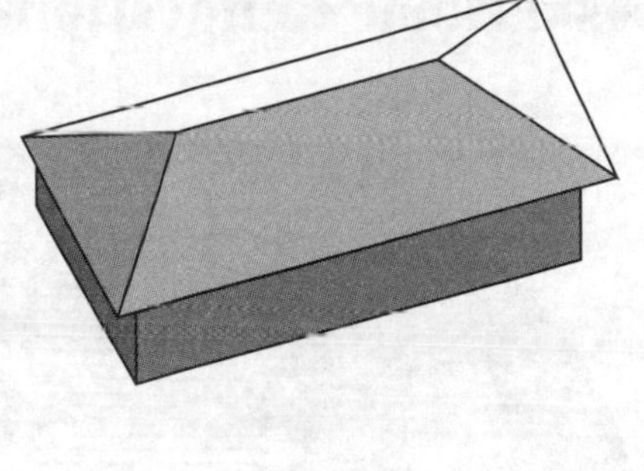

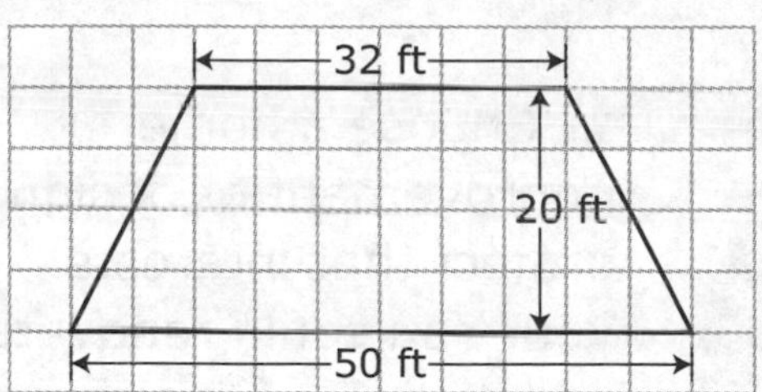

a) On the diagram, divide the side of the roof into regular shapes.

b) Determine the area of the side of the roof.

c) One bundle of shingles covers 32 square feet. How many bundles do you need to cover the side of the roof?

d) Shingles come in different qualities. High quality shingles that are supposed to last 25 years cost $17.99 per bundle. Determine the before-tax cost of the shingles needed to cover the side of the roof.

e) What is the after-tax cost of the shingles?

978-0-07-090894-9

Task: Home Renovations

1. Choose a home improvement or design project that interests you. You could renovate a room in your home or landscape an area in your neighbourhood. You will have a budget of $2000.

Project:

2. Make a list of the steps involved in the project. For example, to renovate your bedroom, you might repaint the walls, replace or install carpet, replace the electrical fixtures, replace windows, and refurnish the room.

 978-0-07-090894-9

Glossary

amortization period number of years it takes to pay off a mortgage. Most mortgages have **amortization periods** of 25 or 30 years. Also see **mortgage** and **term**.

balanced budget when the money coming in equals the money going out. If you make $200/week and you spend $200/week, your budget is balanced. Also see **budget**, and **budget template**.

budget organized income and spending plan. Also see **balanced budget** and **budget template**.

budget template list of common sources of income and expenses used to help you organize your expenses. Also see **balanced budget** and **budget**.

Canada Pension Plan (CPP) provides income for retired workers. People who have paid into CPP receive a regular income from the government when they retire. Also see **Canada Revenue Agency**, **Employment Insurance**, and **TD1**.

Canada Revenue Agency (CRA) federal government agency that collects taxes. The taxes pay for federal and provincial programs and services, such as health care and education. Also see **Canada Pension Plan**, **Employment Insurance**, and **TD1**.

capacity greatest amount a container can hold. The **capacity** of a large carton of milk is 2 L. Also see **volume**.

composite shape a shape made of more than 1 shape. The drawing below is made of a square and a triangle.

deposit money given as part payment when signing a lease. Usually, the **deposit** is equal to one month's rent. The first cheque to a landlord usually includes this amount plus the first month's rent. This is often referred to as paying "the first and last month's rent."

down payment part of a home price that is not financed by a mortgage. First-time buyers need a **down payment** of 5% of the price of the house. A first-time buyer who wanted to buy a $250 000 house would need at least $12 500 for a down payment. Also see **mortgage**.

Employment Insurance (EI) provides income for unemployed workers while they look for a new job. Also see **Canada Pension Plan, Canada Revenue Agency**, and **TD1**.

978-0-07-090894-9

Glossary

essential expenses purchases that are not optional. Food is an **essential expense**. If we do not eat, we cannot live. Also see **fixed expenses**, **non-essential expenses**, and **variable expenses**.

equivalent fractions have the same value. For example, $\frac{1}{2} = \frac{2}{4}$.

exchange rate value of $1 CDN when you buy money from another country. The value of $1 CDN can vary. For example, on January 21, 2002, the exchange rate was quite low. $1 CDN was equal to about 62¢ US, or, $0.62 US. On November 7, 2007, the exchange rate hit a record high. $1 CDN was equal to about $1.10.

experimental probability chance of something happening based on experimental results. If you roll a die 100 times and get thirty-seven 6s, the **experimental probability** of rolling a 6 is $\frac{\text{number of 6s rolled}}{\text{number of times die rolled}} = \frac{37}{100}$. Also see **theoretical probability** and **odds**.

fixed expenses expenses that do not change from month to month. Rent is a **fixed expense**. Also see **essential expenses**, **non-essential expenses**, and **variable expenses**.

fixed rate mortgage interest rate is set for the term of the mortgage. The payments stay the same for the length of the term. Also see **mortgage**, **term**, and **variable rate mortgage**.

fixed term a set length of time, usually 1 year, for which a lease or other business agreement is in effect. Also see **lease** and **tenancy agreement**.

gross pay total earnings before any deductions are taken off. An employee who makes $7.25/h and works 40 h has a **gross pay** of $290. Also see **net pay**.

landlord person who provides a rental unit. This is also called the lessor. Also see **lease**, **lessee**, **tenancy agreement**, and **tenant**.

lease a written agreement between a landlord and a tenant. Also see **landlord**, **lessee**, **lessor**, **tenancy agreement**, and **tenant**.

lessee person paying for renting a unit. Another term is **tenant**.

lessor person or company that owns the rental unit. This is also called the **landlord**.

mortgage loan used to buy property. Mortgages are repaid in regular payments over a set period of time. Also see **amortization period**, **fixed rate mortgage**, **term**, and **variable rate mortgage**.

net flat, 2-dimensional model representing a 3-dimensional object. This is a net of a cube.

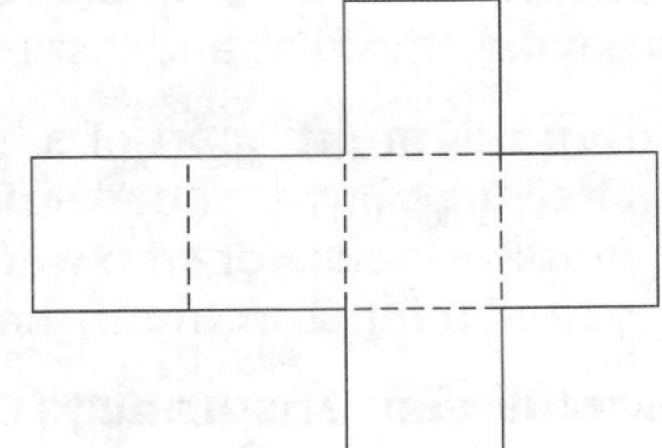

net pay the amount left from gross pay after all deductions have been taken off. Also called take-home pay. If your gross pay is $350 and you have deductions of $25, your **net pay** is $350 – $25 = $325. Also see **Canada Pension Plan (CPP)**, **Employment Insurance (EI)**, **gross pay**, and **TD1**.

non-essential expenses optional purchases. In many urban areas, vehicles are a **non-essential expense** because people can get around easily using public transportation. Also see **essential expenses**, **fixed expenses**, and **variable expenses**.

odds ratio of the probability of an event happening to the probability of an event *not* happening. For example, the **odds** of rolling a 6 if you roll one die are 1 : 5. That is because there is one 6 on the die, and 5 other numbers. Also see **experimental probability** and **theoretical probability**.

ON428 form used to calculate the amount of provincial tax a taxpayer owes. Also see **Schedule 1** and **T1**.

parties people involved in a rental agreement: the lessor and the lessee(s). Also see **lessor**, **lessee**, **tenant**, and **landlord**.

personal reference in measurement, this refers to using a familiar object or part of your body to estimate a specific length in metric or Imperial units. For example, the width of many people's thumbs is about 2 cm or $\frac{3}{4}$".

population all of the people in a group being studied. For example, the **population** of a school consists of the students plus all of the staff, including teachers, counsellors, maintenance workers, and kitchen staff. Also see **sample**.

post-dated cheque cheque that has been written with a date in the future and cannot be cashed until then. A tenant will often give a landlord **post-dated cheques** for rent.

premium money paid for an insurance policy. Many renters buy insurance to protect their belongings against damage or theft.

random number generator tool that picks numbers so that each number has an equal probability of coming up on each try. You can use a TVM solver as a **random number generator**.

real estate land and all buildings on the land. For example, houses, empty building lots, and buildings that hold businesses are all **real estate**.

sample small group of results taken from a larger group. Surveying 10% of your class is a **sample** of the class. Also see **population**.

scale drawing reduced or enlarged picture of an object. A blueprint is a reduced **scale drawing**. A drawing of a cell as seen through a microscope is an enlarged **scale drawing**.

Schedule 1 form used to calculate the amount of federal tax a taxpayer owes. You need to complete this form to claim tax credits. Also see **ON428**, **T1**, and **tax credit**.

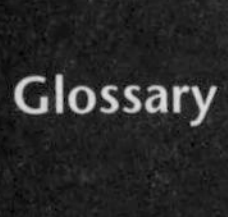

simulate model with an experiment. If traffic lights were programmed to show red, yellow, and green for the same amount of time, you could **simulate** the chance of a traffic light being green by spinning a spinner with 3 equal sectors.

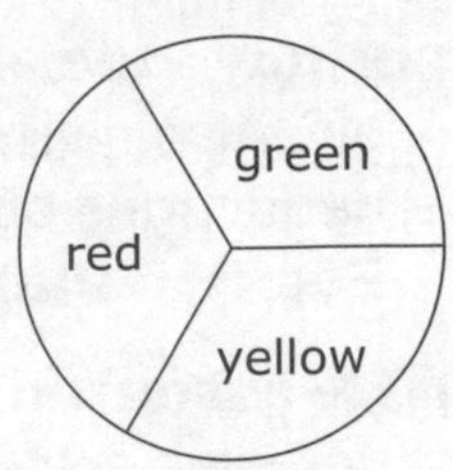

surface area number of square units needed to cover the outside of an object. To calculate the **surface area**, find the area of each outer surface or face and add them together. The area of one face of the cube is $3 \times 3 = 9$ cm². The cube has 6 faces. The cube's surface area is $9 \times 6 = 54$ cm².

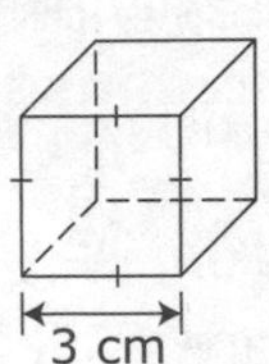

T1 annual tax return that a taxpayer submits to the Canada Revenue Agency. The main parts of the **T1** are identification, total income, net income, taxable income, and refund or balance owing. Also see **Canada Revenue Agency**, **ON428**, **Schedule 1**, and **taxable income**.

T4 form an employer submits to the Canada Revenue Agency showing an employee's payroll deductions for 1 year. The employer is responsible for giving the employee a copy of the **T4**. Also see **Canada Pension Plan**, **Canada Revenue Agency**, and **Employment Insurance**.

taxable income amount left over after all tax deductions have been subtracted from gross income. This is the amount you pay taxes on. Also see **gross income**, **T1**, and **tax deduction**.

tax credit a percent of an expense subtracted from taxes owing. Tuition fees, medical expenses, and charitable donations can be used as **tax credits**. Also see **Schedule 1**, **T1**, **taxable income**, and **tax deduction**.

tax deduction an expense subtracted from gross income to calculate taxable income. For example, if you contribute $5000 to a registered retirement plan, you can subtract $5000 from your gross income so that you do not pay taxes on that $5000. Child care expenses, moving expenses, and union dues are tax deductions. Also see **gross income**, **T1**, **taxable income**, and **tax credit**.

TD1 form an employer uses to determine the amount of federal and provincial tax to deduct from an employee's pay. Also see **Canada Pension Plan**, **Canada Revenue Agency**, and **Employment Insurance**.

tenancy agreement a written or oral contract between a landlord and a tenant. Also see **landlord**, **lease**, **lessee**, **lessor**, and **tenant**.

tenant person who pays rent to a landlord and lives in a rental unit. This is also called the lessee. Also see **landlord**, **lease**, **lessee**, **lessor**, and **tenancy agreement**.

theoretical probability chance of something happening in a perfect world. The **theoretical probability** of rolling a 6 when you roll 1 die is $\frac{\text{number of 6s rolled}}{\text{number of possible rolls}} = \frac{1}{6}$. Also see **experimental probability** and **odds**.

term length of a current mortgage agreement. Most **terms** are 5 years. When the **term** expires, you can either pay the balance of the mortgage or sign a new mortgage agreement. Also see **amortization**, **fixed rate mortgage**, **mortgage**, and **variable rate mortgage**.

unit price cost of a single item in a group, even when a single item cannot be purchased. If the price of lemons is 3 for $1.00, the **unit price** is $0.33 because it costs that much for 1 lemon.

utilities basic services such as electricity, gas, and water.

variable expenses costs that change in amount or how frequently they are paid. Entertainment is a variable expense. Also see **essential expenses**, **fixed expenses**, and **non-essential expenses**.

variable rate mortgage interest rates can change every month. In a **variable rate mortgage**, the payments can change as the interest rates change. Also see **mortgage** and **fixed rate mortgage**.

volume The amount of space an object takes up. Also see **capacity**.

Date

Centimetre Grid Paper

978-0-07-090894-9

Date

Date

978-0-07-090894-9

Date ______________________

Formulas

Item	Hint	Example
Perimeter		
Of an item with straight sides	• Add the lengths of all of the sides.	6 ft 3 ft $6 + 3 + 6 + 3 = 18$ The perimeter is 18 ft.
Of a circle (The perimeter of a circle is also called the circumference.)	• Multiply the diameter by 3.14.	4 m The diameter is 4 m. $4 \times 3.14 = 12.56$ The circumference is approximately 12.6 m.
Area		
Of a rectangle or square	• Multiply the length by the width. • The answer will be in square units. The answer here is 49 square metres or 49 m^2.	7 m length = 7 m width = 7 m $7 \times 7 = 49$ The area is 49 m^2.
Of a triangle	• Multiply the base by the height. • Divide the answer by 2. • Show the answer in square units.	4 m 1.80 m base = 1.80 m height = 4 m $1.80 \times 4 = 7.2$ $7.2 \div 2 = 3.6$ The area is 3.6 m^2.
Of a circle	• Square the radius. • Multiply by 3.14. • Show the answer in square units.	3 m The diameter is 3 m. The radius is half the diameter, or 1.5 m. $1.5 \times 1.5 = 2.25$ $2.25 \times 3.14 = 7.065$ m The area is approximately 7.1 m^2.

978-0-07-090894-9

Conversion Tables

Metric Length

mm → cm → m → km
10 mm = 1 cm
100 cm = 1 m
1000 m = 1 km

Metric	Imperial
1 mm	0.0393 in.
1 cm	0.393 in.
1 m	3.28 ft
1 km	0.621 mi $\frac{5}{8}$ mi

Imperial Length

inch → foot → yard → mile
12 in. = 1 ft
36 in. = 1 yd
3 ft = 1 yd
5280 ft = 1 mi
1760 yd = 1 mi

Imperial	Metric
1 in.	25.4 mm
1 in.	2.54 cm
1 ft	30.48 cm 0.305 m
1 mi	1.609 km $\frac{8}{5}$ km

Metric Capacity

mL → L
1 mL = 1 cc
1000 mL = 1 L

Metric	Imperial
1 mL	0.034 oz
1 L	33.81 oz
1 L	4.23 cups
1 L	2.11 pints
1 L	1.07 quarts
1 L	0.26 gallon

Imperial Capacity (United States)

ounce → cup → pint → quart → gallon
8 oz = 1 cup
2 cups = 1 pint
32 oz = 1 quart
2 pints = 1 quart
4 quarts = 1 gallon

Imperial	Metric
1 oz	29.57 mL
1 cup	236.56 mL
1 pint	473.12 mL
1 quart	0.95 L
1 gallon	3.79 L

Metric Weight

mg → g → kg → tonne
1000 mg = 1 g
1000 g = 1 kg
1000 kg = 1 tonne (or 1 metric ton)

Metric	Imperial
1 g	0.0353 oz
1 kg	2.2046 lb

Imperial Weight (United States)

ounce → pound → ton
16 oz = 1 lb
2000 lb = 1 T

Imperial	Metric
1 oz	28.35 g
1 lb	0.4536 kg

Note that 1 metric ton does not equal 1 Imperial ton!